AN OPEN COURTROOM

AN OPEN COURTROOM
Cameras in New York Courts

NEW YORK STATE
COMMITTEE TO REVIEW
AUDIO-VISUAL COVERAGE
OF COURT PROCEEDINGS

Fordham University Press
New York
1997

Copyright © 1997 by FORDHAM UNIVERSITY PRESS
All rights reserved.
LC 97–16512
ISBN 0-8232-1809-0 (*hardcover*)
ISBN 0-8232-1810-4 (*paperback*)

Library of Congress Cataloging in Publication Data

An open courtroom : cameras in New York courts / New York State Committee to Review Audio-Visual Coverage of Court Proceedings.
    p. cm.
Includes bibliographical references.
ISBN 0-8232-1809-0 (hc : alk. paper). —
ISBN 0-8232-1810-4 (pbk. : alk. paper)
    1. Conduct of court proceedings—New York (State)   I. New York (State). Committee on Audio-Visual Coverage of Court Proceedings.
KFN5955.064   1997
347.747'0504—dc21   97-16512
                                                                  CIP

COMMITTEE TO REVIEW AUDIO-VISUAL COVERAGE OF COURT PROCEEDINGS

The New York State Committee to Review Audio-Visual Coverage of Court Proceedings consists of the following members:

Hon. Fritz W. Alexander, II, counsel, Epstein, Becker & Green and former Associate Judge, New York Court of Appeals

Richard Alteri, President, Cable Television and Telecommunications Association of New York

Professor Jay C. Carlisle, II, Pace University School of Law

Veronica Gabrielli Dumas, Assistant District Attorney, Office of the Albany County District Attorney

John D. Feerick, Dean, Fordham University School of Law (Chair)

Diane Kennedy, President, New York Newspaper Publishers Association

Henry G. Miller, Senior Partner, Clark, Gagliardi & Miller and former president, New York State Bar Association

Leonard Noisette, Director, Neighborhood Defender Service of Harlem

Michelle Rea, Executive Director, New York Press Association

Professor James M. Tien, Chair of the Department of Decision Sciences and Engineering Systems, Rensselaer Polytechnic Institute

Monte I. Trammer, President and Publisher of the *Saratogian & Community News*

Alissa Pollitz Worden, Associate Dean, School of Criminal Justice, State University of New York at Albany

CONTENTS

Acknowledgments	xi
EXECUTIVE SUMMARY	xv
I. INTRODUCTION	1
II. OVERVIEW OF THE COMMITTEE'S WORK	5
III. SUMMARY OF CURRENT LAW	9
A. Section 218 of the Judiciary Law	9
1. Judicial Discretion	9
2. Safeguards for Defendants in Criminal Proceedings and Parties in Civil Proceedings	11
3. Safeguards for Witnesses	11
4. Safeguards for Children	13
5. Safeguards for Jurors	13
6. Other Safeguards	13
7. Pretrial Conference	14
8. Equipment and Personnel Restrictions	14
9. Appeals	15
B. Rules of the Chief Administrative Judge	15
IV. OVERVIEW OF CAMERA COVERAGE LAWS IN OTHER STATES AND IN FEDERAL COURTS	19
A. State Courts	19
1. 50-State Overview	19
2. California	20
B. Federal Courts	22
V. SUMMARY OF THE COMMITTEE'S RECORD	27
A. Public Benefits	27
1. Public Education about the Courts	28

CONTENTS

    2. Judicial Accountability and Public Scrutiny of the Judicial System — 31
    3. Cathartic and Deterrent Effects — 33
    4. Other Benefits — 34
    5. Opponents' Views — 36
        a. Nature of Televised Coverage — 37
        b. Effect on Witnesses — 39
        c. Fair Trial Implications — 41
        d. Privacy Concerns — 43
  B. Compliance by Trial Judges and the Media — 44
    1. Compliance by Trial Judges — 44
        a. Testimony and Public Comment — 44
        b. Results of the Committee's Judicial Survey — 46
        c. Office of Court Administration Data — 49
    2. Compliance by the Media — 49
  C. Effect of Audio-Visual Coverage on the Conduct of Participants in Court Proceedings — 52
    1. Effect on Jurors — 53
    2. Effect on Witnesses — 58
    3. Effect on Lawyers — 62
    4. Effect on Judges — 64
        a. Inside the Courtroom — 64
        b. Outside the Courtroom — 67

VI. COMMITTEE'S ASSESSMENT AND CONCLUSIONS — 69
  A. Public Benefits — 69
  B. Compliance by Trial Judges and the News Media with the Safeguards of Section 218 of the Judiciary Law — 71
    1. Judges — 71
    2. News Media — 74
  C. Effect of Audio-Visual Coverage on the Conduct of Participants in Court Proceedings — 74
    1. Jurors — 76
    2. Witnesses — 77
    3. Lawyers — 78
    4. Judges — 79
  D. Defendant's Consent — 80

VII. RECOMMENDATIONS 83

1. Cameras Should Be Permitted in New York State Courts on a Permanent Basis with All of the Safeguards of Current Law for Parties, Prospective Witnesses, Jurors, Crime Victims, and Other Trial Participants 83
2. Defendant Consent Should Be a Prerequisite for Camera Coverage of Bail Hearings 84
3. There Should Be No Separate Rule for Death Penalty Cases 85
4. Judges Should Be Vigilant in Addressing the Safety and Privacy Concerns of Witnesses in Both Criminal and Civil Proceedings 85
5. The Office of Court Administration Should Actively Monitor Camera-Covered Proceedings, Make Periodic Reports, and, If Necessary, Recommend Changes in Section 218 of the Judiciary Law and the Implementing Rules 86
6. The Office of Court Administration Should Develop an Enhanced Judicial Training Program to Familiarize All Judges with the Applicable Statutory and Administrative Provisions and Safeguards 88

APPENDICES

A. Judicial Survey 93
B. Marist Institute for Public Opinion Poll 113
C. Judiciary Law, Section 218 125
D. Rules of the Chief Administrative Judge 133
E. California Rule of Court 980 149
F. Overview of Camera Coverage Laws in the Fifty States 157
G. Jury Consultant Interviews 171
H. Office of Court Administration Data on News Media Applications for Audio-Visual Coverage of Court Proceedings 175
I. Sample Monitoring Instrument for Camera-Experienced Lawyers 191

J. Judicial Training Program Outline 199
K. Selected Bibliography 201

MINORITY REPORT by Leonard E. Noisette 207

ACKNOWLEDGMENTS

The work of this Committee would never have been completed without the dedication of those who selflessly devoted thousands of hours to this project. The Committee is deeply indebted to all of them.

We owe our greatest debt to Alexandra D. Lowe, Esq., a lawyer with experience in both state and local government. She served with singular distinction as the Committee's counsel. We thank her most especially for the commitment and excellence she brought to all of her work for the Committee, making possible the exhaustive nature of the Committee's review of the subject.

Special thanks are due to Taryn V. Shelton, Esq., and Joseph Guglielmelli, Esq., experienced lawyers who volunteered their time to help organize the Committee's public hearings and assist the Committee's information gathering process. Their participation was truly invaluable. Ms. Shelton also provided enormous help in the final stages of the drafting of the Committee's report.

The Committee wishes to express its special gratitude to Professor Edmund Mantell of Pace University's Lubin School of Business, who designed the data base for the Committee's judicial survey and performed the statistical analysis of the data from that survey on a *pro bono* basis. We are greatly indebted to him for his time, his insights, and his commitment to this project.

We are also especially grateful to Dr. Lee M. Miringoff and Dr. Barbara L. Carvalho of the Marist Institute for Public Opinion, who undertook a public opinion poll for the Committee to determine the views of New Yorkers on cameras in the courts. They refined the Committee's poll topics, surveyed the public, and compiled the results at no cost to the Committee. The interpretation of the survey findings is the Committee's.

The Committee received unfailing cooperation from the staff of the Office of Court Administration. Special thanks are due to Chief Administrative Judge Jonathan Lippman, Deputy Counsel for Criminal Justice Lawrence Marks, and the staff of the Jury and Data Services Unit (especially Chester ("Chip") H. Mount, Jr., Gail Miller, David Greenberg, Harvey Cigman, and Gloria Jean

Williams) for their help in compiling information from the news media's applications for camera coverage. OCA also printed over one thousand mailing labels for the Committee's judicial survey, arranged for court reporters to record and transcribe the Committee's five public hearings, and handled the burdensome task of copying those transcripts for the Committee.

Eight Fordham Law School students—Anthony Bolzan, Dickson Chin, Terris Ko, John McCarthy, Mark Sherman, Elisa Shevlin Rizzo, Joan Soares, and Daniel Winterfeldt—logged hundreds of hours in the law library and reached out to dozens of organizations across the country to put together a national perspective on the issue of cameras in the courts. Their continued involvement and insight at every stage of the Committee's proceedings was an invaluable asset. We would also like to thank Scott Welkis, a new lawyer who found time to help assemble and analyze the public comment the Committee received.

Without the logistical support of Marilyn Force, Sarina McGough, and Michelle Sampson of Fordham Law School, the work of the Committee would have ground to a halt. Together, they kept open the channels of communications, scheduling and rescheduling countless meetings, conference calls, interviews, and appointments. They photocopied thousands of pages of materials, faxed and re-faxed documents, assembled hundreds of overnight mail packages, and made sure that the Committee's meetings and public hearings occurred without a hitch.

The Committee's judicial survey was desk-top published by Fordham Law School's Assistant Dean of Admissions, Kevin Downey, over the course of many nights and weekends. His help was enormous. Equal dedication was demonstrated by John Feerick, Jr., who volunteered to enter all of the data from the judicial surveys into the Committee's data base and helped display the final results. Paul Woomer and the other computer specialists at the Fordham University Law School's "Help Desk" made sure that our computers were able to store and retrieve all of the information and data we collected.

Professor Beth Schwartz of Fordham Law School volunteered to interview jury consultants about their experience with cameras in the courtroom. Michele Falkow and Janice Greer, Fordham Law School reference librarians, fielded dozens of last-minute requests for information and research. Christopher Carter of Fordham University's Office of Public Affairs drafted numerous press releases and helped ensure that notice of the Committee's public hearings and meetings was widely disseminated throughout the state.

Still others assisted the Committee in innumerable ways. Ruth Hochberger, chief editor of the *New York Law Journal*, graciously agreed to help the Committee solicit public comments on cameras in the court by running more than half a dozen public service announcements for the Committee. Helen Herman and Scott Lilly oversaw all of the logistical details of the Committee's two public hearings which took place at Fordham Law School. Donna Welensky, Fordham's Law Clinic Administrator, handled the logistics of videotaping the Committee's first two public hearings, ably assisted by camera operators James G. Andary and Esteban Y. Mondoza.

William Carroll and his dedicated staff at the New York State Bar Association (including Robert Millman, Dorothea Salvador, and Terry Scheid) hosted the Committee's November 14, 1996 public hearing in Albany, contributing space and videotaping services and providing refreshments to the Committee. We are grateful to Presiding Justice Dolores Denman of the New York State Supreme Court, Appellate Division, Fourth Department, who offered the Committee the use of the Fourth Department courtroom for the Committee's December 17, 1996 meetings in Rochester, and to Carl Darnall, Clerk of the Appellate Division, Fourth Department, who helped the Committee with the logistics of using that courtroom for a public hearing.

Finally, the Committee would like to express its gratitude to all of the judges who took the time from their crowded court calendars to complete the Committee's judicial survey, and to all those who testified at the Committee's hearings, responded to the Committee's public opinion survey, wrote to the Committee, or contributed their knowledge and expertise to the Committee in telephone interviews and meetings.

EXECUTIVE SUMMARY

Our Committee conducted its work against the background of camera coverage in New York State of civil and criminal proceedings since December 1, 1987. In allowing for an experimental period, the New York State Legislature noted in its 1987 findings that:

> court proceedings are complex, often involving human factors that are difficult to measure. There may be inherent problems in any court proceeding which could possibly be complicated by audio-visual coverage.
>
> [T]he Legislature, remaining sensitive to these concerns, hereby determines that, in order to enhance public familiarity with the workings of the judicial system, while not interfering with the dignity and decorum of the courtroom, the prohibition of audio-visual coverage of court proceedings should be modified for an experimental period.

Our review of the experiment, the fourth of its kind in New York since 1987, did not find that the presence of cameras in New York interferes with the fair administration of justice. Rather, testimony from over 50 witnesses who spoke at our five public hearings, over 350 responses to our judicial survey, and over 50 letters of public comment from lawyers, bar associations, and interested citizens strongly suggest that the judges of this state have done an excellent job in administering the present law. The many safeguards contained in the law and in the accompanying rules issued by the Chief Administrative Judge have worked well to provide judges with the necessary discretion to deal with potential abuses and to protect the legitimate concerns of parties, prospective witnesses, jurors, crime victims, and other participants in trial proceedings.

The Committee's record includes strong evidence of compliance with the requirements and safeguards of Section 218 of the Judiciary Law by representatives of the electronic news media. Overall, the media appeared to understand and respect the solemnity and dignity of the courtrooms they covered.

In light of the long period of examination of this subject by prior committees and this Committee, we recommend that Section 218 of the Judiciary Law be amended to permit audio-visual coverage on a permanent basis, with all of the safeguards of the current legislation for defendants in criminal proceedings, parties in civil proceedings, witnesses, jurors, crime victims, children and others.[1] We believe that the public nature of a trial and the public's right of access to a trial support the adoption of a law permitting television coverage of court proceedings under the careful control and supervision of trial judges, who must retain their unfettered discretion to determine whether or not to admit cameras to their courtroom, taking into consideration the concerns of trial participants.

In striking this balance, we find instructive judicial decisions on the public nature of a trial and the values served by the principle of openness of the judicial process. These values include promoting confidence in the judicial process, assuring that proceedings are conducted fairly, providing the public with information about the workings of the judiciary, and satisfying the appearance of justice. Although televised coverage could, at times, show the judicial system in an unfavorable light, we do not view that as a detriment. Rather, to the extent that such coverage offers an opportunity for improving the judicial system, we view it as a strength of our democratic system.

It is a fact of life that television has radically changed what is available to the public. Millions now watch inaugurations and other public events previously limited to a few. The courts, like other public institutions, belong to the people, and a principal way for most New Yorkers to view their legal system in action is through television. Certainly, some act differently when they know a camera is upon them. But for every person who shows off, usually to his or her detriment, there are others who will be on their best behavior. For those who are concerned that the public's thirst for stronger punishment might infect the process if criminal trials are televised, there is the compensating safeguard of a courtroom monitored by many members of the community.

While there is no constitutional requirement mandating the presence of cameras in the courtroom, we agree with the findings

---

[1] One Committee member, Leonard Noisette, Esq., does not join in this recommendation and submits a minority report.

contained in the initial 1987 legislative authorization for cameras in New York:

> An enhanced understanding of the judicial system is important in maintaining a high level of public confidence in the judiciary. Public awareness and understanding of judicial proceedings, however, is often limited to the role played as a juror or witness, or as a party in a small claims proceeding. The average law-abiding citizen is not afforded numerous opportunities to participate in civil and criminal court proceedings, or able to attend and observe firsthand the functioning of our legal system. The vast majority of citizens, therefore, rely on reports in the news media for information about the judicial system and accounts of judicial proceedings.

The Committee believes that one of the greatest benefits derived from the presence of cameras in the courtroom is enhanced public scrutiny of the judicial system. The majority of judges who responded to the Committee's survey and a wide array of witnesses who testified at the Committee's hearings agreed that the presence of television cameras in the courtroom enhances public scrutiny of judicial proceedings. It seems clear that television coverage of court proceedings enables the public to learn more about the workings of the justice system, to see directly the conduct of particular cases, and to become more familiar with legal concepts and developments.

In implementing a permanent law in New York on cameras in the courts, we consider it essential that the Chief Administrative Judge actively monitor compliance with the law and its implementing rules, establish a formal mechanism to receive and review complaints about the operation of the law, make periodic reports to the Legislature and, if necessary, recommend changes in Section 218 of the Judiciary Law and the implementing rules.

We strongly recommend that the Chief Administrative Judge develop an enhanced training program for all judges, including town and village judges, to ensure that every judge in the state is familiar with the safeguards of the current law and the implementing rules, and is equipped with the tools necessary to exercise wisely the discretion conferred by the law. In making this recommendation, we note that some judges reflected a misunderstanding that the current statute provides a presumption in favor of cameras in the courtroom.

We also recommend that in order to minimize inadvertent violations of the statute, the Office of Court Administration should develop a new application form which would identify, in plain English, each of the restrictions on camera coverage which are enumerated in the applicable law and administrative rules. Representatives of the news media should be required to sign the form to indicate that they have read and understood the applicable safeguards.

We further recommend that the Legislature extend to bail hearings the same safeguard of defendant's consent which is currently required as a prerequisite to camera coverage of arraignments and suppression hearings. Because widespread pre-trial dissemination of hearsay statements made at bail hearings may have a prejudicial effect on prospective jurors comparable to that of the dissemination of evidence ruled inadmissible at a suppression hearing, the Committee believes that it would be consistent with existing safeguards to add bail hearings to the list of pre-trial proceedings which require a defendant's consent.

The Committee considered whether there should be a special camera coverage rule for death penalty cases insofar as New York State's death penalty statute is new and we have no experience with camera coverage in such cases. The Committee notes that a majority of New York State judges who responded to our survey were not of the view that different rules were needed to govern camera access in capital proceedings, although a sizeable minority favored banning cameras altogether in such proceedings. We find no basis in our consideration of the subject to distinguish such cases from other criminal proceedings. However, we believe that it is important for the trial judge to take account of all relevant factors in deciding whether or not to permit camera coverage in death penalty cases.

The Committee also considered whether a witness' right to insist that his or her image be visually obscured—which is available under current law to non-party witnesses in criminal proceedings—should be extended to non-party witnesses in civil cases. The Committee concluded that it is appropriate to distinguish between these two categories of proceedings, given the heightened safety concerns that may exist in a criminal trial, where threats to witnesses' physical safety could be of serious concern. We also recognize that the privacy concerns of rape and other sexual assault victims are important in criminal proceedings.

We believe that the safety and privacy concerns of witnesses in civil cases deserve the trial judge's careful attention. Some witnesses in civil proceedings may reasonably fear injury to their personal or professional reputation if certain aspects of their past are thrust before a television audience. In accordance with the rules of the Chief Administrative Judge, we believe that trial judges should remain "especially sensitive and responsive to the needs and concerns of all . . . witnesses" and should exercise, if necessary, their statutory discretion to protect the witness in a civil proceeding who raises a valid privacy or safety concern.

Finally, no report about cameras in the courtroom in 1997 would be complete without at least some mention of the O. J. Simpson case. Televised coverage of the Simpson criminal trial has cast a long shadow over the "cameras in the court" debate nationwide. Camera proponents assert that televised coverage of that proceeding made an important contribution to the public's understanding of the judicial process and fundamental legal principles, such as the presumption of innocence, proof beyond a reasonable doubt, and the suppression of illegally seized evidence. Camera opponents have argued that the Simpson case personifies the evils of cameras in the courts: television programming that sensationalized the judicial process and turned a murder trial into a mass-marketed commercial product which, in the eyes of some observers, brought the American legal system into disrepute.

From its inception, this Committee stayed in close contact with the California judicial taskforce charged with re-evaluating California's camera coverage law in the wake of the O. J. Simpson trial. We had several lengthy telephone conferences with the taskforce's senior staff, who shared with us the voluminous set of materials compiled by the California taskforce. Justice Richard Huffman of the California Court of Appeal, who chaired the California study effort, flew to New York to testify at the Committee's hearings. We also heard testimony from one of the criminal defense lawyers who played a pivotal role in the Simpson case. We carefully reviewed the new California court rule on cameras in the court, which gives broad discretion to the trial judge and which provides that there should be no presumption for or against camera access.

In the end, this Committee reaches the same conclusion as California: televised coverage of trials should be left to the sound discretion of the trial judge,[2] unfettered by any presumptions. As required by the current implementing rules, judges in New York should carefully consider "the objections of any of the parties, prospective witnesses, victims or other participants" before deciding whether or not to admit cameras to the courtroom and must remain, throughout the trial,

> especially sensitive and responsive to the needs and concerns of all parties, victims, witnesses and participants in [court] proceedings, particularly where the proceedings unnecessarily threaten the privacy or sensibilities of crime victims, or where they involve children or sex offenses.

With these safeguards in place, the Committee is confident that cameras in the courts of New York State can and will strengthen the public's access to the vital work of the judicial system. We in New York can show the world the benefits of an open system.

In sum, the Committee makes the following recommendations:

1. **Cameras should be permitted in New York State courts on a permanent basis with all of the safeguards of current law for parties, prospective witnesses, jurors, crime victims, and other trial participants.**
2. **Defendant consent should be a prerequisite for camera coverage of bail hearings.**
3. **There should be no separate rules for death penalty cases.**
4. **Judges should be vigilant in addressing the safety and privacy concerns of witnesses in both criminal and civil proceedings.**
5. **The Office of Court Administration should actively monitor camera-covered proceedings, make periodic reports, and, if necessary, recommend changes in Section 218 of the Judiciary Law and the implementing rules.**
6. **The Office of Court Administration should develop an enhanced judicial training program to familiarize all judges with the applicable statutory and administrative provisions and safeguards.**

---

[2] We note that New York provides greater safeguards in pre-trial proceedings than California. We fully support the existing pre-trial safeguards in our law.

In the final analysis, we observe that New York opted in 1987 to open its courts to cameras in both civil and criminal proceedings. Almost 10 years of experience argue in favor of allowing cameras in the courts on a permanent basis so long as a law allowing camera coverage is grounded on judicial discretion, contains all of the safeguards in place during the experimental period and recommended by this Committee, and directs the Office of Court Administration to monitor camera-covered proceedings, make periodic reports, and, if necessary, recommend changes in Section 218 of the Judiciary Law and the implementing rules. It is this Committee's judgment that such an approach, in the context of New York's experiment, respects the public value of openness, the public nature of a trial, and the constitutional principle of a fair trial.

I
Introduction

In January 1995, the New York State Legislature approved the fourth phase of New York's "experiment" with cameras in the courtroom.[1] This experiment, which began on December 1, 1987, gives trial judges discretion to allow televised and still camera coverage of civil and criminal trial court proceedings.[2]

As before, the Legislature created a mechanism for evaluating the latest phase of the experiment, which is scheduled to last until June 30, 1997. The Legislature called for the appointment of a 12-member committee "to review audio-visual coverage of court proceedings."[3] The Legislature directed this Committee to evaluate the efficacy of the experimental program and to assess whether:

1. Any public benefits accrue from the experimental program;

---

[1] The term "experiment" refers to a loosening, on a temporary basis, of the strictures of § 52 of the Civil Rights Law, which prohibits televising proceedings "in which the testimony of witnesses by subpoena or other compulsory process is or may be taken." See Judiciary Law § 218(1).

[2] Although this report most often uses the term "cameras in the court" to refer to televised coverage of court proceedings, still camera coverage is also part of the experiment.

[3] Judiciary Law § 218(9)(a). Richard Alteri, president of the Cable Television and Telecommunications Association of New York, Professor Jay C. Carlisle, II of Pace University School of Law, and Henry G. Miller, Senior Partner, Clark, Gagliardi & Miller, were appointed to the Committee by the Governor. Committee Chair John D. Feerick, Dean of Fordham University School of Law, Hon. Fritz W. Alexander II, counsel, Epstein, Becker & Green, and Veronica Gabrielli Dumas, Assistant District Attorney, Albany County, were appointed by the Chief Judge of New York State. Monte Trammer, president and publisher of *The Saratogian & Community News*, and Professor James M. Tien, Chair of the Decision Sciences and Engineering Systems Department at Rensselaer Polytechnic Institute, were appointed by the Majority Leader of the Senate. Leonard Noisette, director of Neighborhood Defender Service of Harlem, and Alissa Pollitz Warden, Associate Dean of the School of Criminal Justice of the State University of New York at Albany, were appointed by the Speaker of the Assembly. Diane Kennedy, president of the New York Newspaper Publishers Association, was appointed by the Minority Leader of the Senate. Michelle Rea, executive director of the New York Press Association, was appointed by the Minority Leader of the Assembly.

2. Any abuses occurred during the program;
3. The extent to which and the way in which the conduct of participants in court proceedings changes when audio-visual coverage is present;
4. The degree of compliance by trial judges and the media with the requirements of Section 218 of the Judiciary Law;
5. The effect of audio-visual coverage on the conduct of trial judges both inside and outside the courtroom.[4]

As the Committee began its work, it quickly became apparent that it would not be writing on a blank slate. Except for one year during which the experiment was allowed to lapse, cameras have been present in the trial courts of New York State since 1987. Three prior reports had recommended that the state's "cameras in the courts" law be made permanent. A majority of states permit cameras in their trial courts in both civil and criminal proceedings. The U.S. Judicial Conference ended its experiment with cameras in federal civil cases in 1994 and federal law continues to prohibit cameras in federal criminal cases.

Many of the arguments presented to this Committee were presented to prior Committees. Camera proponents, for instance, assert that cameras educate the public about the courts, enhance public scrutiny of the judicial branch of government, improve the quality of justice by discouraging perjury and encouraging knowledgeable witnesses to step forward, increase the accuracy of news reporting about the courts, and help some crime victims or their survivors come to terms with their tragedy.

On the other hand, camera opponents assert that the educational benefits of camera coverage are slight, given the focus of camera coverage, for the most part, on cases involving violent crime, which are frequently depicted in brief segments on the evening news. They further argue that fear of publicity discourages rape and other sexual assault victims from reporting these serious crimes, and that televised coverage of trials affects the fairness of the trial itself, by deterring witnesses from coming forward, by affecting the demeanor and credibility of witnesses who may be intimidated by the presence of cameras, and by creating a danger that hearsay from television news reports and commentary

---

[4] Judiciary Law § 218(9)(c).

will creep into the public consciousness and prejudice potential or actual members of the jury.

Over the course of a 10-month period, the Committee sought to collect information from a wide variety of sources that might shed light on these arguments and concerns. The Committee reached out to every part of the legal community. The Committee's methodology, a summary of the statute and the rules which govern cameras in New York State courts, a short survey of comparable laws across the country, and a detailed overview of the record the Committee has compiled are set forth in sections II through V of this report. The Committee's assessment of the record and its recommendations are set forth in sections VI and VII.

II
Overview of the Committee's Work

The Committee met for the first time on June 25, 1996.[1] The Committee held seven meetings and its members conferred frequently throughout the course of its work. Faced with the challenge created by the absence of any significant funding to discharge its responsibilities, the Committee developed a work plan which sought to take maximum advantage of the *pro bono* resources available to it.

The Committee designed and conducted a written survey to assess the experience of New York judges with cameras in the courtroom.[2] It contacted the Marist Institute for Public Opinion, which agreed to survey public opinion in New York on the issue of cameras in the courtroom.[3] In fulfillment of its statutory mandate to "request participation and assistance from the New York State Bar Association and other bar associations," the Committee wrote to the presidents and executive directors of 150 bar associations in New York, asking for information about the experience of their members with respect to each of the issues the Legislature had directed the Committee to study. In a further effort to reach lawyers with experience trying cases in which cameras were present, the Committee contacted the New York Law Journal, which agreed, as a public service, to run a prominent notice of the Committee's interest in receiving public comment.[4]

---

[1] As of that date, only seven of the 12 members of the Committee had been appointed: Committee Chair John D. Feerick and Hon. Fritz W. Alexander by the Chief Judge, Monte Trammer and Professor James Tien by the Majority Leader of the Senate, Diane Kennedy by the Minority Leader of the Senate, and Leonard Noisette and Alissa Pollitz Worden by the Speaker of the Assembly. As the Committee approached its full complement of members, it decided to open its meetings to the public. Each public meeting was announced in a press release issued by Fordham University's Office of Public Affairs.

[2] The results of the judicial survey are included in Appendix A. The data base for the judicial survey was designed on a *pro bono* basis for the Committee by Professor Edmund Mantell of Pace University's Lubin School of Business, who also performed the statistical analysis of the 351 responses to the survey.

[3] The results of the Marist poll are included in Appendix B.

[4] The notice ran on more than half a dozen occasions, beginning in mid-December 1996 and ending in late January 1997.

Between October 29, 1996 and December 17, 1996, the Committee held four day-long public hearings—two in New York City, one in Albany and one in Rochester—and a shorter public hearing in New York City on February 27, 1997.[5] Each public hearing was announced by a press release, which reiterated the Committee's interest in receiving public comment and which was sent to the Associated Press Daybook, Reuters News Service, UPI, the New York Law Journal, CNN, and New York's daily newspapers.[6] Over fifty witnesses, including representatives of the print and electronic media, civil and criminal trial lawyers who had participated in televised trials, judges, crime victim advocates, law enforcement officials, media scholars, and jurors, testified at the Committee's hearings. In addition, the Committee received numerous communications and letters commenting on the "cameras in the courts" law,[7] a number of which appeared to have been inspired by newspaper coverage of the Committee's hearings.

To understand more fully what kinds of proceedings television cameras covered and what information about the judicial process was conveyed to the public, the Committee sought data from the New York State Office of Court Administration describing the number and kinds of proceedings for which permission to televise was sought and detailing the frequency with which media appli-

---

[5] Transcripts of the Committee's public hearings are on file at Fordham University School of Law and will be available for review in the New York Public Library, the library of the Association of the Bar of the City of New York and the New York State Library in Albany. Throughout this report, these transcripts are referred to as follows: the public hearing in New York City on October 29, 1996 is cited as "NYC-I." The public hearing in New York City on November 12, 1996 is cited as "NYC-II." The public hearing in Albany on November 14 and the public hearing in Rochester on December 17, 1996 are cited, respectively, as "Albany" and "Rochester." The public hearing in New York on February 27, 1997 is cited as "NYC-III."

[6] In addition, the press advisory for the Committee's first public hearing in New York City on October 29, 1996 was also sent through Business Wire, which distributed the advisory to media outlets and daily newspapers throughout New York State. Releases for subsequent public hearings and for the Committee's public meetings were also distributed to broadcast and major print outlets in specific media markets (New York City, Albany, Rochester) where meetings were held. Altogether, Fordham University's Office of Public Affairs prepared and distributed 8 media advisories to publicize the Committee's meetings and public hearings.

[7] Copies of the written public comments sent to the Committee are on file at Fordham Law School.

cations were granted or denied.[8] The Committee also invited television stations around the state to provide samples of their televised courtroom footage to the Committee.[9]

To give the Committee a national perspective on this issue, a team of Fordham law students gathered information on "cameras in the court" laws in the 50 states (including California, which recently undertook a comprehensive review of its own "cameras" law)[10], and collected information about the federal "cameras in the courtroom" pilot project. They also reviewed both the principal decisions of the U.S. Supreme Court on this issue and the legal and psycho-social literature in this field.[11]

The Committee wrote to the deans of all of the law schools in New York State to determine to what extent televised footage from New York cases is used in the classroom and in continuing legal education programs for practicing attorneys. The Committee also wrote to eleven jury consultants to seek information about their experience with the impact of cameras in the courtroom on jurors and other trial participants.[12]

Finally, the Committee conferred informally with media scholars, trial and appellate state court judges from New York and around the country, federal judges who had experience with the federal pilot "cameras in the court" program (including two judges from the U.S. District Court for the Southern District of New York and the former chair of the U.S. Judicial Conference's Executive Committee), camera-experienced trial lawyers in New York State and elsewhere, and a wide variety of organizations,

---

[8] Data from the Office of Court Administration on news media applications for camera coverage is summarized in Appendix H.

[9] COURT-TV, WRGB-TV in Albany, and R-NEWS and WOKR-TV in Rochester responded to the Committee's request.

[10] A table prepared for the Defense Research Institute, which summarizes the camera coverage laws of the 50 states based on information compiled by the Radio And Television News Directors Association, is included in Appendix F. See also Christo Lassiter, *An Annotated Descriptive Summary of State Statutes, Judicial Codes, Canons, and Court Rules Relating to Admissibility and Governance of Cameras in the Courtroom*, 86 Journal of Criminal Law & Criminology 1019 (1996).

[11] A short bibliography of the legal and psycho-social literature on cameras in the courtroom, together with a short list of the principal organizations which supplied background information to the Committee on camera coverage laws in other states, is included in Appendix K.

[12] A memorandum summarizing the jury consultants' responses is included in Appendix G.

ranging from the Courtroom Television Network to the Radio and Television News Directors Association, and from the New York State Bar Association and New York State Defenders Association to the New York State Coalition Against Sexual Assault.

III
Summary of Current Law

A. SECTION 218 OF THE JUDICIARY LAW

Cameras in the courts of New York are governed by the provisions of Section 218 of the Judiciary Law.[1] Compared to the governing law in most states, New York's camera coverage law is quite detailed.[2]

1. JUDICIAL DISCRETION

Section 218 gives trial judges discretion to permit audio-visual coverage of civil and criminal court proceedings upon application by the news media.[3] A judge's decision to grant or deny the news media's request for camera coverage must be in writing and must contain both a list of any restrictions imposed by the judge on camera coverage and a warning to all parties that any violation of the order is punishable by contempt.[4] The judge must also review his or her restrictions and warnings with counsel and with the news media in a pre-trial conference.[5]

The statute identifies five factors which trial judges must take into account when ruling on an application for camera coverage:

1. The type of case involved;
2. Whether the coverage would cause harm to any participant in the case or otherwise interfere with the fair ad-

---

[1] A copy of § 218 of the Judiciary Law is included in Appendix C.

[2] New York's law is also unusual in that cameras in the courts in most states are governed not by statute but by rules of court or codes of judicial conduct.

[3] Judiciary Law § 218(3)(a) & (b). Under § 218(3)(a), requests for audio-visual coverage must be made in writing "not less than seven days before the commencement of the judicial proceeding." The statute, however, allows some leeway in applying the 7-day notice provision. According to 218(3)(a), "where circumstances are such that an applicant cannot reasonably apply seven or more days before the commencement of the proceeding, the presiding trial judge may shorten the time period for requests."

[4] *Id.*, § 218(3)(b).

[5] *Id.*, § 218(4)(b).

ministration of justice, the advancement of a fair trial, or the rights of the parties;
3. Whether any order directing the exclusion of witnesses from the courtroom prior to their testimony could be rendered substantially ineffective by allowing audio-visual coverage that could be viewed by such witnesses to the detriment of any party;
4. Whether such coverage would interfere with any law enforcement activity;
5. Whether such coverage would involve lewd or scandalous matters.[6]

Absent from the list of factors which the judge is specifically directed to consider are any objections raised to the prospect of camera coverage by the parties, their lawyers, their witnesses, or members of the jury. Instead, Section 218(5) provides that "audio-visual coverage of judicial proceedings, except for arraignments and suppression hearings, shall not be limited by the objection of counsel, parties, or jurors, except for a finding of good or legal cause." However, as described in the following section of this report, the implementing regulations promulgated by the Chief Administrative Judge make it clear that, before deciding whether or not to admit cameras, judges must consider the "objections of any of the parties, prospective witnesses, victims or other participants in the proceeding of which coverage is sought."[7]

The exercise of judicial discretion is not limited to the initial decision to permit camera coverage. The statute is clear that "throughout the proceeding," the trial judge has discretion to revoke his or her approval or to limit coverage and "may, where appropriate, exercise such discretion to limit, restrict or prohibit audio or video broadcast or photography of any part of the proceeding in the courtroom, or of the name or features of any participant" in the proceeding.[8] In other words, a judge may decide, in the midst of a trial, to remove cameras from the courtroom or

---

[6] *Id.*, § 218(3)(c).
[7] New York Court Rules, § 131.4(c)(7).
[8] Judiciary Law § 218(7). See also *id.*, § 218(4)(c)("there shall be no limitation on the exercise of discretion under this subdivision except as provided by law. The presiding trial judge may at any time modify or reverse any prior order or determination").

to bar coverage of any witness or exhibit, even if he or she had previously granted permission for coverage.

2. Safeguards for Defendants in Criminal Proceedings and Parties in Civil Proceedings

The statute contains a number of safeguards aimed at protecting the fair trial rights of criminal defendants. Cameras are currently not permitted at arraignments and suppression hearings[9] without the consent of all parties to the proceeding. Defendants who are unrepresented by counsel at the time of the arraignment or suppression hearing cannot consent to camera coverage unless they have been advised of their right to counsel and have affirmatively elected to proceed without counsel at the arraignment or suppression hearing.[10]

Section 218 also contains a number of provisions that limit camera coverage of certain aspects of both criminal and civil trials which take place outside the purview of the jury. For instance, Section 218 prohibits audio pickup and broadcast of discussions between attorneys and their clients and between attorneys and the judge at sidebar. It also prohibits audiovisual coverage of conferences which take place in the judge's chambers.[11]

A judge may not permit camera coverage of either civil or criminal trials if the request is made after the trial has begun, unless counsel for all parties consent to the coverage.[12] An exception has been carved out for requests to cover verdicts and sentencings, which may be granted without the parties' consent.[13]

Finally, the statute expressly provides that "no judicial proceeding shall be scheduled, delayed, reenacted or continued at the request of, or for the convenience of, the news media."[14]

3. Safeguards for Witnesses

Section 218 contains a number of safeguards designed to protect the privacy of witnesses and to encourage witnesses to come for-

---

[9] "Suppression hearings" are broadly defined to include a hearing on a motion made pursuant to § 710.20 of the Criminal Procedure Law, as well as "a hearing on a motion to determine the admissibility of any prior criminal, vicious or immoral acts of a defendant and *any other hearing held to determine the admissibility of evidence.*" Judiciary Law § 218(2)(g) (emphasis added).
[10] *Id.*, § 218(5)(b) & (7)(h).
[11] *Id.*, § 218(7)(a) & (b).
[12] *Id.*, § 218(3)(d).
[13] *Id.*
[14] *Id.*, § 218(7)(I).

ward who might otherwise be reluctant to appear on camera. In criminal (but not in civil) cases, non-party witnesses[15] are entitled to request that their image be "visually obscured"[16] during their testimony—such as with the use of a so-called blue dot.[17] If a witness makes such a request, the statute directs the judge to order the news media "to visually obscure the visual image of the witness in any and all audio-visual coverage of the judicial proceeding."[18] In both civil and criminal proceedings, the judge is further empowered to bar audio-visual coverage if he or she finds that "such coverage is liable to endanger the safety of any person."[19]

New York does not exclude sexual assault cases from camera coverage. It provides a safeguard for the privacy of the complaining witness in a rape case by excluding audio-visual coverage of the victim (unless the victim requests such coverage) and by giving the judge discretion, throughout the proceeding, "to limit any coverage that would identify the victim" in a prosecution for rape, sodomy, sexual abuse, or other sex offense. . . ."[20] Alternately, the victim may request that his or her testimony be filmed but that his or her image be visually obscured by the news media.[21]

New York's statute also contains safeguards aimed at protecting those involved in covert or undercover police operations. Audio-visual coverage is not permitted of covert or undercover witnesses without their prior written consent.[22]

---

[15] A "nonparty witness" is defined by § 218(2)(h) as "any witness in a criminal trial proceeding who is not a party to the proceeding; except an expert or professional witness, a peace or police officer who acted in the course of his or her duties and was not acting in a covert or undercover capacity in connection with the instant court proceeding, or any government official acting in an official capacity shall not be deemed to be a 'nonparty witness'."

[16] "Visually obscured" is defined by the statute to mean that "the face of a participant in a criminal trial proceeding shall either not be shown or shall be rendered visually unrecognizable to the viewer of such proceeding by means of special editing by the news media." Judiciary Law § 218(2)(I).

[17] Judiciary Law § 218(5)(c). Counsel to each party in a criminal case is charged with the duty to advise each non-party witness of their right to request that their image be visually obscured. Id. Counsel are also charged with conveying to the judge at the mandatory pre-trial conference any prospective witnesses' concerns about camera coverage. Id., § 218(4)(b).

[18] Id.

[19] Id., § 218(7)(j).

[20] Judiciary Law § 218(7)(g).

[21] Id.

[22] Id., § 218(7)(e) & (f). The importance of these safeguards was underscored by New York City Police Commissioner Howard Safir in his letter to the Com-

4. Safeguards for Children

Unlike states which specifically exempt divorce and child custody proceedings from camera coverage, New York does not automatically bar camera coverage of domestic relations matters or other cases involving children. However, Section 218 directs the trial judge in any case involving "lewd or scandalous matters" to prohibit audio-visual coverage where necessary "to preserve the welfare of a minor."[23] Section 218 further prohibits camera coverage of any proceedings which by law are closed to the public or which have been closed to the public.[24] This covers many matters which are heard in Family Court, where judges have broad discretion to exclude the public from the courtroom.[25]

5. Safeguards for Jurors

Section 218 prohibits coverage of the selection of the jury.[26] It further prohibits coverage of the jury or of any juror or alternate juror while in the jury box, in the courtroom, in the jury deliberation room during recess, or while going to or from the deliberation room.[27] However, with the consent of the jury's foreperson, the presiding judge may, in his or her discretion, permit audio coverage of the delivery of the verdict.[28]

6. Other Safeguards

Section 218 contains a variety of other safeguards. For instance, in a criminal case, it specifically bars coverage of any family members of a victim or of a party, except when the family member is testifying. Camera personnel are required to make "reasonable efforts" to identify family members so that coverage can be avoided.[29]

---

mittee dated January 24, 1997 ("any audio-visual coverage of . . . undercover officers during court proceedings would potentially threaten their safety and have a chilling effect on their continued ability to investigate criminal activity").

[23] *Id.*, § 218(4)(a).
[24] *Id.*, § 218(7)(k).
[25] *See, e.g.*, 22 NYCRR § 205.4 (authorizing family court judge to exclude any person or the general public from a proceeding in Family Court); *see also* Family Court Act, § 433 (authorizing court to exclude the public from the courtroom).
[26] Judiciary Law § 218(7)(c).
[27] *Id.*, § 218(7)(d).
[28] *Id.*
[29] *Id.*, § 218(7)(l).

Where court proceedings involve "lewd or scandalous matters," Section 218 permits the judge to prohibit audio-visual coverage of any trial participant, a minor, or an exhibit if such a prohibition is needed to "protect any participant or to preserve the welfare of a minor."[30]

7. Pretrial Conference

The statute requires the presiding trial judge to hold a pretrial conference in each case in which camera coverage of the proceeding has been approved.[31] At that conference, the judge must review with the lawyers in the case and the members of the news media the restrictions on camera coverage which she or he intends to impose. Lawyers for the parties are required to convey to the judge any concerns that a prospective witness may have about the prospect of camera coverage of his or her testimony.

8. Equipment and Personnel Restrictions

The statute contains detailed restrictions on the number of cameras and camera-operating personnel who may be present in the courtroom.[32] For instance, no more than two electronic or motion picture cameras and no more than one audio system is permitted, although the statute also gives judges the power to modify these restrictions in "special circumstances."[33] Various broadcasters must enter into "pooling arrangements" and establish procedures for "cost sharing and dissemination of audio-visual material."[34]

The statute also contains detailed restrictions on the type of lighting and sound equipment which may be used in the courtroom. Motorized drives, for instance, are not permitted and only electronic cameras, still cameras, and audio equipment that do not produce distracting sounds or light may be used in court.[35] The judge is required to designate where the cameras, equipment, and

---

[30] *Id.*, § 218(4)(a).
[31] *Id.*, § 218(4)(b).
[32] *Id.*, § 218(6)(a).
[33] *Id.*, § 218(6)(a)(I), (iii) & (iv).
[34] *Id.*, § 218(6)(a)(v). In making these pooling arrangements, "consideration shall be given to educational users' needs for full coverage of entire proceedings." *Id.*
[35] *Id.*, § 218(6)(b).

personnel are to be positioned.[36] Camera personnel are directed not to move about the courtroom or change camera film and lenses except during recesses in the proceeding.[37]

9. Appeals

Section 218(3)(b) of the Judiciary Law provides that an order "for initial access" may be reviewed only by the administrative judge.[38] No further judicial review is available during the pendency of the proceeding.[39]

B. RULES OF THE CHIEF ADMINISTRATIVE JUDGE

Pursuant to Section 218(10) of the Judiciary Law, the Chief Administrative Judge has promulgated rules implementing the state's "cameras in the courts" statute.[40] As the rules make clear, they have two purposes: to comport first "with the legislative finding that an enhanced understanding of the judicial system is important in maintaining a high level of public confidence in the judiciary" and, second, "with the legislative concern that cameras in the court be compatible with the fair administration of justice."[41]

The rules specifically state that "nothing in these rules is intended to restrict the power and the discretion of the presiding trial judge to control the conduct of judicial proceedings."[42] Judges are reminded that in addition to their specific responsibilities under the rules, they must take "whatever steps are necessary to insure that audio-visual coverage is conducted without disruption of court activities, without detracting from or interfering with the dignity or decorum of the court, courtrooms and court facilities, without compromise of the safety of persons having

---

[36] *Id.*, § 218(6)(c).
[37] *Id.*, § 218(6)(d).
[38] *Id.*, § 218(3)(b). *See also New York Times v. Bell*, 135 A.D.2d 182, 523 N.Y.S.2d 807 (1st Dep't 1988) (trial judge's denial of application for camera coverage reviewable by administrative judge, not under CPLR Article 78). But see *P.B. v. C.C.*, 223 A.D.2d 294, 647 N.Y.S.2d 732 (1st Dep't 1996) and *In re Reuben R.*, 219 A.D.2d 117, 641 N.Y.S.2d 621 (1996) (reversing Family Court order denying motion to exclude press and public from courtroom).
[39] *Id.*, § 218(3)(b).
[40] N.Y. Court Rules, Part 131. A copy of the implementing rules is included in Appendix D.
[41] N.Y. Court Rules, § 131.1(a).
[42] *Id.*, § 131.1(d).

business before the court, and without adversely affecting the administration of justice."[43]

For the most part, the implementing rules track the language of Section 218 itself. However, in certain specific instances, the rules provide additional guidance to judges. For instance, the rules make it clear that if a crime victim, a prospective witness, a party, or a child objects to camera coverage, the judge may hold a conference and "conduct any direct inquiry as may be fitting"[44] before ruling on the application for camera coverage.

With respect to the factors to be considered by the presiding judge in deciding whether or not to grant an application for camera coverage, the rules elaborate upon the statutory factors by identifying three additional factors judges must take into account, along with "all relevant factors":

1. The objections of any of the parties, prospective witnesses, victims, or other participants in the proceeding of which coverage is sought;
2. The physical structure of the courtroom and the likelihood that any equipment required to conduct coverage of proceedings can be installed and operated without disturbance to those proceedings or any other proceedings in the courthouse;
3. The extent to which the coverage would be barred by law in the judicial proceeding of which coverage is sought.[45]

In addition, the judge is specifically directed by the rules to "consider and give great weight to the fact that any party, prospective witness, victim or other participant in the proceeding is a child."[46]

The rules also contain a provision directing judges to consider alternatives to denying an application for coverage. Before denying an application, the judge shall consider "whether such coverage properly could be approved with the imposition of special limitations," including, but not limited to:

1. Delayed broadcasting of the proceedings, which is available "only for the purpose of assisting the news media to

---

[43] *Id.*, § 131.1(f).
[44] *Id.*, § 131.4(a).
[45] *Id.*, § 131.4(c)(7), (8) & (9).
[46] *Id.*, § 131.4(c).

comply with the restrictions on coverage provided by law or by the presiding trial judge;"[47]
2. "Modification or prohibition of audio-visual coverage of individual parties, witnesses, or other trial participants, or portions of the proceedings;"
3. "Modification or prohibition of video coverage of individual parties, witnesses or other trial participants, or portions of the proceedings."[48]

The rules contain several other salient features. First, the rules spell out what is to occur at the mandatory pretrial conference. The rules make it clear that the purpose of the pretrial conference is to review with the parties' lawyers and with media representatives "any objections to coverage that have been raised, the scope of the coverage to be permitted, the nature and extent of the technical equipment to be deployed, and the restrictions on coverage to be observed."[49] The rules remind judges that they may include in the conference any person they deem appropriate, including "prospective witnesses and their representatives."[50]

Second, the rules emphasize the judge's continuing duty to supervise audio-visual coverage throughout the course of the proceedings. No camera coverage, for instance, is permitted in the courtroom "when the trial judge is not present and presiding."[51] The rules reiterate that the presiding trial judge "shall have discretion throughout [the] proceedings to revoke [his or her] approval or limit the coverage authorized in any way."[52] In this regard, the rules instruct trial judges to be

> especially sensitive and responsive to the needs and concerns of all parties, victims, witnesses and participants in such proceedings, particularly where the proceedings unnecessarily threaten the privacy or sensibilities of victims, or where they involve children or sex offenses or other matters that may be lewd or scandalous.[53]

The rules place the judge under "a continuing obligation to order the discontinuation or modification of coverage where necessary

---

[47] *Id.*, § 131.4(e)(1).
[48] *Id.*, § 131.4(e).
[49] *Id.*, § 131.6(a).
[50] *Id.*, § 131.6(a).
[51] *Id.*, § 131.9(a).
[52] *Id.*, § 131.9(b).
[53] *Id.*, § 131.9(b).

to shield the identity or otherwise insure the protection of any such person, party, witness or victim, or in order to preserve the welfare of a child."[54]

Third, the rules emphasize the lawyers' obligation to find out whether any of the witnesses they intend to call have any "concerns or objections" about camera coverage. If a witness objects, the lawyer is required to notify the presiding trial judge.[55]

Fourth, the rules make it clear that either the news media applicant or a party, victim, or prospective witness who has objected to camera coverage may seek review by the administrative judge of "any order determining an application for permission to provide [camera] coverage."[56] The administrative judge is directed to uphold the order unless it "reflects an abuse of discretion by the presiding trial judge."[57] The rules further clarify that only the presiding trial judge's initial order is subject to review by the administrative judge. Other orders or decisions of the trial judge relating to camera coverage are not reviewable at this stage in the proceeding.[58]

Finally, the rules identify the types of audio-visual equipment which may be used in a courtroom and prescribe a standard application form for camera coverage and a standard order for ruling on those applications.[59]

---

[54] *Id.*, § 131.9(b).
[55] *Id.*, § 131.9(c).
[56] *Id.*, § 131.5(a).
[57] *Id.*, § 131.5(b).
[58] *Id.*, § 131.5(d).
[59] N.Y. Ct. Rules, Part 131 Forms and §§ 131.12 & 131.13.

IV

Overview of Camera Coverage Laws in Other States and in Federal Courts

Before considering in detail the record developed by this Committee regarding the operation of Section 218, we turn next to a brief overview of the "cameras in the courts" laws in New York's sister states and in the federal court system.

A. STATE COURTS

1. 50-STATE OVERVIEW

Across the country, cameras in the courtroom are governed by a patchwork of statutes, court rules, and codes of judicial conduct. According to information collected by the Radio-Television News Directors Association, 47 states permit some form of television coverage of court proceedings.[1] In some states, coverage is severely limited. Illinois, Delaware, and Louisiana, for instance, permit coverage of appellate courts only, while Maryland and Pennsylvania limit trial coverage to civil cases.[2]

Thirty-seven states permit camera coverage of criminal trials without the consent of the defendant.[3] Thirty-nine states permit

---

[1] See Radio-Television News Directors Association, *News Media Coverage of Judicial Proceedings With Cameras and Microphones: A Survey of the States* (January 1997) (hereinafter "RTNDA Survey") at B-1. The Districts of Columbia, Indiana, Mississippi, and South Dakota do not permit camera coverage. *Id.* at B-2.

[2] RTNDA Survey at B-1, B-2. The Supreme Court of Louisiana recently declined to proceed with a proposal for camera coverage of trial court proceedings which was narrowly approved by its Taskforce to Study Cameras in the Trial Courts of Louisiana. See Order, Supreme Court of Louisiana (Dec. 12, 1996).

[3] RTNDA Survey at B-2, B-10. Alabama, Arkansas, Minnesota, and Okla-

camera coverage of civil trials without the parties' consent.[4] A number of these states exclude certain types of proceedings from their camera coverage laws. Televised coverage of sex crimes, for instance, is excluded in whole or in part in fourteen states.[5] Fifteen states exclude child custody proceedings.[6] Fourteen states exclude divorce proceedings.[7]

2. CALIFORNIA

In the wake of the verdict in the O.J. Simpson criminal trial, California undertook a thorough re-examination of its cameras in the courts law. The Honorable Richard Huffman, Associate Justice of the California Court of Appeal, chaired the California Judicial Council's taskforce charged with re-assessing Rule 980 of California's Rules of Court concerning photographing, recording, and broadcasting in the courtroom. Justice Huffman testified at the Committee's November 12, 1996 hearing about California's experience.

Like this Committee, the California taskforce conducted a statewide survey of judges, solicited the views of many bar groups, hosted a public hearing, and received extensive public comment. It also surveyed public defenders and prosecutors and hosted an educational forum on cameras in the courts.[8]

---

homa require defendant's consent to televise a criminal trial. *Id.* On December 30, 1996, Tennessee removed its defendant consent requirement and committed the question of cameras in the courtroom to the discretion of the trial judge. See Tennessee Supreme Court Rule 30, reprinted in Administrative Office of the Courts, *Report on Cameras in the Courtroom Surveys* (Nov. 4, 1996) (Nashville, Tennessee).

[4] RTNDA Survey at B-13.

[5] *Id.* at B-23. New Jersey, for instance, prohibits camera coverage of proceedings involving "sexual penetration or attempted sexual penetration." *Id.* at A-57. See also New Jersey Supreme Court Guidelines for Still and Television Camera and Audio Coverage of Proceedings in the Courts of New Jersey, New Jersey Court Rules, Guideline 10(b)(1996). Camera coverage of sexual offenses is also prohibited in Connecticut and Virginia. *Id.* at A-17, A-82. See also Va. Code Ann. § 19.2.266 (1992).

[6] RTNDA Survey at B-20.

[7] *Id.* at B-21.

[8] The details of the taskforce's work are laid out in two memoranda from the Taskforce on Photographing, Recording and Broadcasting in the Courtroom to the members of the California Judicial Council: one dated February 16, 1996 and a second dated May 10, 1996. These are referred to below as the "February 16, 1996 California Memorandum" and the "May 10, 1996 California Memorandum" respectively. See May 10, 1996 California Memorandum at 6.

Although a majority of California judges proposed that cameras be barred from courtrooms,[9] judges with television camera experience tended to have more favorable views of cameras. Forty-three percent of camera-experienced judges believed that video cameras affect witness behavior, primarily by promoting guarded testimony or self-conscious, nervous behavior.[10] A large majority of prosecutors and public defenders advocated barring cameras altogether in Los Angeles County criminal cases, as did the representative of the Los Angeles County judiciary on the taskforce.[11]

The taskforce concluded that a total ban on cameras in the courtroom was inconsistent with the California Judicial Council's long-range goal of increasing public access to the courts.[12] According to the taskforce's preliminary report, "today's citizen relies too heavily on the electronic media for information; yet actual physical attendance at court proceedings is too difficult for the courts to countenance a total removal of the public's principal news source."[13]

Instead, the taskforce recommended a ban on coverage of pre-trial proceedings in criminal cases, including arraignments, bail hearings, preliminary hearings, jury selection, and pre-trial actions. It further recommended that in both criminal and civil trials, only those matters which were heard by the trier of fact be televised. These proposals were designed to limit camera access "where the potential for prejudice to the rights of the parties and the ability to influence potential jurors is the greatest."[14]

In the end, the California Judicial Council adopted a rule which left television camera access to both pre-trial and trial proceedings to the "unfettered discretion" of the trial judge.[15] The new Rule 980 provides that "this rule does not create a presumption for or against granting permission to photograph, record or broadcast court proceedings."[16]

In weighing an application for camera coverage, the new Cali-

---

[9] Testimony of Justice Richard Huffman, NYC-II at 137–38.
[10] February 16, 1996 California Memorandum at 24–25.
[11] NYC-II at 137–40.
[12] NYC-II at 140.
[13] February 16, 1996 California Memorandum at 10.
[14] *Id.* at 10–11; see also May 10, 1996 California Memorandum at 12–16 and testimony of Justice Richard Huffman (NYC-II at 146).
[15] NYC-II at 143.
[16] California Rule of Court 980 (a) (effective January 1, 1997). The full text of the new California rule is set forth in Appendix E.

fornia rule directs judges to consider a list of 18 specific factors, as well as any other factor the judge deems relevant.[17] These factors include, among others, the importance of promoting public access to and maintaining public trust and confidence in the judicial system, the parties' support of or opposition to the request for camera coverage, the privacy rights of all participants in the proceeding (including witnesses, jurors, and victims), the effect on any unresolved identification issues and on the parties' ability to select a fair and unbiased jury, the effect of coverage on the willingness of witnesses to cooperate, the difficulty of jury selection if a mistrial is declared, and the nature of the case.[18]

The new rule, which requires 5-day advance notice unless good cause is shown to shorten the time period,[19] includes bans on television coverage of jury selection, jurors, spectators, conferences between an attorney, client, witness, or aide, among attorneys, or between counsel and the judge at the bench.[20] The rule also defines "court" expansively to include not only the courtroom where the televised trial takes place but the courthouse and its entrances and exits, giving judges leeway to regulate cameras in the hallways.[21]

B. FEDERAL COURTS

In contrast with the law in the majority of state courts, federal law prohibits camera coverage of federal criminal proceedings.[22] A narrow exception to this rule was created in 1996 with the passage of the Anti-Terrorism and Effective Death Penalty Act. In order to permit crime victims to watch federal criminal trial proceedings where, as in the Oklahoma bombing case, the trial

---

[17] Rule 980(e)(3).

[18] *Id.*

[19] Rule 980(e)(1). This same provision requires the clerk to "promptly notify the parties that a request has been filed."

[20] Rule 980(e)(6).

[21] Rule 980(b)(3).

[22] Federal Rule of Criminal Procedure 53 provides that "[t]he taking of photographs in the court room during the progress of judicial proceedings or radio broadcasting of judicial proceedings from the court room shall not be permitted by the court." As the RTNDA Survey notes, "by its terms, Rule 53 does not explicitly proscribe television broadcasting, but courts have interpreted it as banning television coverage." See, e.g., *United States v. Hastings,* 695 F.2d 1278, 1279, n.5 (11th Cir. 1983). RTNDA Survey at 4, n.3.

has been moved more than 350 miles out of state, the new federal law requires a trial judge to order closed circuit televising of the proceedings.[23]

On the civil side, the U.S. Judicial Conference ended a three-year pilot project with cameras in the courtroom in September 1994. By a 2-1 majority, the Judicial Conference concluded that "the intimidating effect of cameras on some witnesses and jurors was cause for serious concern."[24] Some members further concluded that "any negative impact on witnesses or jurors could be a threat to the fair administration of justice."[25]

The question of cameras in civil cases in federal courts did not end, however, with the Judicial Conference decision. In March 1996, U.S. District Court Judge Robert J. Ward of the Southern District of New York granted a motion by Court TV to televise a March 4, 1996 oral argument on plaintiff's motion for class certification and defendants' partial motion to dismiss in *Marisol v. Giuliani*, a class action lawsuit brought on behalf of foster children against New York City's child welfare agency.[26] Judge Ward noted that the public interest would be served by granting the application and held that the policy of the Judicial Conference does not supplant the local rules of the Southern District of New York, which give judges discretion to allow cameras in the court.[27]

In April 1996, U.S. District Court Judge Robert W. Sweet granted a similar motion by Court TV to televise a May 1, 1996

---

[23] See Public Law 104–132, approved September 30, 1996 and codified at 42 U.S.C.A. § 10608 (West 1996). The statute makes clear that "no public broadcast or dissemination shall be made of the signal transmitted," which may be viewed only by "persons specifically designated by the court," including "such persons the court determines have a compelling interest in doing so and are otherwise unable to do so by reason of the inconvenience and expense caused by the change of venue." 42 U.S.C.A. § 10608(a)(2), (b)(1) & (c)(2).

[24] See Memorandum from L. Ralph Mecham, Director of the Administrative Office of the United States Courts to All Judges, United States Courts (Sept. 22, 1994).

[25] *Id.* (emphasis in original). See also Molly Treadway Johnson & Carol Krafka, *Electronic Media Coverage of Federal Civil Proceedings: An Evaluation of the Pilot Program in Six District Courts and Two Courts of Appeal* at 14 (Federal Judicial Center 1994). The FJC study, whose recommendations in favor of cameras in civil proceedings were rejected by the U.S. Judicial Conference, was based, in part, on the responses of 41 federal judges who experienced camera coverage under the pilot program.

[26] 929 F. Supp. 660 (S.D.N.Y. 1996).

[27] *Id.* at 661.

oral pre-trial argument in *Katzman v. Victoria's Secret Catalogue*.[28] Like Judge Ward, Judge Sweet found authority in the local district court rules to allow cameras in the court.[29]

Following Judge Ward's decision in the *Marisol* case, the Judicial Conference strongly urged each federal circuit court's judicial council to adopt orders reflecting the September 1994 decision not to permit electronic media coverage of district court proceedings.[30] The Judicial Conference further urged each circuit to abrogate any local rules of court that conflicted with the prohibition on cameras in the trial courts.[31] At the same time, the Judicial Conference approved a resolution allowing each circuit court to decide whether or not to allow cameras in appellate proceedings.[32]

At its June 1996 meeting, the Second Circuit Council took no action to change local rules regarding cameras in the court.[33] Since then, at least two other federal district court judges in New York—Judge Peter K. Leisure in the Southern District of New York and Judge Jack B. Weinstein in the Eastern District of New York—have granted permission to televise civil proceedings.[34]

Judge Gilbert Merritt of the U.S. Court of Appeals for the Sixth Circuit chaired the Executive Committee of the U.S. Judicial

---

[28] 923 F. Supp. 580 (S.D.N.Y. 1996).

[29] *Id.* at 583–85.

[30] *See* Press Release from the Administrative Office of the U.S. Courts (March 12, 1996).

[31] *Id.*

[32] *Id.* The Judicial Conference took no vote on whether the resolution to permit the broadcast of appellate proceedings applied to criminal appeals. See Summary of the Report of the Judicial Conference Committee on Court Administration and Case Management, Agenda F-7 at 5 (September 1996). While some judges thought that Federal Rule of Criminal Procedure 53 prohibited the broadcasting of criminal appeals, others thought that the Judicial Conference left the decision to each circuit. *Id.* To date, the Second and the Ninth Circuit Courts have authorized cameras in appellate courts. See Press Release from the Second Judicial Circuit of the United States (March 27, 1996) (allowing camera coverage for all proceedings in open court, except for criminal matters); Press Release from the Ninth Judicial Circuit of the United States (March 22, 1996) (allowing camera coverage of appellate arguments in all cases except direct criminal appeals and extradition proceedings; coverage also permitted in habeas corpus and death penalty appeals).

[33] Deborah Pines, Circuit Court Leaves Camera Rule Intact, N.Y. L. J., June 14, 1996 at 1.

[34] See *Sigmon v. Parker Chapin Flattau & Klimpl*, 937 F. Supp. 335 (S.D.N.Y. 1996), and *Hamilton v. Accu-Tek*, 942 F. Supp. 136 (E.D.N.Y. 1996).

Conference during the federal pilot program. He informed the Chair of this Committee that although he has serious reservations about televising criminal cases, he personally would like to see the federal courts open to cameras in civil cases, provided that guidelines could be developed that would inhibit so-called "soundbite" coverage, which he views as counterproductive in educational terms.

V
Summary of the Committee's Record

As set forth in the Introduction, the Committee was directed to issue a report to the Legislature, the Governor, and the Chief Judge evaluating five specific aspects of "cameras in the courtroom" in New York State. The Committee was asked to review the efficacy of the program and assess whether:

1. Any public benefits accrue from the experimental program;
2. Any abuses occurred during the program;
3. The extent to which and the way in which the conduct of participants in court proceedings changes when audio-visual coverage is present;
4. The degree of compliance by trial judges and the media with the requirements of Section 218 of the Judiciary Law;
5. The effect of audio-visual coverage on the conduct of trial judges both inside and outside the courtroom.

This section of the report summarizes the information gathered by the Committee on these subjects.

A. PUBLIC BENEFITS

As set forth below, the Committee heard from a wide array of witnesses about a broad range of public benefits that flow from cameras in the courtroom. Proponents of cameras in the courtroom informed the Committee that cameras help educate the public about the courts, allow for enhanced public scrutiny of the judicial system, foster judicial accountability, raise the level of judicial conduct, enhance the quality of justice by discouraging perjury and encouraging knowledgeable witnesses to come forward, increase the accuracy of news reporting about the courts, and help some crime victims and their families come to terms with the tragedy they have experienced. This section provides a detailed summary of this facet of the Committee's record.

1. PUBLIC EDUCATION ABOUT THE COURTS

Heading the list of public benefits articulated by proponents of cameras in the courtroom is the view that cameras in the courtroom demystify the judicial system and allow the public to become better informed about courtroom procedures.[1] Martin O'Boyle, Chief of the New York City Police Department's Organized Crime Control Bureau, testified that cameras give the public a better understanding of the criminal justice system.[2] Thomas Moore, a plaintiff's malpractice attorney in New York City, stated that cameras in the courtroom "give an appreciation of the [American] judicial system."[3] Madeleine Schachter, who chairs the New York State Bar Association's Media Law Committee, emphasized in her testimony that cameras help funnel information about trials to large numbers of people, including cases which attract so much attention that there is not enough seating in the courtroom for all who might wish to attend.[4] Along the same

---

[1] *See* John Corporon, former news director, WPIX-TV (NYC-I at 151). See also letter from Doris Aiken, founder, RID ("Remove Intoxicated Drivers") (with the emergence of home cable channels devoted solely to live broadcasts of current cases, the general public now takes an interest in "everything from the initial voir dire to the final summation") (Nov. 20, 1996); testimony of Janet Dubin (television coverage of trials allows people to see what a juror's responsibility entails) (NYC-III at 53–54).

[2] NYC-II at 47. See also Bud Carey, general manager, WCBS-TV (NYC-II at 229) (camera coverage educates the public not just about a particular case, but about the justice system itself); Christopher Bruner, executive assistant news director, WNYT-TV (camera coverage dispels the Perry Mason image of trials; educates viewers about important emerging legal developments, such as the use of DNA evidence in a serial rape case) (Albany at 9–10); Hon. Howard Relin, Monroe County District Attorney (more people learn how real trials are conducted when cases are on television) (Rochester at 10); Hon. Patricia Marks, Supervising Judge, Criminal Courts, Seventh Judicial District (camera coverage familiarizes first-time jurors with court proceedings) (Rochester at 37–38); Judith Condo, director, Albany County Rape Crisis Center (camera coverage with current restrictions counteracts astounding lack of public information about the criminal courts) (Albany at 128); letter dated November 13, 1996 from Scott Karson, Esq., to John L. Juliano, president, Suffolk County Bar Association ("the policy behind the First Amendment, *i.e.* a well-informed public, is best served by permitting televised coverage of court proceedings").

[3] NYC-I at 169.

[4] NYC-II at 63–64. See also letter dated October 23, 1996 from Irwin S.

lines, Anthony Lewis of *The New York Times* wrote to the Committee on November 11, 1996 to say that, "cameras faithfully recording what is seen by jurors are far less likely to prejudice the legal process than much other journalism, and far more likely to educate citizens."

A similar view was articulated by the New York State Committee on Open Government, which, in its recent annual report, concluded that "with appropriate safeguards, the law authorizing the use of cameras in the courtroom should be made permanent" because "television, as a means of educating the public and promoting understanding of the judicial process, has significant potential value."[5]

Not only do cameras educate the public about the courts in general, say camera proponents, but they shed light on major societal problems. Judge Harold Rothwax, who presided over the Joel Steinberg trial, testified that cameras opened a "window into the whole area of child abuse."[6] Jeanne Mullgrav, director of court programs at the Victims Services Agency, testified that cameras in the courtroom educate the public about domestic violence and other problems formerly "swept under the rug"[7] and that the resulting exposure has helped speed the passage of legislation in the area of sexual assault and domestic violence.[8]

Surviving family members of homicide and drunk-driving victims were particularly outspoken on the issue of educational benefits. Patricia M. Gioia, chapter leader of the Capital District

---

Davison, executive director, New York County Lawyers Association (according to a report adopted by the Association's Board of Directors on February 14, 1994, "when compared with the way the public learns of cases in the print media, it seems certain that the public gets a more complete view of the judicial process when there is audio-visual coverage of trials, as opposed to mere articles in newspapers or reports by television news correspondents on the courthouse steps").

[5] New York State Committee on Open Government, Annual Report, p. 10 (December 1996). See also Committee for Modern Courts, "Citizens' Bill of Rights for the Court System," p. 2 (1997). The Chair of this Committee, John D. Feerick, also chairs the Committee for Modern Courts. He did not participate in the development of Modern Courts' policy statement, which predated his tenure. He also has recused himself from participating in Modern Courts' implementation of its policy.

[6] NYC-I at 11. See also Joseph Reilly, President, New York State Broadcasters Association (televising the Steinberg case helped expose "the horrors of domestic violence") (Albany at 143).

[7] NYC-I at 248.

[8] *Id.* at 254–55.

Chapter of Parents of Murdered Children & Other Survivors of Homicide Victims, informed the Committee that camera coverage "has created a heightened interest in the presentation by victims (or in cases where the victim is deceased, a family member) of an oral victim impact statement at the time of sentencing a convicted defendant." She noted that "when victims have seen—even if only through a small segment on the nightly television news—another family having the courage to give their impact [statement] before the [j]udge and jury, it is a morale builder and inspiration for them to do the same."[9]

Finally, the Committee surveyed the deans of New York State law schools to determine to what extent law schools use videotaped court proceedings for educational purposes. Ten law schools responded to the Committee's inquiry. Among the five schools which regularly used videotapes of court proceedings, tapes of New York State Court of Appeals arguments appear to have received the widest use. Several schools mentioned using Court TV videos of trial court proceedings, although it was not clear from the responses whether those materials involved New York state trials or trials which took place in other states. Those schools which made widespread use of videotaped court proceedings were enthusiastic about this material, noting that "tapes are wonderful teaching tools" and "serve an important educational value."[10]

Among the law schools not currently using videotapes of court

---

[9] See letter dated December 8, 1996 from Patricia M. Gioia. See also letter dated January 2, 1997 from Linda Campion ("cameras in the courtroom serve as a crucial educational tool to bring awareness of the criminal justice system proceedings and shed light on the rights of crime victims" including "the right of the victim to speak at sentencing"); Christopher Bruner, executive assistant news director, WNYT-TV (cameras record victim impact statements in drunk driving proceedings, which are no longer "dismissed with a wink") (Albany at 10); Carole Mulhern, Director of Victim and Witness Services, Monroe County District Attorney's Office (televised coverage of sentencings and victim impact statements lets crime victims know that they are entitled to have a say in the judicial process) (Rochester at 19); letter dated December 23, 1996 from Renee Barchitta, coordinator, Delaware County STOP-DWI Program (among other things, cameras in the courtroom address a "lack of knowledge of victims rights").

[10] See, e.g., letter dated October 30, 1996 from Daan Braveman, Dean, Syracuse University College of Law. But see letter dated February 19, 1997 from Richard L. Ottinger, Dean, Pace University School of Law (experienced trial practice teacher believes that videotapes of court proceedings "have very little educational value").

proceedings, several mentioned that they would be interested in making greater use of videotaped court proceedings if the materials were made as user-friendly as possible and tailored to the needs of the classroom instructor.[11]

2. JUDICIAL ACCOUNTABILITY AND PUBLIC SCRUTINY OF THE JUDICIAL SYSTEM

At the Committee's hearings and in their written comments, many shared the belief of Harry Rosenfeld, editor-at-large of the *Albany Times Union*, in the "overriding importance" of the principle of "opening government agencies to the fullest public scrutiny."[12] He added that "[o]f all the governmental agencies, it is our courts that require the most openness, because they directly touch the lives of all our people."[13]

Several criminal defense counsel testified that "justice is better served by opening the courtroom wide."[14] Terence Kindlon, a criminal defense lawyer in Albany, testified that when he served as an assistant public defender, he was "crushed like a bug" by judges "who pushed us around, limited our trial rights, and made it almost impossible to defend" unpopular clients.[15] He noted that that "really is something that doesn't happen when a camera is in the room." With a television audience looking over their shoulder, Kindlon testified, "everybody behaves. The defense lawyers behave better, the prosecutors behave better, the judges behave better and even the defendants behave better and the witnesses behave better."[16]

Along the same lines, criminal defense attorney Ira London, past president of the New York State Association of Criminal Defense Lawyers, noted that, in his view, "a courtroom devoid of spectators or observers is a courtroom where there is less attention to justice."[17] A similar view was expressed by criminal defense

---

[11] See, e.g., memorandum dated October 23, 1996 from Larry Grossberg to Harry Wellington, Dean, New York Law School.
[12] NYC-I at 198.
[13] *Id.* at 201.
[14] See testimony of Terence Kindlon, Esq. (Albany at 56).
[15] Albany at 45–46.
[16] *Id.* at 47, 66.
[17] NYC-II at 279. Mr. London was careful to point out that the professional association which he formerly headed opposes cameras in the courtroom without the consent of the defendant. *Id.* at 284.

lawyer John Condon of Buffalo in a telephone conference with the Chair of this Committee.

Several homicide victims' relatives also argued that public scrutiny of the judicial system is served by cameras in the courtroom. Patricia M. Gioia, chapter leader of the Capital District Chapter of Parents of Murdered Children & Other Survivors of Homicide Victims, wrote to the Committee:

> In former years when no coverage was available inside the courtroom, there was a greater tendency for pushing through plea bargains by district attorneys and defense attorneys, with absolutely no victim participation. Having a television camera available at the proceeding will better ensure that victims and their families are present not only at the trial but at any plea bargain that has been worked out.[18]

Similar views were stated by a number of journalists. "Widening the window of public scrutiny of judicial procedure is in and of itself an important ingredient of our democracy," said John Corporon, WPIX-TV's former news director.[19] His views were echoed by Professor Jay Wright of the S. I. Newhouse Communications Center at Syracuse University, who testified that cameras belong in the courtroom because "what happens in a trial is a public matter."[20]

Steven Brill, President, Courtroom Television Network, took issue with the criticisms of cameras in the courtroom based on the O. J. Simpson criminal trial. If "lots of lawyers and lots more judges feel that the verdict [in that case] made the system look bad," said Brill, "the system deserved to look bad. . . . It is ridiculous to criticize journalism because journalism covers a public function and makes it look bad. If the system looked bad in that

---

[18] Letter dated December 8, 1996. See also letter dated January 2, 1997 from Linda Campion ("cameras are needed in our courtrooms in DWI homicide cases as defense attorneys in some counties throughout the state are accustomed to making back door deals with little accountability and no visibility for their clients") and testimony of Linda Campion (Albany 135–40).

[19] NYC-I at 154.

[20] NYC-I at 79. See also testimony of New York State Supreme Court Justice Donald J. Wisner, Monroe County (he approves most applications for camera coverage "in keeping with the fact that the courts are open and we are about the public business") (Rochester at 139). For a different perspective see Don Hewitt, executive producer, *60 Minutes*, "Pencils, Yes; Cameras, No," *The New York Times*, June 20, 1996, Section A at 15; Nina Totenberg, legal affairs correspondent, *National Public Radio, Chicago Law Bulletin*, p. 1 (Oct. 10, 1996).

case, that is a benefit of cameras."[21] In a letter dated January 30, 1997, Laura R. Handman, Chair of the Committee on Communications and Media Law of the Association of the Bar of the City of New York, stated that:

> Blaming courtroom cameras for the systemic problems that the Simpson trial may have highlighted confuses the messenger with the message. Audio-visual coverage that raises questions about the effectiveness of the process—in the Simpson trial or elsewhere—is part of the solution, not the problem.

Finally, a plea for open courtrooms was made by Michael Posner, executive director of the Lawyers' Committee for Human Rights. Posner testified that if New York opens its courtrooms to cameras, it would provide an additional precedent which his organization and others could invoke in their efforts to open the courts of repressive regimes around the world to cameras and to official accountability.[22]

A sixty-three percent majority of the approximately 350 New York State judges who responded to the Committee's judicial survey agreed that television coverage fosters public scrutiny of judicial proceedings.[23] Twenty-five percent of responding judges agreed that television coverage had a positive effect on the state's criminal justice system.[24] Twenty percent of the 616 New York State registered voters surveyed by the Marist Institute for Public Opinion agreed that cameras in the courtroom had a positive effect on New York's justice system.[25]

3. Cathartic and Deterrent Effects

Based on testimony presented to the Committee, it appears that sentencings in criminal cases have become an important feature of television coverage of court proceedings. Hon. Patricia Marks, Supervising Judge of the Criminal Courts in the Seventh Judicial District, testified that most of the applications she has received

---

[21] NYC-II at 14. See also Committee for Modern Courts, "Citizens' Bill of Rights for the Court System," p. 2 (1997).
[22] NYC-II at 119.
[23] Judicial Survey, Question 4(e).
[24] *Id.* at Question 4(k).
[25] Marist poll, Question 5. 35% of black respondents, 36% of regular TV-trial watchers, 23% of men and 17% of women agreed that television cameras have a positive effect on New York's justice system.

from the media recently "have been for sentencing."[26] As part of her testimony, Judy Sanders, WRGB-TV's Albany news chief, aired a videotape of WRGB coverage of the sentencing of four local criminal cases. As she described the segments:

> In the first two, Albany County Court Judge Thomas Breslin uses the bench to teach two young men a message that their conduct is unacceptable to society. In the second two, families used the court system as a civilized forum in which to express their rage and confronted defendants who have committed crimes against their loved ones. These cases deal with important social issues that had strong impacts on their communities, and television was a compelling way in which to convey that.[27]

According to some Committee witnesses, coverage of sentencing lets the public know that the personal tragedies caused by the defendant are taken into account.[28] Aside from the cathartic effect of camera coverage, Joseph Kelner, past president of the New York State Trial Lawyers Association and the Association of Trial Lawyers of America, suggested that "televised trials have the potential power to deter viewers from criminal or wrongful acts" because "televised trials are living educational demonstrations relating to criminal and civil liability derived from illegal activities."[29] According to Thomas Neidl, an assistant public defender in Albany County, if "a parent or a young person see[s] a person as young as he standing before a court getting ten years, or two years for something, they might focus in and say, 'I could really go to jail if I do something.' "[30]

4. OTHER BENEFITS

Witnesses and others described a number of further benefits. Hon. Howard Relin, Monroe County District Attorney, testified that

---

[26] Rochester at 47. Although the Office of Court Administration does not require media applicants to specifically identify the type of proceeding for which coverage is sought, OCA's analysis of copies of the media applications which were forwarded to it during the period January 31, 1995 through September 1, 1996 suggests that requests to cover sentencings accounted for the second largest identifiable category of specific proceedings covered, following arraignments. See Appendix H, Table 7.
[27] Albany at 174.
[28] Testimony of Bud Carey, general manager, WCBS-TV (NYC-II at 228).
[29] Letter from Joseph Kelner, Esq. to the Committee (Dec. 20, 1996).
[30] Albany at 188–89. See also Steven Brill, president, Courtroom Television Network ("one of the bedrock purposes of the criminal justice system . . . is . . . the embarrassment of the guilty. That is part of what deterrence is all about") (NYC-II at 42).

camera coverage has prompted witnesses to come forward who did not realize the potential significance of their testimony until they saw a case on television.[31] It was also suggested to the Committee that witnesses are "more likely to overcome the temptation to perjure themselves in public proceedings" at which cameras are present.[32]

Others asserted that by allowing the public to see and hear for themselves the actual testimony of the witnesses and other trial participants, cameras allow news to be reported "with greater accuracy and insight."[33] Along these same lines, it was suggested that camera coverage helps the public understand and accept the outcome of controversial cases, including cases where defendants are acquitted or are given what might otherwise appear to be "light" sentences.[34]

The judges who responded to the Committee's survey were evenly divided on the question of whether cameras in the courtroom increase the accuracy of press coverage of judicial proceedings. Forty-seven percent of judges agreed that television coverage increases the accuracy of news accounts of judicial proceedings. Forty-seven percent of judges disagreed.[35] It is worth noting that, although only 23% of judges agreed that *televised nightly news* coverage of court proceedings accurately represents

---

[31] Rochester at 15. See also testimony of Paul Conti, news director, WNYT-TV (publicly reported testimony is capable of bringing forth witnesses to dispute or add to what has been presented) (Albany at 15). The U.S. Supreme Court has recognized that this is an important reason to keep courts open to the press generally. See *Richmond Newspapers, Inc. v. Virginia*, 448 U.S. 555 (1980).

[32] Testimony of Paul Conti, news director, WNYT-TV (Albany at 15).

[33] Testimony of Bud Carey, General Manager, WCBS-TV (NYC-II at 225–26). See also George Freeman, Assistant General Counsel, *The New York Times* ("the more the viewer can see actual testimony, the fewer questions there can be about the reporter's accuracy") (NYC-II at 79); John Miller, reporter, WNBC-TV (presence of TV cameras enhances accuracy of reporting because, otherwise, reporters have to rely on their notes for quotes from witnesses) (NYC-II at 217–18); Erin Moriarty, CBS correspondent (fairer to the defendant on the stand to report his actual words rather than to try to paraphrase them) (NYC-II at 331); Ed Miller, reporter, Fox News (cameras increase accuracy; viewer no longer dependent on someone else's version of what was said) (NYC-II at 334, 339–40); Christopher Bruner, executive assistant news director, WNYT-TV (Albany 10–11); Hon. Patricia Marks (Rochester at 38–39).

[34] Testimony of Bud Carey, general manager, WCBS-TV (camera coverage helped public understand why a "light" sentence was handed down in the shooting of a black plain-clothed police officer by a white police officer in the subway) (NYC-II at 229).

[35] Judicial Survey, Question 4(a).

what actually takes place in New York courtrooms, 63% agreed that televised *gavel-to-gavel* coverage of court proceedings accurately represents what takes place in court.[36]

Twenty-eight percent of those surveyed by the Marist Institute agreed that cameras in the courtroom increase the accuracy of news coverage.[37]

5. Opponents' Views

Contrasting with the testimony and public comments the Committee received about the public benefits of cameras in the courtroom were the strong reservations voiced by some judges and members of the public about the educational benefits of cameras in the courtroom. Although 45% of the 350 New York State judges who responded to the Committee's judicial survey agreed that television coverage has enhanced public understanding of New York's judicial system, 52% of the responding judges disagreed with that statement.[38] Sixty-one percent of the overall public surveyed in the Marist Institute poll indicated that they thought that cameras in the courtroom are a "bad idea," though a majority of black respondents (54%) thought cameras are a "good idea." Women surveyed had a less favorable view than men: 65% of women compared to 56% of men disfavored cameras.[39]

It was also suggested to the Committee that the educational benefits of camera coverage are slight, given the focus of camera coverage on cases involving violent crime, which are often depicted in brief segments on the evening news. In addition, a number of individuals and organizations raised questions as to whether

---

[36] *Id.*, Questions 5(j) & 5(k).

[37] Marist Poll, Question 2. As in other respects, the answer to this question varied by race, gender, and frequency of TV trials watched. Among black respondents, 49% felt that television cameras increase the accuracy of news coverage of trials; 24% of women, 32% of men and 52% of regular TV-trial watchers agreed. *Id.*

[38] Judicial Survey, Question 4(b). See also Judicial Survey, Question 4(c) (80% of judges agreed that television coverage of court proceedings is more likely to serve as a source of entertainment than education for the viewing public); Marist Poll, Question 3 (61% of respondents thought that television cameras in the courtroom were more a source of entertainment than a vehicle for increasing the public's understanding of the judicial system).

[39] Marist Institute poll, Question 1. See also Question 3 (32% of all respondents, 50% of black respondents, 51% of regular TV-trial watchers, 35% of men, and 30% of women thought that television cameras in the courtroom increase the public's understanding of the justice system).

the televised coverage of trials affects the fairness of the trial itself, by deterring witnesses from coming forward, by affecting the demeanor and credibility of witnesses who may be intimidated by the presence of cameras, and by creating a danger that hearsay and inadmissible evidence will "creep into the public consciousness"[40] and prejudice prospective or actual members of the jury. Some of these concerns are outlined in Section V(C) below, along with our assessment. This Section provides an overview of those concerns which are not addressed in that section.

a. Nature of Televised Coverage

With the exception of COURT-TV, which appears to have covered a fairly even mix of New York civil and criminal cases over the past several years,[41] the information submitted to the Committee suggests that the vast preponderance of cases which received audio-visual coverage were criminal, often involving a homicide or other crime "at the high end of the sentencing structure."[42] This testimony is consistent with data compiled by the Office of Court Administration, at the request of this Committee, from copies of media applications forwarded to it during the period January 31, 1995 to September 1, 1996: 94% of the proceedings in which camera coverage was sought were criminal cases.[43]

The Committee heard from a number of individuals and organizations to the effect that only "sensational" cases attract televised coverage, which, they stated, convey "a very false impression of what justice is all about and what courtroom procedures and trials are all about."[44] It was suggested to the Commit-

---

[40] Testimony of Hon. Norman E. Joslin, past president, New York State Association of Supreme Court Justices (Rochester at 127).

[41] According to information supplied by Court TV, 45% of the 49 New York trials and hearings aired on Court TV through November 1996 were civil cases. See Courtroom Television Network, "New York Trials and Hearings Aired To Date (as of November 11, 1996)."

[42] Testimony of Terence Kindlon, Esq. (Albany at 70). See also testimony of Hon. Joseph Harris, who supports cameras in the courts, Supreme Court Justice, Albany County ("I have had over two dozen cameras in the courtroom and every single case was a criminal case") (Albany at 151).

[43] OCA was able to further analyze 183 of the 540 media applications to determine what kind of criminal proceedings attracted media attention. OCA found that 59% involved violent crime (exclusive of sex-related offenses), 7% involved sex-related offenses, and 34% involved non-violent crime. See Appendix H, Table 5B.

[44] Letter dated November 1, 1996 from Philip Learned, Chemung Bar Associ-

tee that the reduction of lengthy, complex trials to brief segments on the evening news is more misleading than helpful in conveying information about the justice system[45] and that much of the commentary that accompanied televised news coverage of trials was subjective.[46]

Opponents of cameras raised a further objection, taking issue with the assertion that a camera faithfully records in an accurate and neutral fashion what takes place in a courtroom. George Gerbner, former Dean of the Annenberg School of Communications at the University of Pennsylvania, suggested that television creates the deceptive "illusion of actually seeing [a trial] when, in fact, what you are seeing are camera angles, camera selections, editing etc."[47] Richard Sexton, Esq., wrote to the Committee to point

---

ation. We received a similar expression of this point of view from several other bar associations, as well. See letter dated October 28, 1996 from Verner M. Ingram, Jr., President, St. Lawrence County Bar Association, summarizing the comments of Hon. Eugene L. Nicandri; letter dated January 9, 1997 from Deborah A. Elsasser, Westchester Women's Bar Association, forwarding comments of ten members of the Association; letter dated November 14, 1996 from Edward R. Marinstein, President, Rensselaer County Bar Association; letter dated January 23, 1997 from Frank A. Gulotta, Jr., President, Bar Association of Nassau County. See also letter dated December 19, 1996 from Acting Supreme Court Justice Martin H. Rettinger (suggesting that there should be audio-visual coverage of "less than 'newspaper cases' " since "the great bulk of trials deal with lower degree felonies" and "most proceedings deal with matters that have no spectacular content—they do not deal with public figures in high and glamorous positions").

[45] See testimony of Professor Barry Scheck, Cardozo Law School (NYC-I at 144–45). However, a number of reporters and several judges took issue with the "soundbite" critique. They argued that even a soundbite can have a "very positive impact" on the public and that over the course of a one-week or two-week trial, the short segments add up to a "fairly long and extensive body of reporting." See testimony of Hon. Patricia Marks (Rochester at 37) and testimony of Christopher Bruner, executive assistant news director, WNYT-TV (Albany at 30). See also testimony of Paul Conti, news director, WNYT-TV ("Is a person going to become educated about the court process because they view a one-minute story about the court process? No. But over 365 days, if they see 80 of them, they might be") (Albany at 32). For a different perspective, see memorandum dated September 22, 1994 from L. Ralph Mecham, Director, Administrative Office of the United States Courts to All Judges, United States Courts. See also Federal Judicial Center, *Electronic Media Coverage of Federal Civil Proceedings: An Evaluation of the Pilot Program in Six District Courts and Two Courts of Appeals* at p. 36 (1994).

[46] Testimony of Professor Barry Scheck, Cardozo Law School (NYC-I at 121–23). See also testimony of Frank Bensel, Esq. (NYC-III at 8–9).

[47] NYC-I at 55. Dean Gerbner's testimony received confirmation from Henry Simon, a former television news reporter and producer who serves as a court analyst in the chambers of the Hon. Joseph Mattina, Erie County Surrogate, and

out that "the images which appear on the TV set are those selected by the cameraman, director, producer and advertising sponsor. . . . [Viewers] think that they know enough about the imaged persons to make a judgment of them." As a result, he argued, "images and emotional responses supplant the ordered presentation of facts as limited by the rules of evidence."[48]

A concern that the television-viewing audience will usurp the role of the jury was raised by Max Frankel, former executive editor of *The New York Times*. Speaking for himself only, Frankel testified that cameras in the courtroom give viewers "the illusion" that they are "entitled to reach a judgment."[49] Similarly, one comment received by the Committee expressed a concern that cameras in the courtroom allow viewers who have not watched the entire trial to "make [a] judgment" without seeing all of the evidence, as the jury does.[50]

b. Effect on Witnesses

The Committee heard from several spokespersons for crime victims who expressed the opinion that there is a "significant risk" that cameras will have a chilling effect on a victim's or a witness' willingness to report a crime or testify in court.[51] Jeanne Mullgrav, Director of Court Programs for the Victims Services Agency, said that the impact of publicity was particularly acute in the case of victims of sex offenses, domestic violence, and child abuse, and for family members of victims.[52] Even with the current safeguards, she told the Committee, "the details and sensitive nature of the case are still televised and can subject the family and the victim to public scrutiny and public attention."[53]

---

is a strong supporter of cameras in the courtroom. Mr. Simon testified that "it's very easy to say the camera doesn't lie but it's lying constantly," depending on what camera angle is used and whether or not a defendant, witness, or judge has incurred the dislike of the camera person, who could make that person "look like hell." Rochester at 109–10.

[48] Letter from Richard Sexton, Esq., pp. 3–5 (Jan. 9, 1997).

[49] NYC-I at 191. He also noted that the defendant has a constitutional right not to testify at trial and yet he can be required to sit there and "let every bullet of sweat be examined by the entire country."

[50] Letter from Brenda Fair Stevens (Dec. 18, 1996).

[51] Testimony of Jeanne Mullgrav, Director of Court Programs, Victim Services Agency (NYC-I at 250).

[52] *Id.*

[53] *Id.*

Her views were shared by Professor Elizabeth Schneider of Brooklyn Law School, who voiced her concern that "audio-visual coverage could become an additional impediment to and disincentive for women pursuing legal remedies for sexual assault and/or battering."[54] Along the same lines, Tonia St. Germain, director of public policy for the New York State Coalition Against Sexual Assault, said that "high profile rape cases negatively impact on the survivor's willingness to report." She told the Committee that "the consent of the rape victim-witness must be the overriding factor governing judicial discretion in allowing live television coverage" of a trial.[55]

Concern about the deterrent effect of cameras on prospective witnesses went beyond the area of sexual assault. Hon. Howard Relin, Monroe County District Attorney, although strongly supportive of cameras in the courtroom, testified that he had observed in court proceedings generally "a very disturbing trend" of witness intimidation, in the form of threats of witnesses' physical safety, over the past several years.[56] As a result, he pointed out, some witnesses are reluctant to have their face and voice disseminated on television.[57]

---

[54] Letter dated December 9, 1996 from Brooklyn Law School Professor Elizabeth Schneider. See also testimony of Professor Elizabeth Schneider (NYC-II at 292, 303–06) (possibility of televised coverage may impact on the initial decision of a rape victim or a victim of domestic violence on whether to go forward and press charges). But see testimony of Judith Condo, director, Albany County Rape Crisis Center (although there is a "gross underreporting of sexual assault and domestic violence," she was not certain that cameras in the courtroom are a major contributor to victims' failure to report) (Albany at 129, 134).

[55] Letter from Tonia St. Germain (September 25, 1996), who said that "the traditional considerations that apply to any witness, such as the likelihood that the witness would be intimidated or distracted by the cameras while testifying are magnified for the sexual assault survivor because of the explicit nature of her testimony. In addition, the victim's right to privacy, the probability that she would be subjected to excessive public attention, and the fact that this attention encourages victim-blaming, presents a safety and well-being issue for the survivor, her family and her children." But see testimony of Paul DerOhannesian, assistant district attorney, Albany County District Attorney's Office (he has been "surprised" in sexual assault cases at how willing complainants have been to allow coverage of their trial or of their testimony as long as they are not identified, because they feel that the exposure is helpful) (Albany at 92).

[56] Rochester at 31–32. See also testimony of Jeanne Mullgrav, director of court programs, Victims Services Agency (in criminal cases generally, victim and witness intimidation is a problem of "enormous magnitude," making additional reference to the commission of crimes in the Bronx. (NYC-I at 248–49).

[57] Rochester at 31. See also letter dated October 28, 1996 from Verner Ingram, President, St. Lawrence County Bar Association (summarizing views of

c. Fair Trial Implications

The Marist Institute poll commissioned by the Committee reveals concern among the public about the fair trial implications of cameras in the courtroom. Sixty-two percent of respondents think that television cameras in the courtroom get in the way of a fair trial, while 29% think that television coverage decreases the possibility that courts will be unjust.[58] Among black respondents, 47% were of the view that cameras get in the way of a fair trial; and 44% thought cameras decrease injustice. Among regular TV-trial watchers, 39% thought that they get in the way of a fair trial, while 46% thought that television cameras in the courtroom decrease injustice. Sixty-five percent of women thought that cameras get in the way of a fair trial, as did 58% of men.

According to the Marist poll, seventy percent of respondents would not want their trial televised if they were a party to a civil lawsuit.[59] Sixty-eight percent would not want the trial televised if they were the victim of a crime;[60] and sixty-nine percent would not want their trial televised if they were a criminal defendant.[61]

Concerns about the fair trial implications of cameras in the courtroom lay at the heart of much of the opposition to cameras voiced by a number of judges and criminal defense attorneys at

---

Hon. Eugene L. Nicandri of St. Lawrence County, who has not detected any change of conduct of participants in "covered proceedings" with the possible exception of heightened nervousness, but speculated that "cameras might be a further impediment to certain victims' willingness to come forward in the first place"); testimony of Ira London, Esq. ("The blue dot is not going to calm the fears of a nervous witness. . . . A witness who's going to be intimidated in his or her testimony is going to be intimidated by the presence of a camera focusing even if there is a blue dot there") (NYC-II at 283); testimony of Erin Moriarty, CBS correspondent (blue dot can be "disconcerting"; works with witnesses to make them feel more comfortable, i.e., by agreeing to film their hands instead) (NYC-II at 342).

[58] Marist poll, Question 4. Question 4 asked respondents: "Which statement comes closer to your opinion: one, television cameras in the courtroom decrease the possibility that the courts will be unjust, or two, television cameras in the courtroom get in the way of a fair trial?"

[59] Marist poll, Question 7. 59% of black respondents would not want their civil lawsuit televised. Neither would 73% of women and 52% of regular TV-trial watchers. *Id.*

[60] Marist poll, Question 12. Among black respondents, the comparable figure was 59%. 76% of women and 48% of regular TV-trial watchers would not want the trial televised if they were a victim of a crime.

[61] Marist poll, Question 11. 31% of black respondents would not want their criminal trial televised, nor would 75% of women and 43% of regular TV-trial watchers.

our hearings. Presiding Justice Francis T. Murphy of the New York State Supreme Court, Appellate Division, First Department, pointed to the absence of proof that the defendant will not be prejudiced by cameras in the courtroom and testified that the burden of proof should be on camera proponents to show by a fair preponderance of the evidence that the defendant will get a fair trial if cameras are present.[62] Hon. Norman E. Joslin, past president of the New York State Association of Supreme Court Justices, has suggested that "selective editing and repetitive broadcasting of video clips . . . influences the proof and distorts the process."[63]

According to Jack Litman, Esq., prejudice to the defendant is real, even if it is difficult to prove:

> How is the defendant to prove that the prosecutor acted differently than he ordinarily would have, that defense counsel was more concerned with impressing prospective clients than with the interests of the defendant, that a juror was [so] concerned with [how he appeared on] television [that his] mind [continually] wondered from the proceedings, or that an important defense witness made a bad impression on the jury because he was playing to a television audience, or that the judge was more lenient or more strict than he might usually be because he's subject to re-election.[64]

To address this perceived prejudice to the defendant, Litman and other witnesses proposed that Section 218 of the Judiciary Law be amended to require the consent of the defendant as a prerequisite to televising a criminal trial.[65]

Finally, it was suggested that televising bail hearings raises the likelihood that prejudicial information will taint the prospective pool of jurors. California's Associate Justice Richard Huffman testified that prosecutors have a legitimate purpose in pointing out,

---

[62] NYC-I at 88, 101.

[63] See Norman E. Joslin, "Justice Loses to TV in O.J. Trial," *Buffalo News* (Sept. 7, 1995).

[64] NYC-I at 46, citing *Estes v. Texas*, 381 U.S. 532, 579 (1965) (Warren, C. J., concurring). It was also suggested that one potential drawback of gavel-to-gavel coverage is the ability of witnesses to watch the trial testimony of other witnesses. See testimony of Paul DerOhannesian, Albany County assistant district attorney (Albany at 87). But DerOhannesian, like Terence Kindlon, Esq., said that that issue can be addressed on cross-examination. (Albany at 87–88).

[65] NYC-I at 29. See also, e.g., testimony of Jonathan Gradess, executive director, New York State Defenders Association (NYC-I at 222); testimony of Norman Effman, Wyoming County Public Defender (Rochester at 213).

at a bail hearing, "all the evil [things]" the defendant has done.[66] He said that if statements which may be inadmissible as evidence at trial are broadly disseminated on television, any incremental benefit in terms of information about the system "is vastly outweighed by the prejudice to the fair trial interests of both sides."[67]

d. Privacy Concerns

Another concern voiced at the Committee's hearings was that cameras invade a zone of privacy which trial participants may have even in court. Eleanor Alter, Esq., a matrimonial lawyer, testified that in New York, which still has a fault-based divorce law, the presence of cameras "publicize[s] aspects of people's lives that most every other state has recognized should not be publicized . . . in a courtroom."[68] According to Alter, television coverage is especially hard on young children, who may watch (or whose friends may watch) their parents "testifying about the terrible things [they] did or did not do."[69] Alter testified that television is more graphic because it provides the exact words and demeanor of witnesses and other trial participants and has a negative impact on their families.[70]

Frank Bensel, defense counsel in the Libby Zion case, raised a different privacy concern. He questioned the wisdom of forcing private litigants in a civil case to air their dispute on commercial television, where coverage of the three-month long trial competed with the afternoon soap operas.[71] His co-counsel, Luke Pittoni, who favors cameras in the court, after having initially opposed them, voiced concern for the potential harm to the pro-

---

[66] NYC-II at 157, 170. See also testimony of Isaiah Gant, board member, Tennessee Association of Criminal Defense Lawyers (pre-trial footage of defendant gets played over and over again and is viewed by members of the potential jury pool) (NYC-I at 233–34).

[67] Id. at 170–71.

[68] NYC-II at 180.

[69] Id. at 207–08.

[70] Id. at 208. Alter also noted that cameras hinder judge-made settlements and the resulting publicity makes it harder for people to get on with their lives. (NYC-II at 180–81). They also have, she said, a "chilling effect" on witnesses in child custody cases if the witness lacks proper "mmigration status." Id. at 182–83. It is our understanding that Family Court proceedings are rarely open to the public.

[71] NYC-III at 7–9. Bensel suggested that "here should be some requirement of consent by the litigants"before a civil trial could be televised. Id. at 8.

fessional reputation of litigants in a televised medical malpractice suit even if they ultimately prevail at trial.[72]

Finally, it has been suggested that the ability of a camera to zoom in from a distance to provide an extreme close-up image of the witness's face is an invasion of the witness' privacy.[73]

B. COMPLIANCE BY TRIAL JUDGES AND THE MEDIA

We next turn to whether "any abuses occurred during the program" as well as "the degree of compliance by trial judges and the media" with the provisions of Section 218 of the Judiciary Law. Because these two facets of the Committee's mandate are related, they are considered together below.

1. COMPLIANCE BY TRIAL JUDGES

a. Testimony and Public Comment

The Committee received only two specific complaints about the way in which trial judges administered the provisions of Section 218 of the Judiciary Law, only one of which appeared to fall within the period of our legislative mandate.[74] Christopher

---

[72] NYC-III at 10–11.

[73] M. David Lepofsky, *Cameras in the Courtroom: Not Without My Consent*, 6 National J. of Constitutional Law 161, 171 (1996), who stated that "To obtain such a view in the courtroom, the spectator would have to walk up to the witness stand and place him or herself inches from the witness' nose—something that no presiding judge would permit. Hence, the camera can electronically invade and violate the court participant's personal space in a fashion that no spectator can."

[74] The two complaints received by the Committee include: (1) An allegation that a judge refused to enforce his order that the media not photograph a rape victim on court property, including entering and leaving the building and in the parking area (See letter from Tonia St. Germain, Director of Public Policy for the New York State Coalition Against Sexual Assault [Dec. 13, 1996]. It appears from subsequent staff discussions with the rape victim's attorney that this incident, which occurred in 1996, involved, at least in part, an issue of whether the rape victim had standing to seek contempt sanctions for the news media's alleged violations of the court's order); (2) An allegation that a judge permitted camera coverage of an adjournment at which the defendant was scheduled to appear to consent to AIDS testing, with no notice to defense counsel (Testimony of Michelle Maxian, Director of Special Litigation, Legal Aid Society, Criminal Defense Division [NYC-II at 249–50]. This incident, according to Ms. Maxian, took place more than three years ago. In the end, the media agreed not to film the defendant's face. *Id.* at 269–70).

Bruner, executive assistant news director of WNYT-TV in Albany, testified that he was aware of instances when town justices allowed cameras to cover the arraignments of unrepresented defendants, an apparent violation of Section 218(5)(b) of the Judiciary Law.[75] He testified that "several times, I personally had to quietly inform town justices and my fellow members of the media that we had to refuse the invitation" of town justices to let the cameras in under those circumstances.[76] Bruner further testified that he has advised reporters to destroy tapes and not to air material where town justices have permitted camera access they should not have.[77]

The Committee received a substantial amount of testimony from reporters and attorneys which suggested that judges have discharged their obligations under Section 218 quite responsibly. Christopher Bruner testified that in his experience, "if a witness, a non-material witness, expressed any misgivings whatsoever about having the camera in the courtroom, the judge would immediately tell us that he was inclined not to allow us to take pictures."[78] His views were shared by Carol De Mare, a reporter with 25 years' experience at the *Albany Times Union*, who testified that in her experience, judges "have all been extremely familiar with the guidelines and safeguards governing cameras [and] . . . have exhibited the utmost control of the situation."[79]

Paul DerOhannesian, assistant district attorney in Albany County, testified that judicial compliance in the child homicide and sexual assault cases that he handles has been "excellent."[80] DerOhannesian testified that "when there are abuses, I have found the judges that I have practiced before . . . are very willing to exercise . . . control."[81] Thomas Neidl, an assistant public de-

---

[75] Albany at 11. § 218(5)(b) provides that an unrepresented defendant cannot consent to coverage of an arraignment unless he or she "as been advised of his or her right to the aid of counsel" and "as affirmatively elected to proceed without counsel."

[76] Albany at 11–12.

[77] *Id.* at 34–35.

[78] Albany at 26. See also testimony of John Miller, reporter, WNBC-TV (he has seen trial judges instruct cameras to be pointed at something else if a witness does not want to be televised and has seen judges shut off the cameras when undercover agents testify) NYC-II at 221).

[79] Albany at 111. She noted further that "udges at least in this county have bent over backward to accommodate us." *Id.* at 113.

[80] Albany at 71.

[81] *Id.* at 80.

fender in Albany County, also testified that he had "complete satisfaction" with the way trial judges have complied with the law's safeguards.[82]

Reporters were appreciative of the "latitude" judges have given them on the 7-day notice provision, which, according to John Miller, a reporter for WNBC-TV, "is completely applicable" for trials but not for hearings and other proceedings "that come up suddenly."[83] In this regard, Miller testified, "judges have been flexible."[84]

b. Results of the Committee's Judicial Survey

This willingness of judges to be flexible with respect to the 7-day notice provision is borne out by the Committee's judicial survey. Seventy-one percent of the 205 judges who responded to the relevant portion of the Committee's survey reported that they had "shortened or waived the statutory seven-day notice period in granting an application for camera coverage."[85] Asked to explain their willingness to waive the 7-day notice period, some judges noted the impracticability of complying with the 7-day notice period in cases involving "breaking news."[86] Others commented that "every single application I have ever gotten has been filed the day of the proceedings"[87] and that the "media usually and habitually disregard the requirement."[88] Others noted the ab-

---

[82] *Id.* at 194. See also letter dated January 23, 1997 from Frank A. Gulotta, President, Bar Association of Nassau County (although the majority of the Association's Executive Committee and Board of Directors voted to recommend that cameras in the courtroom be discontinued in both civil and criminal cases, they felt that "judges have done their jobs well both in complying with the safeguards included in the State's camera coverage law and in their conduct both inside and outside the courtroom").

[83] NYC-II at 234–35.

[84] *Id.* See also testimony of Judy Sanders, Albany news chief, WRGB-TV News ("by and large, the judges do give us some latitude"on the 7-day notice provision) (Albany at 185).

[85] Judicial Survey, Question 14(a). § 218(3)(a) of the Judiciary Law gives judges discretion to shorten the notice period "where circumstances are such that an applicant cannot reasonably apply seven or more days before the commencement of the proceeding."

[86] *See* Judicial Survey, Question 14(b), written comments of Judge #311. See also comments of Judges #159 ("impossible to have 7 days notice to cover preliminary hearings which happen within 6 days"); #164 ("immediate request made, just after arrest"); #271 ("not enough time between arrest and court appearance to give 7-day notice").

[87] Judicial Survey, Question 14(b), written comments of Judge #45.

[88] Judicial Survey, Question 14(b), written comments of nine judges.

sence of objections as a reason for waiving the 7-day notice period.[89]

The Committee's Judicial Survey sheds further light on how trial judges handle applications for camera coverage. Part II of the survey, which sought information only from judges who had, at any time, received an application to permit television coverage in their courtroom, was completed by 226 judges. Nearly 90% of responding judges stated that they hold oral argument to determine whether camera coverage should be permitted,[90] 7% hold an evidentiary hearing and 21% allow counsel to brief the issue.[91]

Two hundred and five judges—91% of Part II respondents—had granted at least one application for televised coverage in their courtroom. The most common reason given for granting an application for television coverage was the "absence of objections," followed in close succession by "the importance of maintaining public trust and confidence in the judicial system" and "the importance of promoting public access to the judicial system."[92] Others mentioned that they felt constrained to grant the application because they interpret Section 218 to contain a "presumption" in favor of access,[93] requiring that "we must provide audio-visual access unless there are compelling reasons not to do so."[94]

Forty-eight percent of 186 responding judges stated that they had permitted camera coverage over the objections of the defense in criminal cases (other than arraignments and suppression hearings, where defendant consent to camera coverage is required).[95] Explaining their decision to override defense objections, judges pointed most often to the "importance of promoting public access to the judicial system" and of "maintaining public trust and confidence" in that system. Judges also mentioned that they were

---

[89] Judicial Survey, Question 14(b), written comments of Judges #187, 195, 216, 244. On the other hand, 62 judges identified "application untimely" as a factor which had led them to *deny* an application for camera coverage. See Judicial Survey, Question 12(b)(iv).
[90] Judicial Survey, Question 15(a)(ii).
[91] *Id.*, Question 15(a)(I) and 15(a)(iii).
[92] *Id.* Question 11.
[93] *Id.*, Question 13(c)(vii), written comments of Judges #28, 304. See also Question 13(d), written comments of Judge #106 (under the current law, "the presumption favors the presence of audio-visual coverage and provides little, if any, discretion to the court").
[94] Judicial Survey, Questions 11(b)(viii), 13(c)(vii) and 13(d), written comments received from five judges.
[95] Judicial Survey, Question 13(a).

more willing to override a defendant's objections to camera coverage if they believed that the objection was "pro forma."[96]

Fifty-eight percent of the judges stated that they had denied at least one application for camera coverage.[97] In criminal cases, the most common reasons for denying an application were the objections of the defense (a factor mentioned by 80% of 121 judges who had denied an application), objections of the prosecution (mentioned by 61% of judges), objections of witnesses and the effect on witnesses' willingness to cooperate, including the risk that coverage will engender threats to the health or safety of any witness (mentioned by 55% of judges), possible interference with the defendant's right to a fair trial (55%), the type of case involved (52%), and the untimeliness of the news media's application (51%). The possibility that coverage might unfairly influence or distract the jury was mentioned by 39% of judges. At the other end of the scale, only 8% of judges cited administrative or financial burdens as grounds for denying an application and only 12% mentioned the difficulty of jury selection if a mistrial were declared.[98]

Approximately one-fourth of the responding judges (23%) have exercised their discretion to impose restrictions on camera coverage in criminal cases in addition to those expressly required by Section 218 of the Judiciary Law and the implementing rules promulgated by the Chief Administrative Judge.[99] For instance, several judges mentioned that they do not allow the media to televise the defendant's face; others imposed limits on televising in the corridors or parking lot of the courthouse[100] or have ruled that television "could film all the witnesses or none of them but could not film some and not others."[101] Several judges mentioned that they "maintain control over where the camera is positioned"[102] and do not allow shots of spectators.[103]

---

[96] Judicial Survey, Question 13(c)(vii), written comments of Judge #336.
[97] Judicial Survey, Question 12(a).
[98] Judicial Survey, Question 12(b).
[99] Judicial Survey, Question 16(a). The Chief Administrative Judge's rules are codified at 22 NYCRR Part 131.
[100] Judicial Survey, Question 16(b).
[101] Judicial Survey, Question 16(b), written comments of Judge #18.
[102] Id., Judge #56. See also id., Judges #62, 190, 209, 249, 316, 336, 345.
[103] See, e.g., id, Judges #28, 61.

c. Office of Court Administration Data

Data compiled by the Office of Court Administration suggests that judges grant a majority of the applications they receive for camera coverage. Of the 540 applications which were forwarded to OCA by the twelve judicial districts around the state during the period from January 31, 1995 to September 1, 1996, 83.5% were approved.[104] Like the Committee's judicial survey, the OCA data suggest that the most common reason given by judges for denying an application for camera coverage was the objection of the defense.[105]

The OCA data further suggests that the most common restrictions on camera coverage imposed by the court are restrictions on the news media's equipment. The second most common restriction was a prohibition on photographing or filming the defendant's face, followed by restrictions on revealing the defendant's name, the victim's name and/or face, and a prohibition on filming spectators.[106]

2. COMPLIANCE BY THE MEDIA

The Committee's record includes strong evidence of compliance by many television reporters and camerapersons with the requirements and safeguards of Section 218 of the Judiciary Law.

Several witnesses testified that they were unaware of any abuses by the media. Professor Jay Wright of the S. I. Newhouse Communications Center at Syracuse University, who chairs New York State's Fair Trial/Free Press Conference, reported to the Committee that no abuses had been brought to his attention over the period of this Committee's mandate.[107] His experience paralleled that of Madeleine Schachter, chair of the New York State Bar Association's Media Law Committee, and Francis D. Phillips II, president of the New York State District Attorneys Association.[108]

---

[104] Appendix H, Table 1.
[105] Appendix H, Table 6.
[106] Appendix H, Table 8.
[107] NYC-I at 80–81.
[108] *See* testimony of Madeleine Schachter (NYC-II at 62); letter dated October 25, 1996 from Francis D. Phillips, president, New York State District Attorneys Association ("to the best of my knowledge, the media has complied with the safeguards included in the law").

Their testimony was bolstered by further evidence of compliance by the media with court rules.[109] The Committee received several letters of public comment from both lawyers and judges which stated that the media had been cooperative with respect to excluding certain witnesses from coverage[110] and "generally compl[ied] with the safeguards" of Section 218.[111]

The Committee's judicial survey asked judges whether they were aware of any violations of Section 218 of the Judiciary Law by the media or any improper or inappropriate use of television footage filmed in a courtroom. Only nine percent of 172 judges answered "yes" to that question.[112] Several responded that the news media had violated a judge's order not to film certain trial participants (i.e., the defendant's family members, a victim's family, a witness, or the jury) or had filmed an attorney's legal pad.[113] A few others complained that the media had done an end-run around the ban on filming arraignments without the defendant's consent, either by filming in the hallway outside the courtroom

---

[109] See testimony of Paul DerOhannesian, assistant district attorney, Albany County (compliance by media has been "exemplary") (Albany at 72); See also testimony of Hon. Patricia Marks (Rochester at 41–42) (media "very cooperative"); letter dated October 29, 1996 from Hon. Guy James Mangano, Presiding Justice, Appellate Division, Second Department (press and television personnel have "comported themselves properly" in covering appellate proceedings in his court).

[110] See letter from Verner M. Ingram, president, St. Lawrence County Bar Association (October 28, 1996).

[111] See letter dated January 9, 1997 from Deborah A. Elsasser, Westchester Women's Bar Association, enclosing members' responses to the Committee's request for comments. See also letter dated December 19, 1996 from Acting Supreme Court Justice Martin H. Rettinger (all rules were followed by camera crew who covered one of his trials).

[112] Judicial Survey, Question 25(a). Question 25 on the judicial survey was not expressly limited to the recent two-year period of the Committee's mandate so that the Committee could not ascertain specifically where and when the alleged instances occurred. Furthermore, the Committee has not independently investigated these allegations and makes no judgment about the specifics of each individual complaint. Indeed, most of the complaints were not particularized so as to permit such an undertaking even if resources had been available.

[113] Judicial Survey, judges' written comments to Question 25. See also additional comments of Judges #47 ("when told not to film a 14-year old rape victim, [the news media] simply stalk her into the parking lot and her sobbing countenance is that night's "lead""); #68 ("the explosion of independent producers in the news magazine TV format create[s] potential for harm. They are not or don't seem to be constrained in any way. Unlike regular TV reporters, they don't worry about pushing or testing the rules because they are not going to be coming back looking for permission to A/V a case").

without the permission of the presiding judge or the administrative judge, or by filming an unrepresented defendant with a bag over his head.¹¹⁴ A few cited alleged "abuses" ranging from "inadvertent violations" to a complaint that "footage was taken in the courtroom of a party [to the proceedings] while the news media representative was applying for permission."¹¹⁵

By far the most common complaint voiced by lawyers was "that we never get seven days notice."¹¹⁶ Although Section 218(3)(a) of the Judiciary Law requires the media to file a written request for camera coverage "not less than seven days before the commencement of the judicial proceeding," failure to provide seven days notice is not necessarily a violation of Section 218, since 218(3)(a) also allows a judge to shorten the notice period "where circumstances are such that an applicant cannot reasonably apply seven or more days before." This might be the case, for example, in circumstances when an unforseen proceeding is scheduled on an expedited basis, and the media does not receive sufficient advance notice of the proceeding. However, criminal defense lawyers testified that they found it burdensome and distracting to "have to argue against the press, about coverage" at the last minute, especially when a trial date has been set well in advance.¹¹⁷

Other complaints raised, but not investigated by the Committee, drew our attention to the quality of some of the sound equip-

---

¹¹⁴ *Id.* According to Paul DerOhannesian, assistant district attorney for Albany County, if an arraignment is closed, the defendant is photographed in handcuffs going to and from the courtroom. Albany at 79, 99–104.

¹¹⁵ Judicial Survey, Question 25(b), written comments of judges #13 and #152.

¹¹⁶ Testimony of Michele Maxian, Director of Special Litigation, New York Legal Aid Society, Criminal Defense Division (NYC-II at 260). *Cf.* testimony of Justice Joseph Harris, New York State Supreme Court, Albany County ("I've never had one make an application on time according to the rules, but they always show up with their camera right at the last minute and ask for permission and you [have] to hold a hearing") (Albany at 152); testimony of Madeleine Schachter, chair of the New York State Bar Association's Media Law Committee ("occasionally there has been some issue about getting the application in within the 7-day statutory period and there may occasionally be some rushing of that time period") (NYC-II at 94).

¹¹⁷ *See* testimony of Michelle Maxian, Director of Special Litigation, New York Legal Aid Society, Criminal Defense Division (NYC-II at 261); See also testimony of Diane Russell, an assistant public defender in the Monroe County Public Defenders Office (Rochester at 58–61).

ment,[118] occasional distracting noises,[119] the behavior of a camera crew,[120] audio-visual coverage of defense counsel's table,[121] and equipment which exceeds the statutory guidelines.[122]

C. EFFECT OF AUDIO-VISUAL COVERAGE ON THE CONDUCT OF PARTICIPANTS IN COURT PROCEEDINGS

At the core of the debate over the wisdom of allowing cameras in the courtroom is the question of whether cameras have an impact

---

[118] See testimony of Terence Kindlon, Esq. (Because of the poor quality of some of the sound equipment, after a judge finishes saying "a lot of really bad things about my client at a sentencing," the TV equipment does not pick up the response of the defendant or his counsel) (Albany at 51).

[119] Schuyler County Judge John P. Callanan wrote to the Committee on December 17, 1996 to report that the camera-covered trials over which he has presided have gone "without interruption with one serious exception. During the sentencing of a 17-year old girl who got 25 years to life in the state prison for murder in the second degree, one of the television cameramen made a series of loud, interrupting noises with his equipment that was very distracting to everyone in the courtroom. The reporter apologized to the Court in chambers after the conclusion of the sentencing."

[120] See letter dated October 23, 1996 from Remy Perot, founder of the Southern Tier Criminal Defense Attorneys Association (describing a televised second-degree murder trial at which, it is alleged, "the crew in the monitoring room . . . had left the feed lead on during breaks and were listening to the conversations of the family of the victim . . .").

[121] Testimony of Diane Russell, assistant public defender, Monroe County Public Defender's Office (use of microphones on counsel table) (Rochester at 61–62). See also the testimony of Henry J. Simon, a member of the staff of Erie County Surrogate Joseph S. Mattina, regarding a local cameraman employed by Court TV shooting a video of still pictures of minors left on counsel table. Rochester at 93–95. The Committee has examined this matter and is satisfied that the cameraman's mistake was corrected and that the footage in question was never aired. We also received a copy of a November 27, 1995 letter of Justice Mattina's to Steven Brill, stating that "[a]pparently there were several occasions that led to some disagreement as to the suitability of videotaping certain material provided by some of the parties. Your producers were, after discussion and explanation, understanding of the wishes and intentions of the court. They are to be commended for outstanding work in logistically difficult circumstances and for demonstrating high ethical standards." The letter accompanied a memorandum to the Chair of this Committee from Jeffrey H. Ballabon, Vice President of Government Relations for Court TV, dated March 28, 1997.

[122] See testimony of Jonathan Gradess, executive director, New York State Defenders Association (asserting that 10 video cameras were present for a proceeding in New York's first death penalty case) (NYC-I at 211). Although § 218(6)(a)(i) through (iii) limit the number of still and video cameras which may be permitted, § 218(6)(a)(iv) allows judges to vary these limits in "special circumstances, so long as [doing so] will not impair the dignity of the court or of the judicial process."

on trial participants—the jurors, the witnesses, the lawyers or the judge—and, ultimately, on the outcome of the case. In an earlier era, the concern included a fear that the camera itself—unwieldy, noisy, and accompanied by glaring lights—might distract the trial participants from the tasks at hand. However, with the advances in technology, those fears have been laid to rest.[123]

What remain very much alive are the concerns about the psychological impact of the camera: how will the realization that their every word and gesture is being transmitted to a vast, unseen audience affect the behavior of trial participants?[124] We turn to the record developed by this Committee on this question.

1. Effect on Jurors

The Committee heard testimony from two jurors: the foreperson and another juror who served on the jury in the Libby Zion malpractice action against New York Hospital and several physicians. Neither juror felt that the presence of television cameras on a daily basis in that three-month long trial affected the outcome of the case.[125] One juror stated that the presence of cameras just for

---

[123] See, however, testimony of Peter Moschetti, Esq. (sometimes the cameras are "right by the jury box . . . there's a lot of hardware . . . I know the jurors look at the cameras when they come in, I know they watch the cameras move at times") (Albany at 249); testimony of Luke Pittoni (the snapping and rewind sounds of still cameras were "extremely distracting" in the Libby Zion trial) (NYC-III at 18–19); testimony of Diane Russell, Monroe County assistant public defender (Rochester at 62).

[124] Perhaps the most comprehensive summary of the concerns about the psychological impact of cameras on trial participants is set forth in the several plurality opinions in *Estes v. Texas*, 381 U.S. 532 (1965). See, e.g., the concurring opinion of Chief Justice Earl Warren, 381 U.S. at 567–70 ("awareness that trial is being televised to a vast, unseen audience is bound to increase nervousness and tension, cause an increased concern about appearances, and bring to the surface latent opportunism that the traditional dignity of the courtroom would discourage"). See also concurring opinion of Justice John Harlan, 381 U.S. at 591 ("In the context of a trial of intense public interest, there is certainly a strong possibility that the timid or reluctant witness, for whom a court appearance even at its traditional best is a harrowing affair, will become more timid or reluctant when he finds that he will also be appearing before a 'hidden audience' of unknown but large dimensions"). See also M. David Lepofsky, "Cameras in the Courtroom: Not Without My Consent," 6 National Journal of Constitutional Law 161 (1996). But see *Chandler v. Florida*, 449 U.S. 560, 579–80 (1981) ("at present, no one has been able to present empirical data sufficient to establish that the mere presence of broadcast media inherently has an adverse effect on the [judicial] process").

[125] Testimony of Janet Dubin (NYC-III at 56–57); testimony of Edgar Greene (NYC-III at 57–59).

one witness or one aspect of a proceeding could send a signal to the jurors "about the importance of one aspect over another aspect of the proceedings."[126]

Janet Dubin, the foreperson in the Zion case, felt that there were benefits and drawbacks to cameras in the courtroom. On the one hand, she testified that television allows people to become "more familiar with what is going on in the courtroom" and that it is important for the public to see what jurors' responsibilities entail.[127] On the other hand, after the trial was over, she watched televised videotapes of the trial, which she felt was "so different" from being at the trial.[128] She also felt that the commentary that accompanied the televised trial footage "does not give the public the experience of what it looks like to be a juror and to just go with what's given in the trial."[129]

Edgar Green, her fellow juror, expressed his view that cameras in the courtroom "are generally not helpful."[130] He noted a concern of his about the rights of parties, especially defendants in civil cases, whom he felt should be able to say "I don't want to be displayed before a multinational audience of millions of people."[131] According to Green, jurors in the Zion case, in which he participated, noticed the camera.[132] However, he also felt that cameras had no impact on the jurors in that case as they worked their way through the lengthy set of questions the trial judge asked them to answer.[133] He also expressed a general concern that jurors might inadvertently see televised coverage of a case,[134] although he said there was no indication that any juror did so in the 3-month-long Zion trial.

Diane De Bellis, a third juror in the Libby Zion case, wrote to the Committee to convey her "strong feelings in favor of and against the videotaping and airing of trials." She believes that televised trials provide some educational benefits, may encourage witnesses to be truthful if they know that "their testimony will be shared with, potentially, millions of television viewers" and

---

[126] *Id.* at 66–67.
[127] *Id.* at 53–54.
[128] NYC-III at 62.
[129] *Id.* at 53.
[130] *Id.* at 54–55.
[131] *Id.* at 54–55.
[132] *Id.* at 58.
[133] *Id.* at 59.
[134] *Id.* at 64.

may provide an incentive for lawyers to work "more competently . . . knowing their work will be scrutinized by colleagues and potential clients alike."[135] She stated the view that the presence of cameras during a trial is "invasive and disruptive," especially for those who "experience a sense of discomfort when in front of a camera." She said that televised witnesses might withhold information out of fear of "criminal or professional retribution." She also believes that "many attorneys and witnesses play to the camera and add unwarranted drama" which may be a "major obstacle in the pursuit of the truth."[136]

With respect to jurors, two concerns were voiced at the Committee's hearings: first, that jurors will watch televised coverage of the case (or will speak to family members, friends, and colleagues who have watched the televised coverage) and will be influenced either by commentary about the case or by evidence which was ruled inadmissible and thus not presented to the jury, and second, that jurors will be influenced in their deliberations by their realization that the eyes of the general public are upon them and will be reluctant to reach a verdict which is "unpopular" with the community to which they will return after the trial.

Only 17% of judges who had received an application for camera coverage agreed that jurors in televised trials were more likely to have communications with people who have seen coverage of the case.[137] Thirty percent of camera-experienced judges agreed that "jurors were more likely to be aware of the implications of their verdict in cases in which TV cameras were present."[138] Twenty-one of the 167 judges who answered this question disagreed and 48% had no opinion.

The idea that television coverage heightens jurors' perception of the implications of their verdict was expressed by Professor Barry Scheck of Cardozo Law School, one of the defense lawyers in the Simpson criminal case. Scheck testified that in televised trials, jurors will have to explain their verdicts in ways that are different from the past.[139] Scheck also expressed concern about the "second-guessing" of jury verdicts by TV viewers who be-

---

[135] Letter from Diane De Bellis (March 5, 1997).
[136] *Id.*
[137] *See* Judicial Survey, Question 22(b). 24% of the 165 judges who answered this question disagreed and 59% had no opinion.
[138] *Id.*, Question 22(c).
[139] NYC-I at 116.

lieve, based on seeing a short segment of a witness' testimony on television, that they are as capable as the actual jurors of making a judgment about a witness' credibility.[140] His views were consistent with those of George Gerbner, Dean Emeritus of the Annenberg School of Communications at the University of Pennsylvania, who testified that putting a trial on television transports it "into a global tribunal" and "mobilize[s] emotionally an entire community to which judges and jurors must return at the end of the trial.[141] In that environment, he testified, "there is no way that your own future will not weigh as heavily in what you are saying [as] the specific facts of the case."[142]

Professor Beth Schwartz interviewed on behalf of the Committee three jury consultants about their impressions of the impact of cameras on jurors and other trial participants.[143] One was of the opinion that the presence of cameras would exaggerate the importance of the case for jurors and that, in most cases, camera coverage would be harmful to criminal defendants, in part because some defense witnesses may be less forthcoming if cameras are present. A second jury consultant felt that there was very little impact so long as there was only one camera focused on the witness box. During some of the televised trials at which she had been present, she said the jurors appeared to pay little or no attention to the cameras. She felt it was possible that some jurors might be concerned that if there is televised coverage of a trial, they may be asked to account for their verdict. A third jury consultant was concerned about televised coverage that might mislead members of the public who constitute the pool of prospective jurors.[144]

---

[140] *Id.* at 118–19. See also testimony of Max Frankel, former executive editor, *The New York Times* (in the Simpson criminal case, cameras allowed "two-thirds or more of the American people to feel and to believe that they know better than the 12 people who were painstakingly empaneled and who sat through every moment of that trial") (NYC-I at 188–89).

[141] NYC-I at 59–60, 64.

[142] *Id.* at 59. See also testimony of Peter Moschetti, Esq. (jurors in one of his cases were very concerned that they might have been filmed; "if their verdict was an unpopular verdict, then their neighbors and people they see around would know that they sat on that jury") (Albany at 247).

[143] See Appendix G.

[144] In her written comments to the Committee, Elissa Krauss, president of the National Jury Project, asserted that "audio-visual courtroom coverage injects bias into a trial that is difficult to detect or remedy." She voiced a concern that "the presence of cameras in courtrooms increases the widespread predisposition to presume that a person who is accused of a serious crime is probably guilty." She further noted her concern that "the presence of cameras in courtrooms

At its hearings, the Committee heard testimony from several witnesses to the effect that some jurors may be affected by the presence of cameras. Thomas Moore, Esq., a plaintiff's malpractice lawyer who favors cameras in the courtroom, testified that, in his opinion, jury verdicts are more "conservative" when cameras are present than when they are not.[145] "In a plaintiff's case," he explained, that means that there is "more likely to be a verdict against the plaintiff and for the defendant. In a criminal case, [that means] a verdict for the prosecution and [a] finding of guilty against the defendant."[146]

Christopher Bruner, executive assistant news director at WNYT-TV in Albany, took issue with the view that jurors are influenced by camera coverage. He testified that he has interviewed jurors after trials and "ha[s] yet to encounter a juror who said afterward that they found the camera either distracting or the media coverage an impediment to rendering a fair verdict."[147] Mr. Bruner described a high-profile trial in which a town councilman was exonerated of the most severe charge of murder and was convicted of the lesser charge of manslaughter. Although the trial received extensive television coverage, Bruner testified that none of the jurors felt that the camera had any effect.[148] Hon. Patricia Marks reported getting feedback from a juror who said to her, "you told us not to pay attention to the cameras so we didn't."[149]

Norman Effman, the Wyoming County Public Defender, testified that cameras "have an impact" on trial participants, which "has to be recognized and factored in as a strategy question for lawyers" before they decide whether or not to object to an application for camera coverage. In his upstate trials where he typically finds himself defending black and Hispanic prison inmates before all-white juries, he favors camera coverage because he thinks "it's important to open the doors to the courtroom to a much broader community than the community in which the trial is taking place." He wants jurors to feel that "it's not a closed club situation when they go back to the deliberation room and determine what

---

exacerbates privacy and safety concerns." Memorandum from Elissa Krauss, to the Committee (Jan. 23, 1997).
[145] NYC-I at 170–71, 175–76.
[146] *Id.* at 170–71.
[147] Albany at 12.
[148] *Id.* at 25.
[149] Rochester at 41.

to do in a case involving someone who truly isn't from their community."[150]

The Committee also heard opinions on the question of whether jurors are likely to disregard the judge's instructions not to watch televised coverage of the trial or discuss the cases with family members and friends who have, as well as on the question of what effect, if any, such a disregard might have on the outcome of the case.[151] Thomas Neidl, an assistant public defender in Albany County, testified that "clearly, jurors will go home and watch the news whether they're told to or not on occasion." However, Neidl testified that he does not believe that it affects their ability to decide the case.[152]

2. Effect on Witnesses

The Committee heard from several witnesses concerning whether the presence of cameras in the courtroom deters potential witnesses from coming forward.

According to Jacqui Williams, a member of the board of the New York State Coalition Against Sexual Assault, the impact of cameras in the courtroom on sexual assault survivors is "immense" and "create[s] a barrier to any survivor pursuing prosecutorial action."[153] According to Ms. Williams, a study by the National Victim Center suggests that "high profile cases negatively impact on survivors' willingness to report."[154]

New York State Supreme Court Justice Harold Rothwax took issue with the contention that the presence of cameras deters witnesses from coming forward to testify. In his experience, it is not

---

[150] Rochester at 203, 205–06.

[151] Carol De Mare, a reporter of the Albany Times Union, stated that she could see potential prejudice to a criminal defendant if a juror speaks to a spouse who has seen the defendant on television and the defendant has made a poor impression. (Albany at 121–122.) Ms. De Mare further testified that the "same thing could happen" with any witness. She noted that newspaper reporters try to put into context as much as possible of a witness' testimony. "That can't happen on television. The very best line spoken by that witness is what the people see," she told the Committee. "And sometimes the re-cross doesn't get in or a defense lawyer will eventually get up and rehabilitate that witness after that witness has been shot down and that doesn't get on television and it will get into a newspaper." (Id. at 123.) See also testimony of Thomas Moore. (NYC-I at 174.)

[152] Id. at 203–205.

[153] Albany at 219–20.

[154] Id. at 220.

more difficult to get witnesses if cameras are present.[155] His experience is consistent with the views of 42% of the respondents to the Marist public opinion poll, who stated that the presence of a television camera in a criminal case would make no difference in their willingness to testify.[156] However, 54% of all respondents, 45% of black respondents, 41% of regular TV-trial watchers and 64% of women said they would be less willing to testify as a witness to a crime if cameras were present.[157] In contrast, only 20% of all respondents, 16% of black respondents, 20% of regular TV-trial watchers, and 23% of women said they would not be willing to testify if only newspaper reporters were present.[158]

Some lawyers for criminal defendants drew the Committee's attention to the effect of cameras in the courtroom on the willingness of some defense witnesses to come forward in criminal cases. In his testimony, Jonathan Gradess, executive director of the New York State Defenders' Association, related the experience of David Bruck, defense counsel in the Susan Smith murder case in South Carolina, who moved to exclude cameras from that case on the grounds that it would be harder for the defendant's witnesses' "untrammeled, full, nuanced testimony to come across."[159]

On the other hand, Professor Barry Scheck stated that television coverage of the Simpson case led a key defense witness to come forward who might otherwise not have realized the relevance of her testimony.[160]

Peter Moschetti told the Committee that subpoenaing a witness

---

[155] NYC-I at 22. See also testimony of Thomas Neidl, assistant public defender, Albany County ("I have not seen the cameras having any effect on any of my witnesses or my clients" either as a public defender or during his 15 years as a prosecutor) (Albany at 193).

[156] Marist Poll, Question 13. 55% of black respondents and 33% of women said that the presence of cameras would make no difference in their willingness to testify. *Id.*

[157] *Id.*

[158] *Id.*, Question 15. According to the Marist poll, the presence of television cameras in a *civil* case would make no difference in the willingness to testify of 52% of respondents. But 45% of all respondents, 51% of black respondents, 36% of regular TV-trial watchers and 49% of women said they would be less willing to testify as a witness in a non-criminal case if there were cameras in the courtroom. *See* Marist Poll, Question 8. In contrast, only 17% of all respondents, 27% of black respondents, 7% of regular TV-trial watchers and 18% of women said they would not be willing to testify in a non-criminal trial if there were only newspaper reporters in the courtroom (Question 10).

[159] NYC-I at 215.

[160] *Id.* at 130–31.

who is reluctant to testify because of cameras is an option that may "alienate" a witness whom counsel would prefer to put as much at ease as possible.[161] Isaiah Gant, a board member of the Tennessee Association of Criminal Defense Lawyers, gave testimony about adverse effects of cameras on witnesses in the penalty phase of a death penalty case.[162]

Section 218(5)(c) of the Judiciary Law permits non-party witnesses in criminal cases to request that their image be visually obscured[163] and is aimed at reassuring witnesses who are intimidated by the presence of cameras. In this regard, criminal defense attorney Jack Litman testified that even with the blue dot, some witnesses simply will not appear.[164] Other witnesses do not come forward, said Litman, "because they don't know there is a blue dot."[165] According to Litman, the deterrent and intimidating effects of cameras fall disproportionately on defense witnesses, who are typically friends and neighbors of the defendant and are less used to the criminal justice system, he said, than forensic experts or police officers who routinely appear in courtrooms on the prosecution's behalf.[166]

---

[161] Albany at 257. Diane Russell, a Monroe County assistant public defender, testified that a subpoenaed witness did not appear in one of her cases when he became aware that the trial was being filmed on national television (Rochester at 63).

[162] NYC-I at 228. See also testimony of Jack Litman (speaking up for a defendant at the penalty phase of a death case is particularly difficult) (NYC-I at 41).

[163] Under Section 218(5)(c) of the Judiciary Law, the duty to inform a non-party witness of his or her "right to request that his or her image be visually obscured" during the witness' testimony is imposed on counsel in criminal proceedings. Section 218(4)(b) imposes on counsel the duty to convey to the court during the pretrial conference "any concerns of prospective witnesses with respect to audio-visual coverage." The witness' right to insist that his or her image be visually obscured is limited to non-party witnesses in criminal cases. There is no corresponding right in civil cases.

[164] NYC-I at 28. The Committee heard testimony that the blue dot is not always "fail safe." See also testimony of Jacqui Williams, a member of the board of the New York State Coalition Against Sexual Assault, regarding the William Kennedy Smith rape trial in Florida, where the victim's name was inadvertently broadcast (Albany at 222). The Committee was not made aware of any such mishaps taking place in New York, where the rape victim is entitled, under Section 218(7)(g) of the Judiciary Law, to request that his or her testimony not be televised.

[165] NYC-I at 37.

[166] *Id.* at 41. See also testimony of Michelle Maxian, Director of Special Litigation, New York Legal Aid Society, Criminal Defense Division (she said that because government witnesses such as police officers have more experience testifying than defense witnesses, the impact of camera-induced nervousness falls

The Committee also received views that witnesses who do appear at trial may be intimidated by the presence of cameras.[167] Although he favors cameras in the courtroom, Pittoni was of the opinion that the presence of cameras has an effect on witnesses and makes them more nervous.[168] Michelle Maxian of the Legal Aid Society's Criminal Defense Division said that even if witnesses eventually get used to the camera, the defendant in a criminal trial is not entitled to an instant replay. The jury's impression of a witness is formed right from the beginning, Maxian stated. If a nervous witness "hems and haws" or does not answer a question, she opined that that influences the jury's view of the witness's credibility and can influence the jury's fact-finding function.[169]

According to Part II of the Committee's judicial survey (which was completed only by judges who had actually received an application for television coverage in their courtrooms), 40% of the judges agreed that "witnesses were more nervous in the presence of cameras,"[170] although 40% also agreed that "witnesses' testimony was unchanged in the presence of cameras."[171] Thirty-two

---

more heavily on the defendant) (NYC-II at 256); letter dated November 6, 1996 from Peter R. Kehoe, counsel and executive director, New York State Sheriffs' Association Institute (although "none of the responding sheriffs reported the occurrence of any problems during the experimental period, [m]ost expressed a concern that the presence of cameras intimidates some witnesses"); New York State Defenders Association, *The Intrusion of Cameras in New York's Criminal Courts* at 6 (May 12, 1989).

[167] Testimony of Edwin Nowak, Monroe County Public Defender and president of the New York State Defenders' Association (Rochester at 276).

[168] NYC-III at 21. Pittoni suggested that where necessary to protect a witness' livelihood and reputation, witnesses in civil cases be allowed to give their name and address outside of the presence of the jury and to have their visual image obscured. *Id.* at 20–21. Further, although he believed that cameras in the courtroom made some witnesses nervous, he was not convinced that the camera had an adverse effect on the "end product" (*Id.* at 48).

[169] NYC-II at 256.

[170] See Judicial Survey, Question 22(f). 28% of the 173 judges who responded to this question had "no opinion"; 32% disagreed that witnesses were more nervous in the presence of television cameras.

[171] Judicial Survey, Question 22(I). 39% of the 170 judges who responded to this question had "no opinion"; 20% disagreed. See also Eugene Borgida, Kenneth G. DeBono, & Lee A. Buckman, *Cameras in the Courtroom: The Effects of Media Coverage on Witness Testimony and Juror Perceptions*, 14 Law & Human Behavior 489 (1990) (although witnesses and jurors in mock camera-covered trials reported greater witness nervousness, distraction, and awareness than those in mock print media-covered trials, the camera coverage experience did not impair witnesses' ability to accurately recall the details of the crime or the witnesses' ability to communicate effectively).

thought witnesses were distracted by the presence of TV cameras. Twenty-two percent thought witnesses' testimony was more guarded in the presence of cameras.[172] Three percent thought witnesses were more truthful in the presence of cameras.[173] Thirty-two percent thought witnesses' privacy was violated by the presence of cameras.[174]

Some camera proponents said that cameras probably do change participants' behavior, but suggested to the Committee that the effect is no greater than that of a court reporter taking down the witness' every word.[175] While it may be "regrettable" that putting witnesses on television makes them nervous, argued John Corporon, former news director and vice-president, WPIX-TV, "it's part of . . . an open, free system."[176]

One final issue regarding witnesses should be mentioned. It was suggested to the Committee that the presence of cameras invades the privacy of witnesses in ways that are different from print media coverage. According to Professor Barry Scheck of Cardozo Law School, one of the defense lawyers for O. J. Simpson, television coverage conveys a level of intimate personal detail that is usually missing from newspaper coverage. He told the Committee that one of the expert witnesses on DNA contamination in the Simpson criminal case received death threats at his laboratory. Scheck suggested that it would have been unusual for a newspaper to have disclosed, as the television station apparently did, the address of the witness' laboratory.[177] We received no information of an incident of this kind in New York, however.

3. Effect on Lawyers

The experience of lawyers who had tried camera-covered cases ran the gamut from one lawyer who wrote to the Committee to

---

[172] *Id*. Questions 22(e) & 22(h).

[173] *Id*. Question 22(g). 49% of the 174 judges who responded to this question had no opinion; 47% disagreed. In a separate interview, Thomas Moore said that, in his experience, expert witnesses were more truthful in the presence of cameras, avoiding "outlandish and outrageous" claims and statements.

[174] *Id*. Question 22(d). 21% of the 172 judges who responded to this question had no opinion; 47% disagreed.

[175] Testimony of John Corporon, former news director, WPIX-TV (NYC-I at 155–56). See also testimony of Carol De Mare, *Albany Times Union* reporter ("undoubtedly, some witnesses have been inhibited by cameras. I have observed this. It's usually a passing reaction. . . . I think they soon forget that that camera is trained on them.") (Albany at 110).

[176] NYC-I at 162.

[177] NYC-I at 127–30.

SUMMARY OF THE COMMITTE'S RECORD 63

say that the presence of cameras made everyone "extremely self-conscious"[178] to another who testified that it never even occurred to him that the camera was there during a highly sensational murder trial.[179] In between was one lawyer who testified that some lawyers are more conscious of the cameras than he would like them to be[180] and another who expressed his view that "there are a number of my colleagues who believe that television in the courtroom represents essentially free advertising and I think that many times that affects the way they present the case."[181]

Thirty-five percent of the judges who responded to Part II of the Committee's survey agreed that lawyers came to court better prepared in cases in which TV cameras were present.[182] Most judges also felt that compared to similar cases covered only by the print media, about the same number of motions, witnesses, and objections were made in camera-covered cases and about the

---

[178] See members' comments forwarded to the Committee by Deborah A. Elsasser of the Westchester Women's Bar Association (Jan. 9, 1997).

[179] Testimony of Thomas Neidl, assistant public defender, Albany County (Albany at 192). On the other hand, he stated that "there [are] a lot of lawyers who play to the cameras somewhat," although he "did not think that has been really damaging" (Id. at 196–97).

[180] Testimony of Thomas Moore, Esq. (NYC-I at 186).

[181] Testimony of Peter Moschetti (Albany at 243–44). See also letter dated January 28, 1997 from Stephan J. Siegel, Esq. (In the presence of television cameras in the courtroom, "defense lawyers tend to posture and say more about their case than is good for their client. I have even seen lawyers reveal what I thought to be confidences of clients. Prosecutors posture and tend to pronounce grandiloquent platitudes to the detriment of the judicial proceedings"); letter dated January 23, 1997 from Frank A. Gulotta, Jr., President, Bar Association of Nassau County, N.Y., Inc. (Members of his Association felt that "attorneys knowing a case is being televised try . . . to impress the television audience with their flamboyance and antagonistic approach in hopes of attracting future clients"). But see testimony of Pete Dobrovitz, News Director R-News. ("I think the attorneys by nature are performing in a courtroom, and it's still a performance for the jury. And the fact that there are a couple cameras there I don't think affects them differently") (Rochester at 188).

[182] Judicial Survey, Question 22(k). See also testimony of John Miller, reporter, WNBC-TV (when cameras are present, defense lawyers are "better prepared because they know that they are not just defending their clients, but, in a sense, they are selling themselves and their work as highly competent")(NYC-II at 220); testimony of Terence Kindlon, Esq. (when cameras are present, "the defense lawyers behave better, the prosecutors behave better, the judges behave better and even the defendants behave better and the witnesses behave better. Everybody acts the way that they're really supposed to act.")(Albany at 47); letter dated January 22, 1997 from Paul A. Callan, Esq. ("attorneys are generally on their best behavior and are better informed and more forceful advocates when cameras are monitoring the proceedings").

same amount of evidence and argument was presented in both kinds of cases. Thirty-three percent of 147 responding judges were of the view that more arguments were made in camera-covered cases and 26% of 141 responding judges were of the view that more objections were made in camera-covered cases.[183]

A different concern was voiced by several defense counsel. One criminal defense lawyer suggested that "on occasion, decisions are made as to whether there should be a trial or a plea based on sometimes the need or the desire for publicity that's generated as a result of the case that's going to have cameras in the courtroom, and I think that many times that works to the detriment of the defendant."[184] Another defense lawyer, specializing in civil cases, expressed the view that there was a greater probability that a products liability defendant might settle a case if it were to be televised.[185] Finally, several criminal defense lawyers noted that arguing over whether or not cameras should be permitted constituted a last-minute distraction from the job of preparing to try their case.[186]

4. Effect on Judges

a. Inside the Courtroom

With near unanimity, witnesses and interested citizens agreed that the presence of cameras had some effect on judges.[187] There was disagreement over whether the effect was beneficial or harmful.

There was ample testimony and public comment that cameras raised the level of performance of judges. One lawyer who wrote

---

[183] Judicial Survey, Question 23.

[184] Albany at 255.

[185] NYC-III at 77–79. See also testimony of Edgar Green (because a video camera reaches "so deeply in the courtroom, it might influence the way that litigation is brought about") (NYC-III at 55).

[186] See, e.g., testimony of Peter Moschetti, Esq. (when the press makes their application, "you're trying a murder case, you're worried about the rights of the accused, the prosecution is worried about presenting a case in the manner that's going to result in a just decision, and not whether cameras should be in the courtroom and whether there should be a filming") (Albany at 245–46).

[187] See, e.g., testimony of Justice Harold Rothwax (after his wife pointed out that he appeared angry on videotapes of the Steinberg trial, he became more mindful of the way he appeared) (NYC-I at 15); testimony of John Miller, reporter, WNBC-TV (in the presence of cameras, judges may be "more alert") (NYC-II at 220). See Testimony of Hon. Patricia Marks (after the first couple of minutes, "you forget [the camera] is there") (Rochester at 50).

to the Committee suggested that cameras serve as "court watchers" and have an ameliorating effect on judicial conduct.[188] This sentiment was echoed by Terence Kindlon, who testified that when cameras come into court, "the judges behave better"[189] and by Jerry Garguilo and Madeleine Fitzgibbon, co-chairs of the Suffolk County Bar Association's District Court Committee, who concluded that "the effect of camera coverage on the conduct of trial judges both inside and outside the courtroom is indeed positive" since cameras in the courtroom tend to "enhance the behavior of both professional and civil participants in court proceedings."[190]

Joseph Kelner, past president of the New York State Trial Lawyers Association, agreed. In his written comments, he pointed out to the Committee that

> some judges have pro-plaintiff or pro-prosecutor leanings in civil or criminal cases while others occasionally activate their pro-defendant proclivities. Under the glare of television, such excesses are likely to be remedied.[191]

Along similar lines, Luke Pittoni testified that cameras have a "watchdog" impact on judges and ensure that they carefully consider motions and rulings which they might otherwise treat in a more *pro forma* fashion.[192]

Several witnesses reminded the Committee that judges are elected officials who stand to benefit from the publicity a televised

---

[188] Anonymous letter from a former prosecutor who has done "substantial criminal defense work as well" (Dec. 31, 1996) (cameras "act as incentives for judges whose courtroom demeanor and treatment of the participants is normally horrid to behave more properly"). See also testimony of Luke Pittoni (NYC-III at 38–39) (a camera in the courtroom may make the judge "spend more time thinking about his or her ruling").

[189] Albany at 47. See also testimony of Thomas Moore, Esq. (with cameras present, "some judges rise to the occasion and are even better judges") (NYC-I at 186); letter from Francis D. Phillips II, President, New York State District Attorneys Association (October 25, 1996) (when cameras are present, "I have personally witnessed the conduct of judges rise to a higher level"); testimony of Norman Effman, Wyoming County Public Defender (cameras counteract the dangers of a closed society and expose improper judicial practices) (Rochester at 212–13). The Chair's telephone conference with John Condon, Esq. was to the same effect.

[190] Letter dated October 30, 1996 from Jerry Garguilo and Madeleine A. Fitzgibbon to John Juliano, president, Suffolk County Bar Association.

[191] Letter from Joseph Kelner, Esq. (December 20, 1996).

[192] NYC-III at 39.

trial generates. Justice Norman E. Joslin, past president of the New York State Association of Supreme Court Justices, testified that some elected judges welcome the exposure that cameras offer, noting that some judges "will volunteer for . . . a criminal term the year before they're up for re-election. You get a lot more exposure than you will get in the civil term."[193] Justice Joslin testified further that while most judges are very conscientious, "there are a few [who] will showboat" and that "showboating" can affect the fairness of the trial.[194]

Several criminal defense lawyers suggested that the desire for publicity may adversely affect a judge's rulings or his or her conduct at sentencing. Peter Moschetti noted that judges are elected officials and that "to maintain a spot on the bench, it's my belief that you must come across as a law-and-order judge." Moschetti testified that:

> When there's a camera in the courtroom . . . We see more name-calling, words like "predator" and calling them "sick individuals" and "less than human." I have had judges say on the bench, "if the death penalty were available, that person should get it." . . . [T]hose are comments you just didn't hear before the cameras were placed in the courtroom.[195]

His views were echoed by Michelle Maxian, Director of Special Litigation, New York Legal Aid Society, Criminal Defense Division, who testified that judges "want to appear more popular when they are televised" and "right now, what's popular is being tough." According to Ms. Maxian, it takes "a very courageous woman or man who can stand up there and give a ruling that they know will be . . . vilified in the press"[196]

---

[193] Rochester at 126.

[194] Rochester at 126–28.

[195] Albany at 244–45. Mr. Moschetti stated further that the language which the judge places on the record at the time of sentencing may subsequently influence decisions about parole. Albany at 251–53. See also letter from Stephan J. Siegel, Esq. (Jan. 28, 1997) (when cameras are present, "judges tend to react by being much tougher than they regularly are in an effort to show that they are tough on crime").

[196] NYC-II at 255. See also testimony of Thomas Neidl, assistant public defender, Albany County ("I think there [have] been judges who want to move from one bench to another and have used the camera for that purpose. But I think that's a rare example. . . . [T]he judge may be speaking a little longer than he has to, showing himself to be firmer than he has to, because I believe that it's popular for judges running for office to show themselves as tough judges in today's world") (Albany at 189–90).

The Committee's judicial survey sought to elicit judges' views on this issue. Fifty-two percent of 350 judges disagreed with the proposition that cameras in the courts "tend[ ] to cause judges to issue rulings they might otherwise not issue," although 37% agreed with that statement.[197]

b. Outside the Courtroom

The Committee also sought to obtain information about the effect of cameras on the conduct of judges outside the courtroom, including how frequently judges appeared on television or radio to comment on televised cases.

Fourteen percent of the 344 judges who answered the relevant portion of the Committee's judicial survey stated that they had been interviewed on television or radio about a televised court proceeding.[198] The subject matter of the interviews included, among others, a discussion of child abuse and the role of child protective services agencies, the nuts and bolts of housing court proceedings, and the fairness of drunk driving plea bargains, as well as such celebrated cases as the Bernard Goetz, Tawana Brawley, Joseph Buttafuoco, Colin Ferguson, Baby Jessica, and O. J. Simpson cases.[199] Despite the huge amount of publicity surrounding the latter, only two judges stated that they were interviewed about the Simpson case.

---

[197] Judicial Survey, Question 4(g).

[198] Judicial Survey, Question 9. Several of the respondents noted that the interviews occurred before they became judges.

[199] Although criminal cases constitute the overwhelming majority of cases for which applications for audio-visual coverage were forwarded to the Office of Court Administration, civil cases represented approximately one-third of the cases in which judges identified the subject matter of their television or radio interview in response to the Committee's judicial survey.

VI

Committee's Assessment and Conclusions

In assessing each aspect of its legislative mandate, the Committee is mindful that its record contains a great deal of information based on opinions and surveys. The information was received in the form of public testimony, interviews, responses to the Committee's judicial survey, a public opinion poll sponsored by the Marist Institute for Public Opinion, and communications from bar associations, judges, lawyers, law school deans, and interested citizens. The Committee did not undertake extensive controlled studies to measure the difference, if any, in outcomes between trials in which cameras are present and comparable cases in which cameras are not present. Even if funds had been appropriated by the Legislature for such studies, the Committee seriously doubts that any such analysis could or will resolve the fundamental clash of interests and values which underlie the issue of cameras in the court.

The Committee is satisfied that it has heard a broad spectrum of points of view from a wide range of persons with experience and expertise in this field and organizations with a vital interest in this issue. Based on the record it has developed over the course of its work, the Committee reaches the following conclusions about the operation of Section 218 of the Judiciary Law since January 31, 1995.

A. PUBLIC BENEFITS

The Committee believes that one of the greatest benefits derived from the presence of cameras in the courtroom is enhanced public scrutiny of the judicial system. The majority of judges who responded to the Committee's survey and a wide array of witnesses who testified at the Committee's hearings agreed that the presence of television cameras in the courtroom enhances public scrutiny of judicial proceedings.

The record developed by the Committee also suggests that there have been educational benefits to the public in general from the state's experiment with cameras in the courts. It seems clear that television coverage of court proceedings, especially where it is gavel-to-gavel or extended, enables the public to learn more about the workings of the justice system, to see directly the conduct of particular cases, and to become more familiar with legal concepts and developments. The fact that many view television coverage as a form of entertainment does not deprive it of educational content, since education and entertainment are not mutually exclusive.

The record before the Committee does not establish to what extent the presence of cameras in New York State courts has actually enhanced the public's understanding of New York's judicial system. The judges of the State, according to our survey, were split on the question. The record suggests that civil cases are often not covered by the major media and that in criminal proceedings, coverage is focused largely on violent crimes. With rare exceptions, coverage on the evening news takes the form of a brief segment, which is by itself hardly sufficient to promote a detailed understanding of the judicial system. At the same time, there is little doubt that television coverage has drawn the public's attention to major societal problems, such as domestic violence and child abuse, and has served a cathartic purpose for the families of some homicide victims.

The record also contains opinions that the presence of cameras may operate as a disincentive for some victims of sex crimes, domestic violence, or child abuse either to report such crimes or to participate as witnesses in judicial proceedings involving those crimes. According to the Marist poll commissioned by the Committee, a majority of the public would not want their trial televised if they were a party to a proceeding or the victim of a crime. As for the claim that camera coverage may encourage witnesses to come forward, the specific evidence in support of that contention during the experimental period is slight.

Weighing the question of public benefits is not a simple matter. After having carefully reviewed the record, the Committee believes that the benefits that flow from televised coverage of the judicial process are so important that they ought not to be sacrificed by barring cameras from the courtroom across-the-board. The Committee agrees with the view expressed by one witness that "what happens in a trial is a public matter"[1] and should be accessible to as many interested New Yorkers as possible. Video and photographs have become important tools in presenting news to the public, many of whom now rely on television as their principal source of information about public affairs.

Openness of public institutions, including the judiciary, is a key ingredient in our democracy. Among the many values served by openness are promoting public confidence in government, providing the public with information about the workings of the judiciary, assuring the fairness of court proceedings, and satisfying the appearance of justice.

As the New York State Legislature stated in its findings in 1987:

> The average law-abiding citizen is not afforded numerous opportunities to participate in civil and criminal court proceedings, or able to attend and observe firsthand the functioning of our legal system. The vast majority of citizens, therefore, rely on reports in the news media for information about the judicial system and accounts of judicial proceedings.[2]

The Committee considers it of the utmost importance that judges have unfettered discretion to decide in each case whether or not to allow cameras, taking into account the benefits of coverage as well as all of the objections to such coverage, whether those objections are raised by parties, their counsel, prospective 3znwitnesses, crime victims, or other trial participants.

B. COMPLIANCE BY TRIAL JUDGES AND THE NEWS MEDIA WITH THE SAFEGUARDS OF SECTION 218 OF THE JUDICIARY LAW

1. JUDGES

The record strongly suggests that New York State trial judges have discharged with care their responsibilities under Section 218 of the Judiciary Law and have acted appropriately both inside and outside the courtroom. The Committee received few complaints about the way in which trial judges have administered Section 218. Nor has the Committee's research revealed any published

---

[1] Testimony of Syracuse University Professor Jay Wright, executive director, New York State Fair Trial/Free Press Conference (NYC-I at 79).

[2] Chapter 113, Laws of New York, 1987 Regular Session, approved June 15, 1987, codified as § 218 of the Judiciary Law.

appellate decisions overturning a judgment, verdict, or conviction based on the presence of cameras at trial.[3] The evidence, rather, reflects a high degree of compliance by judges with the requirements of Section 218.

We find instructive the evidence from the Committee's judicial survey that many judges have applied the safeguards of Section 218 to deny camera coverage and that some, while granting coverage, have exercised their statutory judicial discretion to impose restrictions in addition to those expressly mandated by Section 218. We note that judges who granted applications for coverage cited "the absence of objections" as the most common reason for doing so and that those who denied coverage frequently did so because of objections by the defense, the prosecution, or witnesses.

According to the Committee's judicial survey, some judges who granted coverage indicated that they felt obligated to do so because they understood Section 218 to contain a presumption in favor of camera coverage. We would note that Section 218 of the Judiciary Law does not contain a presumption of access. Although the statute provides that "audio-visual coverage . . . shall not be limited by the objection of counsel, parties, or jurors, except for a finding by the presiding trial judge of good or legal cause," it expressly states that "presiding trial judges, in their discretion, may permit audio-visual coverage of civil and criminal court proceedings."[4]

The wide discretion of the trial judge in deciding whether or not to permit camera coverage lies at the core of Section 218 and its implementing rules. The statute instructs the judge to evaluate:

1. The type of case involved;
2. Whether the coverage would cause harm to any participant in the case or otherwise interfere with the fair administration of justice, the advancement of a fair trial, or the rights of the parties;
3. Whether any order directing the exclusion of witnesses from the courtroom prior to their testimony could be rendered substantially ineffective by allowing audio-visual

---

[3] See, e.g., *New York v. Shattell*, 179 A.D.2d 896, 578 N.Y.S.2d 694 (3d Dep't 1992) (rejecting defendant's claim that he was denied a fair trial as a result of alleged mismanagement of television cameras at his trial).

[4] Judiciary Law § 218(3)(b) & 218(1).

coverage that could be viewed by such witnesses to the detriment of any party;
4. Whether such coverage would interfere with any law enforcement activity;
5. Whether such coverage would involve lewd or scandalous matters.[5]

In addition, under the rules promulgated by the Chief Administrative Judge, judges must take into account "the objections of any of the parties, prospective witnesses, victims or other participants in the proceedings of which coverage is sought" and must give "great weight" to the fact that a child may be involved.[6]

Judges are further directed to protect all participants and to preserve the welfare of minors, where necessary, by prohibiting coverage of testimony or exhibits, particularly in cases involving "lewd or scandalous matters." The law imposes no limits on this authority and further enables judges to modify or reverse any earlier order or determination. In other words, a judge can decide mid-trial to remove cameras from the courtroom or bar coverage of any witness or exhibit, even if he or she previously indicated coverage would be allowed.

If a judge elects to grant permission to cover a trial, he or she must make a written order granting permission for coverage and include this order in the record of the proceedings. The order must contain the judge's restrictions and a warning to all parties that a violation of the restrictions is punishable by contempt. The judge must also go over his or her restrictions and warnings with counsel and the media in a pre-trial conference.

We conclude, in the absence of any hard evidence of judicial abuses in any of the cases televised during the experimental period, that there is no basis in the record to bar outright all televised coverage of court proceedings based on the potential for such abuse. However, the discretion of the trial judge is of critical importance in handling requests for camera coverage and in striking the appropriate balance in each case between the principles of public access and a fair trial. We stress again that judges must have wide discretion to weigh the benefits and objections to camera coverage in each individual case. By a wide margin, our judicial

---
[5] Judiciary Law § 218(3)(c).
[6] N.Y. Court Rules § 131.4(c)(7).

survey shows that judges favor broad discretion in this area.[7] It should remain unfettered.

2. News Media

The Committee's record includes strong evidence of compliance with the requirements and safeguards of Section 218 by representatives of the electronic news media. Reporters and photographers who testified before the Committee appeared to understand and respect the solemnity and dignity of the courtrooms they covered. The most common complaint heard by the Committee was the absence of 7-days notice of the media's intent to film or photograph a court proceeding. It appears that in some cases the 7-days notice was not given. In some instances, judges have exercised their statutory discretion to shorten the notice period (i.e., where 7-day notice was not possible because the court proceeding was scheduled at the last minute) or have denied coverage altogether because of the absence of adequate notice.

The Committee's record revealed several individual complaints about the media, ranging from filming of arraignments without the consent of the defendant to filming material on counsel table without permission of the court or counsel. It appears that some of the *alleged* violations may have been inadvertent, although not all of the complaints can be excused on this ground. Other complaints regarding the use of televised footage fell outside the scope of Section 218 and took issue with editorial decisions regarding such footage.

We believe that in order to minimize inadvertent violations of the statute, it would be important for the Office of Court Administration to develop a new application form which would identify, in plain English, each of the restrictions on camera coverage that are enumerated in the applicable law and administrative rules. Representatives of the news media should be required to sign the form to indicate that they have read and understood the applicable safeguards.

C. EFFECT OF AUDIO-VISUAL COVERAGE ON THE CONDUCT OF PARTICIPANTS IN COURT PROCEEDINGS

Central to the debate over cameras in the courtroom are concerns about the psychological impact of the camera. Will critical wit-

---

[7] Judicial Survey, Questions 5(a) & 5(f).

nesses be deterred from coming forward by the fear of publicity? Will witnesses be so nervous or guarded in the presence of television cameras that the jury will mistake that nervousness for a lack of credibility? Will jurors avoid reaching unpopular verdicts for fear of public reaction? Will lawyers "showboat," wasting the court's time with frivolous arguments, unnecessary motions, cumulative witnesses? Will judges, with an eye on the upcoming elections, tailor their rulings and their sentencings to suit the views of the television audience scrutinizing their performance?

Undoubtedly, it is human nature to act differently when our conduct is under public scrutiny. But the question for this Committee is how differently do we act in the presence of cameras, and is that difference (whatever it might be) significant enough to justify ending the use of cameras in the courtrooms of New York State?

Prior Committees, reviewing earlier surveys of judges, lawyers, and other trial participants, concluded that evidence of impact on trial participants was too slight to outweigh the benefits of cameras. The majority of states which permit camera coverage of court proceedings have reached similar conclusions.[8] The U.S. Judicial Conference brought its "cameras in the court" pilot project to a halt because "the intimidating effect of cameras on some witnesses and jurors was cause for concern."[9]

The record developed by this Committee does not show that the fears regarding the impact of cameras on trial participants have been realized in New York during the experimental period. In our judgment, if subject to judicial discretion and accompanied by appropriate safeguards for trial participants, audio-visual coverage does not impair the search for justice. The many safeguards contained in Section 218 of the Judiciary Law and the implementing rules issued by the Chief Administrative Judge, along with the

---

[8] *See* Molly Treadway Johnson, "Supplemental Report to the Federal Judicial Center, Electronic Media Coverage of Courtroom Proceedings: Effects on Witnesses and Jurors" at 4 (January 18, 1994) (overview of 12 state studies of the impact of cameras on witnesses and jurors suggests that the majority of jurors and witnesses who experience media coverage do not report negative consequences or concerns).

[9] See memorandum dated September 22, 1995 from L. Ralph Mecham, Director, Administrative Office of the United States Courts to All Judges, United States Courts. Some members of the Judicial Conference of the United States, who voted by a 2-1 margin to disapprove the request to permit cameras in the federal courts in civil proceedings, "believed that *any* negative impact on witnesses or jurors could be a threat to the fair administration of justice." *Id.*

recommendations in this report, if properly applied, address the fair trial concerns that have been raised. We therefore conclude that any impact cameras may have on trial participants does not justify an across-the-board ban of cameras in courtrooms.

1. Jurors

Although under the current statute no audio-visual coverage of jurors is permitted,[10] two major concerns were voiced at the Committee's hearings with respect to jurors: first, that jurors will watch televised coverage of the case (or will speak to family members, friends, and colleagues who have watched the televised coverage) and will be influenced either by commentary about the case or by evidence which was ruled inadmissible and thus not presented to the jury; and second, that jurors will be influenced in their deliberations by their realization that the eyes of the general public are upon them and will be reluctant to reach a verdict which is "unpopular" with the community to which they will return after the trial.

The Committee has not received any hard data to support these claims. No one has drawn the Committee's attention to a specific case in New York in which jurors had improper communications regarding a televised case or in which jurors disregarded a judge's instructions not to watch televised coverage of the proceedings. Nor has it been suggested to us that the outcome of a particular case in New York was altered by the presence of cameras. Judges, of course, are equipped with a variety of tools which they can use to minimize the impact of trial publicity. They can instruct the jury not to watch televised coverage of the case and can give those instructions repeatedly throughout the trial. In extraordinary cases, they can sequester the jury.

We recognize that fears that jurors will be influenced by televised coverage of a case or will shy away from reaching unpopular verdicts are not wholly imaginary. But we believe that judges, exercising their discretion under the statute, are capable of taking these factors into account when they consider whether to grant

---

[10] Judiciary Law § 218(7)(d) prohibits audio-visual coverage of jurors while in the jury box, in the courtroom, in the jury deliberation room during recess, or while going to or from the deliberation room, except that upon the consent of the foreperson "of a jury, the presiding trial judge may, in his or her discretion, permit audio coverage of such foreperson delivering a verdict."

or deny an application for camera coverage in a particular case. In this regard, we note that a number of New York State judges reported that in denying an application for television coverage, they typically take into account whether the coverage might unfairly influence or distract the jury.

2. WITNESSES

It is the possible effect of the presence of cameras on witnesses that lies at the heart of some of the opposition to cameras in the courtroom. Concerns were voiced by some at the Committee's hearings that if cameras are present, witnesses will be deterred from coming forward to testify. For example, a prospective witness may be concerned that certain aspects of his or her past will be made public before a television audience. It was said that the victim of a rape and sexual assault may fear the invasion of privacy that follows in the wake of a highly publicized trial and may refrain from prosecuting a case because of the attendant publicity. It was also said that a witness may fear retribution and physical retaliation. It was suggested that witnesses who do come forward will be intimidated by the presence of cameras, and that their initial nervousness may be misinterpreted by the jury as a lack of credibility. Where the witness' testimony is highly personal in nature, concerns were voiced that the presence of cameras will make it more difficult for witnesses to tell their story fully and honestly.

It is difficult for this Committee to segregate the effect on witnesses of the presence of television cameras from the effect of being called to testify in any public trial (especially a highly publicized trial) which is covered by the print media alone, or, for that matter, in any public trial before a judge and jury. The Marist poll suggests that members of the public have a greater aversion to testifying in the presence of cameras than in the presence of conventional media, although there is an aversion to the latter as well. The Committee's judicial survey suggests that many judges believe that witnesses' testimony is unchanged in the presence of cameras.

The Committee concludes from its review of the evidence that witness intimidation is neither borne out by the record in New York nor sufficiently strong to warrant barring cameras from the courtroom across-the-board. Such witness concerns are adequately addressed, in our view, by all of the current safeguards in Section 218 and in the implementing rules. In deciding whether to permit cameras, judges need to be mindful, as they have been during the experimental period, of the potential effects of coverage on witnesses. Where camera coverage is permitted in criminal proceedings, judges should ensure that counsel have advised witnesses of their right under Section 218 to request that their image be visually obscured and, if necessary, reiterate that admonition themselves. In addition, Section 218 accords judges the power in both civil and criminal proceedings to insist that the face—and the voice, if necessary—of a witness not be transmitted beyond the courtroom.[11]

In the final analysis, we observe that New York opted in 1987 to open its courts to cameras in both civil and criminal proceedings. Almost 10 years of experience argue against an across-the-board ban on cameras so long as a law allowing camera coverage is grounded on judicial discretion, contains all of the safeguards in place during the experimental period, and directs the Office of Court Administration to monitor camera-covered proceedings, make periodic reports, and, if necessary, recommend changes in Section 218 of the Judiciary Law and the implementing rules. It is this Committee's judgment that such an approach, in the context of New York's experiment, respects the public value of openness, the public nature of a trial, and the constitutional principle of a fair trial.

3. Lawyers

The experience of lawyers who have tried camera-covered cases ran the gamut from those who were self-conscious to whose who told the Committee that they were unaware of the camera. For the most part, it appears that lawyers who are initially self-conscious often become so absorbed in the task of trying their case that the camera fades into the background. There is some indication that lawyers may come to court better prepared in camera-covered cases.[12]

Concern was voiced that prosecutors, knowing that a case is being televised, will make decisions (i.e., whether or not to offer a plea bargain, for instance) with an eye to the favorable publicity

---

[11] Judiciary Law § 218(2)(I), 218(5)(c), 218(7).
[12] Judicial Survey, Question 22(k).

that might attend a televised trial. Others expressed concern that attorneys in a televised case will seek to impress the television audience in hopes of attracting future clients.

According to the Committee's judicial survey, most judges felt that compared to similar cases covered only by the print media, lawyers made about the same number of motions, objections, and arguments in camera-covered cases and presented about the same amount of evidence and witnesses.[13]

One objection voiced by lawyers about the impact of cameras on their own performance was that arguing over whether or not cameras should be permitted constituted a last-minute distraction from the job of preparing to try their case. For this reason, the Committee believes that it remains important that lawyers receive adequate notice of the media's application for permission to televise a trial, especially one that has been scheduled in advance.

As for the claim of lawyers seeking to "showboat" or call attention to themselves in televised cases, we cannot discount these possibilities. On the other hand, we do not believe that it is fair to the public to construct a policy against cameras based on a presumption that lawyers will not handle their roles professionally. We recognize that some may not, with or without cameras, but we have no basis from our review to conclude that lawyers in camera-covered cases in New York State have failed to serve their clients and the public responsibly. The evidence from the record before this Committee is that they have met their professional obligations.

4. JUDGES

The Committee's record establishes that the presence of cameras has an effect on some judges. There was ample testimony and public comment that cameras raised some judges' performance and had a positive impact on judicial demeanor. Some suggested to the Committee that cameras serve as "court watchers" and deter judicial abuses. A few witnesses suggested, however, that cameras encourage "showboating" and can adversely affect a judge's rulings, particularly at the time of sentencing. Thirty-seven percent of the 350 judges who responded to the Committee's judicial survey agreed that the presence of television cameras

---

[13] *Id.*, Question 23.

in the courtroom tends to cause judges to issue rulings they otherwise might not issue, with 52% disagreeing with that statement.

The Committee has wrestled with the meaning of the response to this survey question. While it is possible that some judges may issue substantively different rulings when cameras are present, we think that it is at least equally plausible that the presence of cameras may simply cause some judges to proceed with greater caution and to issue written rulings instead of ruling from the bench on a variety of objections and evidentiary issues. Without further information, it is difficult to draw any firm conclusion from this survey response.

As for the argument that the presence of cameras causes judges to make harsher comments at the time of sentencing or even to impose harsher sentences, we find it difficult, if not impossible, to segregate the impact of cameras from the overall pressure of the times for judges to be "tough on crime" regardless of whether or not cameras are present.

In the end, we are left with a record heavily weighted with opinions which suggest that judicial conduct may improve rather than worsen in the presence of cameras. There is no basis in this record to conclude that judges will not faithfully discharge their responsibilities if courtrooms are open to cameras. The evidence before this Committee is that they have met their obligations with a high degree of competence.

D. DEFENDANT'S CONSENT

A number of criminal defense lawyers who testified before the Committee urged us to recommend that Section 218 of the Judiciary Law be amended to require the consent of the defendant in a criminal trial before television cameras are admitted to the courtroom. They argue that it is the defendant's Sixth Amendment right to a fair trial which is at stake in a criminal proceeding and that the defendant ought therefore to have a say in whether or not the trial is televised. They further argue that if witnesses are deterred by the presence of cameras from coming forward, if witnesses are intimidated by the presence of cameras, or if jurors will be influenced by televised coverage of the trial, the defendant—whose liberty and whose life is at stake—should have a voice in determining whether or not cameras will be present.

We note that New York, by imposing a defendant consent requirement for two major categories of pre-trial proceedings, has already gone further in the direction of protecting the rights of criminal defendants than most states. Under Section 218 of the Judiciary Law, neither arraignments nor suppression hearings may be covered by cameras unless the defendant consents to the coverage. Of the 37 states which permit camera coverage in criminal proceedings without the consent of the defendant at trial, it appears that New York is the only one to explicitly limit coverage of arraignments.[14] New York also is one of only a handful of states to explicitly limit coverage of motions *in limine* and hearings on the admissibility of evidence.[15]

Precluding camera coverage of an arraignment without the defendant's consent minimizes the likelihood that witnesses in subsequent "line ups" and other identification procedures will be influenced in their identifications and perceptions by images broadcast from an arraignment. Similarly, exclusion of cameras from suppression hearings minimizes the possibility that prospective jurors will be exposed to information and evidence which a judge has ruled to be inadmissible at trial.

In order to more fully protect the defendant's fair trial rights, we believe that it would be consistent with the existing statutory safeguards to add bail hearings to the list of pre-trial proceedings which require defendant consent. Wide dissemination of hearsay statements made by prosecutors at bail hearings may have a prejudicial effect on prospective jurors comparable to that of broad dissemination of inadmissible evidence.

With these pretrial safeguards in place, together with all of the other statutory and administrative safeguards and the wide discretion granted to the trial judge, we do not believe that a defendant consent requirement is needed at trial, or appropriate. In our view, one of the gravest dangers to a defendant's fair trial rights is created by pretrial publicity and, particularly, by publicity regarding inadmissible evidence. At the trial stage, we believe that openness and the public access to information about trials afforded by television works as a safeguard, not a threat, to the defendant's

---

[14] Radio and Television News Directors Association, *News Media Coverage of Judicial Proceedings with Cameras and Microphones: A Survey of the States* at B-26 (January 1997).
[15] *Id.* at B-25, B-26.

rights. As the U.S. Supreme Court ruled in *Richmond Newspapers, Inc. v. Virginia*, 448 U.S. 555 (1980), an open trial

> giv[es] assurance that the proceedings were conducted fairly to all concerned and discourage[s] perjury, the misconduct of participants, or decisions based on secret bias or partiality.[16]

As for death penalty cases, the Committee discussed whether there should be a special rule to take account of the fact that the state's death penalty law is new and that we have had no experience with camera coverage in such cases. The Committee noted that a majority of the 323 New York State judges who responded to the relevant portion of its survey were not of the view that different rules were needed to govern television camera access in capital cases, although a sizeable minority favored banning cameras in death penalty cases.[17] We find no basis from our consideration of the subject to distinguish such cases. We believe it important to emphasize again, however, that the trial judge must take account of all relevant factors in the particular case.

---

[16] 448 U.S. at 569. The case did not involve camera coverage of a trial.
[17] Judicial Survey, Question 8(b).

VII

Recommendations

1. Cameras Should Be Permitted in New York State Courts on a Permanent Basis with All of the Safeguards of Current Law for Parties, Prospective Witnesses, Jurors, Crime Victims, and Other Trial Participants

Our Committee conducted its work against the background of camera coverage in New York State of civil and criminal proceedings since December 1, 1987. In allowing for an experimental period, the New York State Legislature noted in its 1987 findings that:

> court proceedings are complex, often involving human factors that are difficult to measure. There may be inherent problems in any court proceeding which could possibly be complicated by audio-visual coverage.

> [T]he Legislature, remaining sensitive to these concerns, hereby determines that, in order to enhance public familiarity with the workings of the judicial system, while not interfering with the dignity and decorum of the courtroom, the prohibition of audio-visual coverage of court proceedings should be modified for an experimental period.

Our review of the experiment, the fourth of its kind in New York since 1987, did not find any evidence that the presence of cameras in New York cases has actually interfered in a particular case with the fair administration of justice. Rather, testimony from over 50 witnesses who spoke at our five public hearings, over 350 responses to our judicial survey, and over 50 letters of public comment from lawyers, bar associations, and interested citizens strongly suggests that the judges of this state have done an excellent job in administering the present law. The many safeguards contained in the law and in the accompanying rules issued by the Chief Administrative Judge have worked well to provide judges with the necessary discretion to deal with possible abuses and to protect the legitimate concerns of parties, prospective witnesses, jurors, crime victims, and other participants in trial proceedings.

In light of the long period of examination of this subject by prior committees and our committee, we recommend that Section 218 of the Judiciary Law be amended to permit audio-visual coverage on a permanent basis, with all of the safeguards of the current legislation for defendants in criminal proceedings, parties in civil proceedings, witnesses, jurors, crime victims, children, and others. We believe that the public nature of a trial and the public's right of access to a trial support the adoption of a law permitting television coverage of court proceedings under the careful control and supervision of trial judges, who must retain their unfettered discretion to determine whether or not to admit cameras to their courtroom, taking into consideration the concerns of trial participants.

In striking this balance, we find instructive judicial decisions on the public nature of a trial and the values served by the principle of openness of the judicial process. These values include promoting confidence in the judicial process, assuring that proceedings are conducted fairly, providing the public with information about the workings of the judiciary, and satisfying the appearance of justice. Although televised coverage may, at times, show the legal system in an unfavorable light, we do not view that as a detriment. Rather, to the extent that such coverage offers an opportunity for improving the judicial system, we view it as a strength of our democratic system.

2. Defendant Consent Should Be a Prerequisite for Camera Coverage of Bail Hearings

We further recommend that the Legislature extend to bail hearings the same safeguard of defendant's consent which is currently required as a prerequisite to camera coverage of arraignments and suppression hearings. Because widespread pre-trial dissemination of hearsay statements made at bail hearings may have a prejudicial effect on prospective jurors comparable to that of the dissemination of evidence ruled inadmissible at a suppression hearing, the Committee believes that it would be consistent with existing safeguards to add bail hearings to the list of pre-trial proceedings which required defendant's consent.

3. There Should Be No Separate Rule for Death Penalty Cases

The Committee considered whether there should be a special camera coverage rule for death penalty cases in light of the fact that New York State's death penalty statute is new and that we have no experience with camera coverage in such cases. We find no basis in our consideration of the subject to distinguish such cases. However, we believe that it is important for the trial judge to take account of all relevant factors—including even slight evidence of a prospective witness's intimidation and nervousness—in deciding whether or not to permit camera coverage in death penalty cases.

4. Judges Should Be Vigilant in Addressing the Safety and Privacy Concerns of Witnesses in Both Criminal and Civil Proceedings

The Committee considered whether a witness's right to insist that his or her image be visually obscured—which is available under current law to non-party witnesses in criminal cases—should be extended to non-party witnesses in civil cases. The Committee concluded that it is appropriate to distinguish between these two categories of proceedings, given the heightened safety concerns that could exist in a criminal trial, where threats to witnesses' physical safety may be of serious concern. We also recognize that the privacy concerns of rape and other sexual assault victims are important in criminal proceedings.

We believe that the safety and privacy concerns of witnesses in civil cases deserve the trial judge's careful attention. Some witnesses in civil proceedings may reasonably fear injury to their personal or professional reputation if certain aspects of their past are suddenly thrust before a television audience. In accordance with the rules of the Chief Administrative Judge, we believe that trial judges should remain "specially sensitive and responsive to the needs and concerns of all . . . witnesses" and should exercise, where and if necessary, their statutory discretion to protect the witness in a civil proceeding who raises a valid privacy or safety concern.

5. The Office of Court Administration Should Actively Monitor Camera-Covered Proceedings, Make Periodic Reports, and, if Necessary, Recommend Changes in Section 218 of the Judiciary Law and the Implementing Rules

Although we uncovered no pattern of non-compliance by the media with the safeguards of the law, we heard complaints about inadequate notice of the news media's interest in televising a court proceeding as well as scattered other complaints, ranging from filming material on counsel table without the consent of the court or counsel to violations of judges' orders not to film certain trial participants. (As previously noted, the Committee did not investigate and determine the merit or validity of each complaint.) We also received information of an anecdotal nature that some witnesses might be deterred from coming forward by the presence of cameras in the courtroom, that some of those who did come forward might be intimidated by the presence of cameras, and that their attendant nervousness could be misinterpreted by the jury as a lack of credibility.

We also note that the development of new technology and new media for the coverage of trials (e.g., the Internet, additional cable networks and programs) make it impossible to say with absolute certainty how these expanded types of coverage will affect trials in the future. The recent enactment of the New York death penalty statute introduces a further element of uncertainty into the "cameras in the court" arena, since no death penalty case has yet been tried with cameras in the courtroom. Therefore, in implementing a permanent law in New York on cameras in the courts, we consider it essential that the Office of Court Administration actively monitor compliance with the law and its implementing rules, establish a formal mechanism to receive and review complaints about the operation of the law, make periodic reports to the Legislature and, if necessary, recommend changes in Section 218 and the implementing rules.

We recommend a three-part monitoring approach. First, OCA should develop a formal procedure for receiving and investigating complaints from trial participants, members of the public, and the press. Those who believe that Section 218, or the implementing rules, have been violated need to have somewhere to go with their complaints. A formal mechanism for filing those complaints should be established, together with a procedure for investigating those complaints and publicly reporting the results of those investigations.

Second, the Office of Court Administration should periodically survey lawyers who have participated in camera-covered cases about their experience. A sample survey has been prepared by the Committee and is included in Appendix I to this report. Such a survey would assist OCA in assessing the impact of cameras on witnesses and other trial participants and could serve as the basis for future judicial training programs.

Third, the Office of Court Administration should collect certain basic data on each case in which an application for camera coverage is made and should provide periodic reports to the Chief Judge, the Legislature, and the Governor summarizing its findings. The types of data which should be considered for collection include:

1. the applicant (with pertinent identifying information);
2. the court to which the application was made and the name of the presiding judge;
3. type of case (including whether the case is a civil or criminal proceeding, what the principal crime or cause of action is, and whether the case is one in which the death penalty has been sought);
4. type of coverage sought (gavel-to-gavel or for a particular witness or portion of the proceeding; live television coverage; videotape for later broadcast; still photography; radio broadcast);
5. type of proceeding for which coverage is sought (arraignment, suppression hearing, bail hearing, pre-trial motion, trial, verdict, penalty phase of capital case, sentencing, appeal, etc.);
6. whether objections were made and, if so, by whom and on what grounds;
7. grounds for granting or denying the application;
8. any limitations imposed on coverage;
9. whether approval was subsequently revoked in whole or in part;
10. how many witnesses, if any, requested that their image be visually obscured and, if known, why;
11. names, addresses and telephone numbers for the presid-

ing judge, parties' attorneys, and representatives of the media who applied for permission for camera coverage;
12. whether the decision to grant or deny coverage was subsequently challenged;
13. in criminal proceedings where permission for televised coverage is sought, what level of bail was set, whether the defendant was acquitted or convicted and, if convicted, what sentence was imposed;
14. whether any complaints were filed with the Office of Court Administration and, if so, the results of OCA's investigation of the complaint.

Finally, the Committee recommends that in order to minimize inadvertent violations of the statute, it would be important for the Office of Court Administration to develop a new application form which would identify, in plain English, each of the restrictions on camera coverage which are enumerated in the applicable law and administrative rules. Representatives of the news media should be required to sign the form to indicate that they have read and understood the applicable safeguards.

6. The Office of Court Administration Should Develop an Enhanced Judicial Training Program to Familiarize All Judges with the Applicable Statutory and Administrative Provisions and Safeguards

It is essential that all judges be familiar with the safeguards contained in Section 218 of the Judiciary Law and in the implementing rules promulgated by the Chief Administrative Judge. We recommend that OCA develop a judicial training program for all judges, including town and village judges, to ensure that the entire judiciary of the state is familiar with the safeguards contained in the statute and the rules which are designed to provide judges with wide discretion and to protect parties, witnesses, jurors, crime victims, and other trial participants.

A syllabus for a continuing judicial education program on cameras in the courts is included in Appendix J to this report. Using selected readings, lectures, simulations and roundtable discussions with camera-experienced judges, lawyers, witnesses, jurors, journalists and media scholars, a judicial training program should acquaint all judges with the requirements and safeguards of Section 218 and the implementing rules, and should provide a guide to judges for the informed exercise of their statutory discretion.

                                            Respectfully submitted,[1]

                                            Fritz W. Alexander, II
                                            Richard Alteri
                                            Jay C. Carlisle, II
                                            Veronica Gabrielli Dumas
                                            John D. Feerick, Chair
                                            Diane Kennedy
                                            Henry G. Miller
                                            Leonard Noisette[2]
                                            Michelle Rea
                                            James M. Tien
                                            Monte I. Trammer

April 4, 1997

---

[1] Alissa Pollitz Worden was unable to participate in the work of the Committee and therefore did not express a view.

[2] Leonard Noisette, Esq., submits a minority report.

APPENDICES

APPENDIX A

Appendix A
Judicial Survey

The Committee developed a two-part survey to elicit detailed information about the operation of New York's "cameras in the court" law and to determine the views of New York State judges on this issue. Together with the attached cover letter, the survey was mailed in late October 1996 to 1,108 state-payroll judges, using mailing labels supplied to the Committee by the New York State Office of Court Administration. Judges were invited to return the survey in pre-printed envelopes addressed to the Committee at Fordham Law School.

351 judges (31.7% of those surveyed) responded to Part I of the survey, which was addressed to all judges and was designed to elicit their views on the benefits and detriments of cameras in the courtroom under the current statute. Of these, 226 judges (64.4%) also responded to Part II of the survey, which was addressed only to judges who had received one or more applications to permit television coverage in their courtroom. Part II was designed to elicit specific, detailed information about the courtroom experience of judges who had actually ruled on camera coverage applications and to determine how they interpreted and applied the law.

The statistical analysis of the survey was performed on a *pro bono* basis for the Committee by Professor Edmund H. Mantell of Pace University's Lubin School of Business. The results of the survey are summarized on the following survey form. The number of responses ("N") is indicated for each question and the distribution of responses for each question is stated in percentage terms. For questions with a 5-scale "agreement" response, a weighted mean was also computed by assigning a weight of $+2$ to "strongly agree," a weight of $+1$ to "somewhat agree," a weight of "0" to "no opinion," a weight of -1 to "somewhat disagree" and a weight of -2 to "strongly disagree."

Inasmuch as the 351 responses constitute only a sample—although, compared to other typical surveys, a relatively large sample—of the target group of 1,108 judges, two questions arise:

Are the results statistically significant? Are the results representative of the target group? Statistical tests were performed to assess whether the results are statistically different from an equally likely response (i.e., a 50%-50% response to a 2-outcome question, or a 20%-20%-20%-20%-20% response to a 5-outcome question). Given the relatively large sample size and at a 95% level of confidence, it can be stated that most of the responses in the survey are indeed statistically significant.

The issue of representativeness is harder to address. Certainly, if the 351 responses were randomly drawn from a target group of 1,108 judges, then the responses would be a true representation of the opinions of all 1,108 judges. On the other hand, it could also be possible that only those judges who had a strong opinion responded. In such a case, the survey results would, of course, not be representative. However, the resultant survey results do not indicate respondent bias. This, together with the relatively large response, would suggest that the survey respondents can be considered to be a representative sample of the 1,108 judges.

October 25, 1996

Re: Cameras in the Court

Dear Judge:

    I am writing to ask for your help in connection with the work of the New York State Committee to Review Audiovisual Coverage of Court Proceedings. The Committee, which I chair, is an independent body charged by the New York State Legislature with the task of evaluating New York's experiment with cameras in the courtroom.

    To help us in our work, we have prepared a two-part questionnaire. The first 10 questions invite responses from <u>all</u> judges, regardless of whether or not you have had experience with cameras in your courtroom. The final set of 15 questions is addressed to judges who have received an application for camera coverage in their courtroom.

    Your views and experience are important to our evaluation. The results of the enclosed survey will be reported to the New York State Legislature, the Governor and the Chief Judge and will inform their views about the future of cameras in New York State courts. However, we will report only aggregate responses from the survey. No answers or comments will be attributed to particular individuals.

    We welcome additional comments. If you would like to explain any of your answers, please include your comments in the space provided.

    Thank you in advance for taking the time to complete this survey. We would be most appreciative if you could return it by <u>November 30, 1996</u> to Fordham Law School, Office of the Dean, 140 West 62d Street, New York NY 10023.

Respectfully,

John D. Feerick

NEW YORK STATE
COMMITTEE TO REVIEW AUDIO VISUAL COVERAGE OF COURT PROCEEDINGS
CAMERAS IN NEW YORK COURTROOMS
JUDICIAL SURVEY

The New York State Committee to Review Audio Visual Coverage of Court Proceedings is an independent body chaired by John D. Feerick, Dean of Fordham Law School. The Committee has been charged by the New York State Legislature with the task of evaluating New York's experiment with cameras in the courtroom.

There are two parts to this survey. The first 10 questions invite responses from *all* judges, regardless of whether or not you have had experience with cameras in your courtroom. The final set of 15 questions is addressed to judges who have received an application for camera coverage in their courtroom.

Your views are important to our evaluation. The results of this survey will be reported to the New York State Legislature, the Governor and the Chief Judge and will inform their views about the future of cameras in New York State courts. We will report only aggregate survey responses. No answers or comments will be attributed to particular individuals.

We welcome additional comments. If you would like to explain any of your answers, please check the appropriate box in the right hand margin and include your comments in the space provided or on the blank pages at the end of the survey.

Please complete and return the original by November 30, 1996 to:
Dean John D. Feerick
Fordham University School of Law
140 West 62nd Street
New York NY 10023

New York State
Committee to Review Audio Visual Coverage of Court Proceedings

The New York State Committee to Review Audio Visual Coverage of Court Proceedings consists of the following members:

>Hon. Fritz W. Alexander II, partner, Epstein, Becker & Green and former Associate Justice, New York State Court of Appeals
>
>Richard Alteri, President, Cable Television and Telecommunications Association of New York
>
>Professor Jay Carlisle, Pace University School of Law
>
>Veronica G. Dumas, Assistant District Attorney, Office of the Albany County District Attorney
>
>John D. Feerick, Dean, Fordham University School of Law (Chair)
>
>Diane Kennedy, President of the New York Newspaper Publishers Association
>
>Henry G. Miller, Senior Partner, Clark, Gagliardi & Miller
>
>Leonard Noisette, Director, Neighborhood Defenders Service of Harlem
>
>Professor James M. Tien, Chair of the Department of Decision Sciences and Engineering Systems, Renneselaer Polytechnic Institute
>
>Monte I. Trammer, President and Publisher of the Saratogian & Community News
>
>Alissa Pollitz Worden, Associate Dean, School of Criminal Justice, University of Albany, State University of New York

The Committee was appointed pursuant to section 218(9) of the Judiciary Law by the Governor, the Chief Judge and the leaders of the New York State legislature.

APPENDICES

NEW YORK STATE
COMMITTEE TO REVIEW AUDIO VISUAL COVERAGE OF COURT PROCEEDINGS
CAMERAS IN NEW YORK COURTROOMS JUDICIAL SURVEY

PART I

Questions 1 through 10 invite responses from ALL JUDGES, whether or not you have had experience with cameras in your courtroom.

351 judges responded to Part I of the Survey.

1. Name (optional): _____

2. (a) How many years have you served on the bench? __11.63 (average)__
   (b) Court(s) in which you have presided: _____

Civil	135	Supreme	225
Criminal	153	City	61
District	24	Family	94
County	94	Other	70

   (c) County in which your court is located: _____

3. (a) In approximately how many jury trials have you presided. **N = 351**

   Civil __69 (average)__   Criminal __84 (average)__

   (b) In approximately how many proceedings have you presided in which television cameras were present: Civil __3.4 (average)__   Criminal __9.3 (average)__

                                                               N = 63   N = 157

   (c) Prior to your service on the bench, did you ever serve as a   N

       (i) criminal defense counsel?   Yes **68%**   No **32%**   318

       (ii) criminal prosecutor?   Yes **47%**   No **53%**   301

       (iii) civil litigator?   Yes **86%**   No **14%**   333

APPENDICES   99

4. Do you agree or disagree with the following statements (please check the applicable box):

	Television coverage:	Strongly agree	Somewhat agree	Somewhat disagree	Strongly disagree	No Opinion	N	Weighted Mean
(a)	Increases the accuracy of news accounts of judicial proceedings	9%	38%	24%	23%	5%	349	-0.126
(b)	Has enhanced public understanding of New York's judicial system	10%	35%	27%	25%	3%	350	-0.214
(c)	Is more likely to serve as a source of entertainment than education for the viewing public	41%	39%	15%	3%	2%	350	0.997
(d)	Serves as a deterrent against injustice	3%	22%	29%	39%	8%	346	-0.795
(e)	Fosters public scrutiny of court proceedings	13%	50%	21%	12%	4%	346	0.318
(f)	Transforms sensational criminal trials into mass-marketed commercial products	57%	30%	5%	5%	3%	351	1.299
(g)	Tends to cause judges to issue rulings they might otherwise not issue	10%	27%	24%	28%	11%	350	-0.343
(h)	Poses a potential threat to judicial independence	17%	28%	23%	25%	7%	350	-0.111
(i)	Has impaired judicial dignity or courtroom decorum in New York	17%	22%	23%	27%	11%	350	-0.229
(j)	Has had a positive effect on New York's *civil* justice system	3%	14%	22%	24%	38%	349	-0.507
(k)	Has had a positive effect on New York's *criminal* justice system	5%	20%	30%	29%	16%	350	-0.571

If you would like to comment further, please check the box to the right and include your comments in the space below or on the blank pages at the end of this questionnaire.

_____
_____
_____
_____

2.

APPENDICES

5. Do you agree or disagree with the following statements (please check the applicable box):

		Strongly agree	Somewhat agree	Somewhat disagree	Strongly disagree	No opinion	N	Weighted Mean
Criminal Cases								
(a)	Trial judges should have discretion to allow criminal trials to be televised	62%	23%	6%	7%	2%	345	1.278
(b)	Television cameras should not be allowed in criminal trials unless the defendant consents	29%	14%	21%	31%	4%	343	-0.120
(c)	Television cameras should not be allowed in criminal trials unless both the prosecution and the defendant consent	26%	19%	20%	31%	4%	341	-0.123
(d)	Television cameras should not be permitted in criminal trials	21%	15%	22%	38%	4%	344	-0.387
(e)	Television cameras should not be permitted in criminal trials if the crime victim (or surviving family members) object(s) to camera coverage of the trial	34%	24%	16%	20%	5%	339	0.360
Civil Cases								
(f)	Judges should have discretion to allow civil trials to be televised	59%	22%	6%	5%	8%	340	1.241
(g)	Television cameras should not be allowed in civil trials unless both parties consent	29%	20%	17%	24%	10%	333	0.132
(h)	Television cameras should not be permitted in civil trials	15%	15%	21%	38%	11%	343	-0.504

If you would like to comment further, please check the box to the right and include your comments in the space below or on the blank pages at the end of this questionnaire. ☐

3.

		Strongly agree	Somewhat agree	Somewhat disagree	Strongly disagree	No opinion	N	Weighted Mean
5.	**Accuracy of coverage**							
(j)	In the majority of cases, *televised nightly news* coverage of court proceedings accurately represents what actually takes place in New York courtrooms	2%	21%	35%	34%	7%	349	-0.768
(k)	In the majority of cases, televised *gavel-to-gavel* coverage of court proceedings accurately represents what actually takes place in New York courtrooms	17%	46%	16%	8%	14%	351	0.464
(l)	In the majority of cases, *televised* coverage of court proceedings in *news feature programs* (such as "Prime Time Justice" or "American Justice") accurately represents what actually takes place in New York courtrooms	1%	19%	25%	31%	24%	346	-0.662
(m)	In the majority of cases, *newspaper* coverage of court proceedings accurately represents what actually takes place in New York courtrooms	4%	31%	39%	23%	3%	349	-0.464
(n)	I am concerned about the commercial exploitation of judicial proceedings by the *television* industry	52%	28%	8%	4%	9%	349	1.149
(o)	I am concerned about the commercial exploitation of judicial proceedings by *newspaper* companies	30%	28%	22%	9%	11%	349	0.467

If you would like to comment further, please check the box to the right and include your comments in the space below or on the blank pages at the end of this questionnaire. ☐

_____
_____
_____
_____

4.

APPENDICES

6. (a) Does section 218 of the Judiciary Law need modification?   Yes __43%__   No __57%__   N = 230

   (b) If yes, what provisions should be modified and what specific changes should be made?   ☐
   (You may use the space below, or, if more space is needed, please check the box on the right

   _____
   _____
   _____
   _____
   _____

7. If television cameras are permitted in criminal trials, do you favor:

	Yes	No	
(a) delayed broadcasting (i e after the verdict) instead of contemporaneous broadcasting?	50%	50%	N = 326
(b) giving the judge a "kill switch" which would allow you to stop all audiovisual coverage at appropriate moments?	72%	28%	N = 328
(c) installation of a ten-second time delay device to prevent inadvertent transmission of certain prohibited testimony or images?	77%	23%	N = 319
(d) other (please specify) _____			

   _____
   _____

	Yes	No	
8. (a) In your opinion, are different rules needed to govern television camera access in cases in which the *death penalty* is sought?	31%	69%	N = 320
(b) Do you favor banning television cameras in *death penalty* cases?	42%	58%	N = 323
(c) If you favor special rules for television cameras in *death penalty* cases, please explain	26%	74%	N = 158

   (You may use the space below, or, if more space is needed, please check the   ☐
   box on the right and use the blank sheets at the end of this questionnaire)

   _____
   _____

5.

APPENDICES   103

	Yes	No	
9. Have you ever been interviewed on television or radio about a televised court proceeding? If yes, please identify:	14%	86%	N = 344

(a) the case about which you were interviewed _____

(b) the name of the television or radio station on which you appeared _____

(c) the name of the program on which you appeared _____

(d) the subject matter of the interview _____

(e) the date of the interview _____

10. Overall, how do you feel about:

	Strongly in favor	Somewhat in favor	Somewhat opposed	Strongly opposed	No opinion	N	Weighted Mean
(a) Television coverage of *criminal* trials	16%	33%	18%	30%	3%	348	- 0.118
(b) Television coverage of *civil* trials	15%	33%	19%	24%	10%	345	- 0.043
(c) Television coverage of oral pre-trial arguments in *criminal* cases	10%	25%	22%	40%	3%	346	- 0.566
(d) Television coverage of oral pre-trial arguments in *civil* cases	10%	25%	22%	31%	11%	344	- 0.404

If you have additional comments, including noteworthy experiences with cameras in your courtroom, please check the box to the right and include your comments on the blank pages at the end of this questionnaire ☐

If you would like to be contacted for a more detailed telephone interview, please check the box to the right and provide us with your name and telephone number ☐

Name _____

Phone number (_____) _____ -- _____

Most convenient time of day to contact you. _____

Thank you very much for taking the time to complete this portion of the survey If you have, at any time, received an application to permit television coverage in your courtroom, please proceed to **PART II**, questions 11 through 25

NEW YORK STATE
COMMITTEE TO REVIEW AUDIO VISUAL COVERAGE OF COURT PROCEEDINGS
CAMERAS IN NEW YORK COURTROOMS JUDICIAL SURVEY
PART II

Questions 11 through 25 should be completed ONLY if you have, at any time, received an application to permit television coverage in your courtroom.

226 judges responded to Part II of the Survey.

N = 226

11. (a) Have you ever *granted* an application for television coverage in your courtroom? Yes __91%__ No __9%__

    (b) If so, in *granting* an application for television, what factors do you typically take into account? (please check all that apply)

    N = 205

	Criminal	Civil
(i) absence of objections	74%	32%
(ii) educational value of the proceedings	32%	20%
(iii) importance of promoting public access to the judicial system	54%	27%
(iv) importance of maintaining public trust and confidence in the judicial system	55%	26%
(v) strength of public's interest in the proceedings	36%	21%
(vi) strength of print media's interest in the proceedings	19%	11%
(vii) public's need to understand my judicial philosophy	9%	3%

    (viii) other (please specify)

    _____

    _____

12. (a) Have you ever *denied* an application for television cameras in your courtroom? Yes __58%__ No __42%__

    N= 207

7.

(b) In *denying* an application for television coverage (other than for an arraignment or suppression hearing), what factors do you typically take into account? (please check all that apply):

		N = 121	Criminal	Civil
(I)	objections of defense		80%	18%
(II)	objections of prosecution		61%	12%
(III)	objections of witnesses		55%	12%
(IV)	application untimely		51%	12%
(V)	effect on witnesses' willingness to cooperate, including risk that coverage will engender threats to the health or safety of any witness		55%	12%
(VI)	effect on excluded witnesses who would have access to televised testimony of prior witnesses		24%	8%
(VII)	whether coverage might unfairly influence or distract the jury		39%	16%
(VIII)	implications for selecting a fair and impartial jury		28%	10%
(IX)	difficulty of jury selection if a mistrial is declared		12%	7%
(X)	type of case involved		52%	17%
(XI)	possible interference with defendant's right to a fair trial		55%	13%
(XII)	possible interference with law enforcement activities		30%	5%
(XIII)	presence of lewd or scandalous matters		30%	10%
(XIV)	undue administrative or financial burden to the court		8%	5%
(XV)	other (please specify)			

_____

_____

13. (a) In a *criminal* case (other than an arraignment or suppression hearing), have you ever permitted television coverage over the objections of the defense? Yes 48% No 52% N=186

(b) If yes, in how many criminal cases where television coverage was sought have you overruled defense objections to coverage? (5) cases (average) N = 78

(c) If yes, what factors have you taken into account in granting permission for television coverage over the defense's objection?

N = 89

(I) educational value of the proceedings — 34%

(II) importance of promoting public access to the judicial system — 76%

(III) importance of maintaining public trust and confidence in the judicial system — 73%

(IV) strength of public's interest in the proceedings — 46%

(V) strength of print media's interest in the proceedings — 19%

(VI) public's need to understand my judicial philosophy — 10%

(VII) other

_____
_____

(d) Have you ever denied an application for television coverage in a *criminal* case where the defendant requested or consented to camera coverage? Yes 5% No 95%

N=185

(e) If yes, please explain:

_____
_____
_____
_____
_____
_____
_____
_____

9.

APPENDICES

14.(a) Have you ever shortened or waived the statutory seven-day
notice period in granting an application for camera coverage? Yes __71%__ No __29%__ N=205

(b) If yes, why? _____

_____

_____

(c) If yes, please state how many days' notice was typically provided in cases in which you shortened the seven-day notice period. (1.7) days. (average) N = 112

15. (a) To determine whether television coverage should be permitted, do you typically:

		Yes	No	
(i)	Allow counsel to brief the issue	21%	79%	N=170
(ii)	Hold oral argument	89%	11%	N=201
(iii)	Hold an evidentiary hearing	7%	93%	N=163

(b) If you permit counsel to brief the issue of whether television coverage should be permitted, how many days do you typically allow counsel to prepare briefing papers on this issue? (3 days). (average) N = 42

16. (a) In *criminal* cases, have you imposed restrictions on television coverage in addition to those required by section 218 of the Judiciary Law and 22 NYCRR Part 131? Yes __23%__ No __77%__ N=166

(b) If yes, what type of additional restrictions have you imposed?

_____

_____

_____

_____

_____

_____

_____

10.

APPENDICES

(c) In *civil* cases, have you imposed restrictions on television coverage in addition to those required by section 218 of the Judiciary Law and 22 NYCRR Part 131?   Yes __7%__   No __93%__   N=121

If yes, what type of additional restrictions have you imposed?

(d) _____

_____

_____

17. How do you assure yourself that televised footage filmed in your courtroom and subsequently broadcast actually complies with the restrictions required by law and any additional restrictions you may have imposed? (please check all that apply):

(a) by monitoring news broadcasts — 32%

(b) by reviewing videotapes provided by the news media — 4%

N =226

(c) information from counsel — 37%

(d) information from court personnel — 35%

(e) other (please specify)

_____

_____

18. (a) In a case in which television cameras are present, do you typically question witnesses under oath to determine if they have viewed televised broadcasts about the trial?   Yes __6%__   No __94%__   N=143

(b) If yes, approximately how many witnesses have acknowledged that they have viewed such broadcasts? (insignificant number of responses).

19. (a) Section 218 (5) (c) of the Judiciary Law imposes on counsel in criminal cases the obligation to advise each nonparty witness that he or she has a right to request that his or her image be visually obscured during testimony. Do you believe it would be better for this admonition to be made by the presiding judge? Please explain.   Yes __53%__   No __47%__   N= 171

11.

APPENDICES

(b) When confronted with a witness who is reluctant to testify before television cameras, are you more likely to (check one):

(i) question the witness about his or her reservations 28%

N = 226

(ii) proceed directly to order the cameras to obscure the witness' image 34%

(iii) other (please specify) _____

_____

_____

(c) Approximately how many witnesses in your courtroom have requested that their image be visually obscured? (2-3). (average) N= 115

(d) In approximately what percent of cases in which television cameras were present in your courtroom has a witness requested that his or her image be visually obscured? (10%) (average) N= 103

20.(a) Before the beginning of a televised trial, do you typically say anything to the prospective jurors about the presence of the cameras? Yes 76% N = 119
No 24%

(b) If yes, what do you typically say and what, if any, other precautions do you take to ensure that the jury is not affected by the presence of cameras? _____

_____

21. Do you agree or disagree with the following statements (please check the applicable box):

	Strongly agree	Somewhat agree	Somewhat disagree	Strongly disagree	No opinion	N	Weighted Mean
(a) My administrative/supervisory burden was significantly increased by the presence of television cameras in my courtroom	12%	39%	18%	23%	8%	181	-0.011
(b) I have experienced a significant decrease in the public's willingness to serve as jurors in cases in which television cameras are present in the courtroom	3%	6%	20%	32%	39%	175	-0.726
(c) Trials in which television cameras were present were significantly longer than comparable cases covered only by the print media	7%	15%	18%	28%	32%	177	-0.443

12.

22. Do you agree or disagree with the following statements (please check the applicable box):

		Strongly agree	Somewhat agree	Somewhat disagree	Strongly disagree	No opinion	N	Weighted Mean
(a)	Jurors were more attentive in cases in which TV cameras were present	4%	14%	17%	18%	48%	169	-0.308
(b)	In cases in which TV cameras were present, jurors were more likely to have communications with people who have seen coverage of the case	4%	13%	10%	14%	59%	165	-0.170
(c)	Jurors were more likely to be aware of the implications of their verdict in cases in which TV cameras were present	8%	22%	10%	11%	48%	167	0.060
(d)	Witnesses' privacy was violated by the presence of TV cameras	10%	22%	24%	23%	21%	172	-0.285
(e)	Witnesses were distracted by the presence of TV cameras	13%	19%	24%	19%	24%	175	-0.171
(f)	Witnesses were more nervous in the presence of TV cameras	12%	28%	19%	13%	28%	173	0.064
(g)	Witnesses were more truthful in the presence of TV cameras	0%	3%	27%	20%	49%	174	-0.638
(h)	Witnesses' testimony was more guarded in the presence of TV cameras	6%	16%	25%	15%	38%	174	-0.276
(i)	Witnesses' testimony was unchanged in the presence of cameras	14%	26%	12%	8%	39%	170	0.265
(j)	In cases in which TV cameras were present, trial participants were sensitive to how the day's events in court would "play" on the evening news and tended to shape their actions accordingly	11%	23%	20%	12%	34%	172	0.012
(k)	Lawyers came to court better prepared in cases in which TV cameras were present	6%	29%	18%	13%	33%	174	-0.017

13.

23. Compared to similar cases covered only by the print media, were there, in the case(s) where you allowed television cameras, more or fewer attempts made to offer unnecessary:

	More	Fewer	About the same	N
a Motions	16%	2%	82%	144
b Evidence	11%	1%	87%	142
c Witnesses	10%	1%	89%	136
d Objections	26%	3%	71%	141
e Argument	33%	3%	65%	147

24. (a) Compared to similar trials covered by the print media, did you notice a change in the behavior of the *spectators* in trials in which television cameras were present?   Yes 17% No 83% N= 151

(b) If yes, please describe.

_____
_____
_____
_____

25. (a) Are you aware of any violations of section 218 of the Judiciary Law by the media or any improper or inappropriate use of television footage filmed in a courtroom?   Yes 9% No 91% N= 172

(b) If so, please describe.

_____
_____
_____
_____

14.

(c) Have you ever withdrawn consent for a television camera in your courtroom? Yes 6% No 94%

(d) If yes, why?   N= 177

_____

_____

_____

_____

Thank you.

If you have additional comments, including noteworthy experiences with cameras in your courtroom, please check the box to the right and include these comments on the blank pages at the end of this questionnaire ☐

If you would like to be contacted for a more detailed telephone interview, please check the box to the right and provide us with your name and telephone number. ☐

Name._____

Phone number: (_____) _____ -- _____

Most convenient time of day to contact you: _____

Please complete and return the original by November 30, 1996 to:

Dean John D. Feerick

Fordham University School of Law

140 West 62nd Street

New York NY 10023

Appendix B
Marist Institute for Public Opinion Poll

Marist Institute for Public Opinion
Marist College • Poughkeepsie, N.Y. 12601 • (914) 575-5050

TELEVISION CAMERAS IN THE COURTS
A Survey of New York State
December, 1996

Background

This survey, conducted by the Marist Institute for Public Opinion of registered voters within New York State, focuses on the public's perceptions of the role of television cameras in courtrooms in New York State. General information was gathered on the public's opinion of television cameras in the courts and specifically the impact the presence of cameras might have on an individual's personal decision to participate in both civil and criminal cases.

The interviews were administered by telephone on October 28 and 29, 1996. Six hundred sixteen registered voters were interviewed in proportion to the voter registration in each county in New York State. The results for the entire sample are statistically significant at ± 4.0°/c. The margin of error increases for sub-groups and for all cross-tabulations.

The results are presented by question for the entire sample beginning on page five of this report. The question wording is given along with the results for each question. The interview sequence of the questions is maintained, unless otherwise noted. Additional results from specific sub-groups are detailed. Questions one through six deal with general perceptions of the impact of television cameras in the courts; questions seven through ten deal specifically with civil lawsuits; and questions eleven though fifteen present the issues in the context of criminal cases.

The goal of a scientifically designed survey sample is to be representative of the population which is being surveyed. The results obtained from a scientific probability survey are not just answers from those individuals who responded but, more importantly, because of the design and methods by which the data is collected, can be used to generalize to the population as a whole. For this survey, the results are an estimate of what would have been obtained, within a certain range, if all registered voters within New York State had been interviewed.

A stratified random digit dial (RDD) probability design was used to draw the telephone numbers for this study. RDD ensures representation of both listed and unlisted telephone numbers. The first eight digits of the sample telephone numbers (which includes the area code, telephone exchange, and the first two digits of a phone number within the exchange) are selected based upon estimates of telephone households within each exchange and the proportion of registered voters within each county of New York State. The last two digits of the telephone numbers are selected through a random generation. During the course of the interviewing process five attempts were made to obtain a completed interview for each telephone number. These callbacks were made on the subsequent evening and/or at different time periods.

When analyzing the survey results, it should be kept in mind that in all surveys each result is an estimate of what would have been obtained had everyone in the eligible population been interviewed, in this instance, New York State residents 18 years of age or older and registered to vote at their current address. This difference between the responses of all registered voters and the survey results is referred to as sampling error and is primarily based upon the number of interviews in the survey sample.

The sampling error the entire sample is ±4% for percentages near 50% at a confidence level of 95%. The sampling error may be interpreted as indicating the probability (95 times out of 100) within which the results of repeated samplings, in the same period, assuming the same sampling procedures, could be expected to fall within a certain range. The sampling error diminishes slightly for questions whose results are at the extremes and the sampling error increases as the number of interviews for a particular group or sub-group within the sample declines.

For example, 55% of those surveyed in this study respond that the presence of cameras in the courtroom makes no difference in their decision to serve as a juror. We may conclude that there is a high probability (95 times out of 100) that the average of repeated samplings of registered voters within New York State will fall between 51% and 59% (±4%).

Sampling error increases for sub-groups within the sample. For instance, 51% of women surveyed say that cameras in the courtroom do not make a difference on their decision to serve on a jury. There are 306 women in the sample who responded to this question, which means that there is a high probability (95 times out of 100) that the average of repeated samplings of registered voters in New York State iwho are women will fall between 45.5% and 56.5% (±5.5%).

NATURE OF SAMPLE: 616 New York State Registered Voters

Race		Party	
White	82.2%	Democrat	45.8%
Black	10.0%	Republican	34.2%
Hispanic	5.2%	Non-enrolled	13.6%
Asian	1.5%	Conservative	3.1%
Other	1.1%	Liberal	2.1%
		Other	1.1%
Religion		**Ideology**	
Protestant	30.0%	Liberal	23.6%
Catholic	50.2%	Moderate	46.8%
Jewish	11.2%	Conservative	29.6%
Other	8.6%		
Age		**Region**	
18–30	14.3%	Upstate	44.5%
31–44	38.7%	New York City	32.8%
45–60	22.3%	Suburbs	22.7%
Over 60	24.7%		
Gender (weighted)		**Watch Trials on TV**	
Men	48.0%	Always or Sometimes	22.6%
Women	52.0%	Seldom or Never	77.4%

*Percentages may not equal 100% due to rounding.

Q1. In New York State, television cameras are now allowed in certain courtrooms so that trials or parts of trials can be shown to the public on television. Do you think it is a good idea or bad idea for courtroom trials to be shown on television?

	Total	Race		Watch Trials on TV		Age				Gender	
		White	Black	Yes	No	18–30	31–44	45–60	Over 60	Men	Women
Good idea	35%	31%	54%	62%	22%	48%	35%	34%	28%	40%	31%
Bad idea	61%	65%	43%	33%	74%	49%	60%	63%	69%	56%	65%
Unsure	4%	4%	3%	5%	4%	3%	5%	3%	3%	4%	4%

Q2. Which statement comes closer to your opinion: one, television in the courtroom increase the accuracy of the news coverage of a trial, or two, television cameras in the courtroom serve more to sensationalize a trial?

	Total	Race		Watch Trials on TV		Age				Gender	
		White	Black	Yes	No	18–30	31–44	45–60	Over 60	Men	Women
Increase accuracy	28%	24%	49%	52%	16%	32%	25%	26%	30%	32%	24%
Sensationalize	65%	70%	44%	43%	78%	62%	69%	64%	64%	60%	70%
Other	7%	6%	7%	5%	5%	6%	6%	10%	6%	8%	6%

Q3. Which statement comes closer to your opinion: one, television in the courtroom increase the public's understanding of the justice system, or two, television cameras in the courtroom are more a source of entertainment?

	Total	Race		Watch Trials on TV		Age				Gender	
		White	Black	Yes	No	18–30	31–44	45–60	Over 60	Men	Women
Increase understanding	32%	30%	50%	51%	23%	33%	29%	34%	38%	35%	30%
Entertainment	61%	64%	43%	43%	71%	60%	66%	56%	56%	58%	63%
Other	7%	6%	7%	6%	6%	7%	5	10%	6%	7%	7%

Q4. Which statement comes closer to your opinion: one, television cameras in the courtroom decrease the possibility that the courts will be unjust, or two, television cameras in the courtroom get in the way of a fair trial?

	Total	Race		Watch Trials on TV		Age				Gender	
		White	Black	Yes	No	18–30	31–44	45–60	Over 60	Men	Women
Decrease injustice	29%	27%	44%	46%	21%	33%	27%	28%	29%	33%	26%
Get in way of fair trial	62%	64%	47%	39%	72%	60%	66%	60%	59%	58%	65%
Other	9%	9%	9%	15%	7%	7%	7%	12%	12%	9%	9%

Q5. Overall, do you think television cameras in the courtroom have a positive effect on New York's justice system, a negative effect, or make no difference?

	Total	Race		Watch Trials on TV		Age				Gender	
		White	Black	Yes	No	18–30	31–44	45–60	Over 60	Men	Women
Positive effect	20%	18%	35%	36%	12%	16%	21%	20%	21%	23%	17%
Negative effect	52%	57%	32%	30%	65%	45%	55%	56%	51%	52%	52%
Unsure	28%	25%	33%	34%	23%	39%	24%	24%	28%	25%	31%

Q6. If there were television cameras in the courtroom, would you be more willing to serve on a jury, less willing, or would the cameras not make any difference to you?

	Total	Race		Watch Trials on TV		Age				Gender	
		White	Black	Yes	No	18–30	31–44	45–60	Over 60	Men	Women
More willing	2%	2%	5%	2%	2%	2%	1%	2%	7%	2%	3%
Less willing	43%	44%	37%	29%	48%	39%	46%	41%	40%	40%	45%
No difference	55%	54%	58%	69%	50%	59%	53%	57%	53%	58%	52%

APPENDICES 119

Q7. If you had a civil lawsuit, would you want the trial to be televised, not want it to be televised, or would it not make any difference to you?

	Total	Race		Watch Trials on TV		Age				Gender	
		White	Black	Yes	No	18–30	31–44	45–60	Over 60	Men	Women
Want it televised	6%	5%	10%	4%	5%	5%	8%	0%	9%	8%	4%
Not want it televised	70%	72%	59%	52%	77%	60%	73%	76%	64%	66%	73%
No difference	24%	23%	31%	44%	18%	35%	19%	24%	27%	26%	23%

Q8. If there were television cameras in the courtroom, would you be willing to testify as a witness in a non-criminal case, less willing, or would the cameras not make any difference to you?

	Total	Race		Watch Trials on TV		Age				Gender	
		White	Black	Yes	No	18–30	31–44	45–60	Over 60	Men	Women
More willing	3%	2%	5%	2%	2%	2%	1%	2%	7%	3%	2%
Less willing	45%	46%	51%	36%	49%	38%	47%	48%	42%	42%	49%
No difference	52%	52%	44%	62%	49%	60%	52%	50%	51%	55%	49%

Q9. If your image was blurred so that viewers could not see your face on television, would you be more willing to testify as a witness in a non-criminal case, less willing or would the blurred image not make any difference to you? (Asked only of those who in the previous question responded that they were less willing to testify as a witness if there were television cameras in the courtroom.)

Asked only of those less willing to testify	Total	Race		Watch Trials on TV		Age				Gender	
		White	Black	Yes	No	18–30	31–44	45–60	Over 60	Men	Women
More willing	18%	17%	25%	39%	14%	15%	21%	15%	21%	16%	21%
Less willing	57%	59%	61%	26%	64%	48%	64%	61%	41%	64%	51%
No difference	25%	24%	14%	35%	22%	37%	15%	24%	38%	20%	28%

Q10. If there were only newspaper reporters, no cameras, in the courtroom, would you be willing to testify as a witness in a non-criminal case, not willing, or would the presence of newspaper reporters not make any difference on your willingness to testify?

	Total	Race		Watch Trials on TV		Age				Gender	
		White	Black	Yes	No	18–30	31–44	45–60	Over 60	Men	Women
Willing	19%	17%	33%	18%	16%	21%	18%	17%	20%	15%	23%
Not willing	17%	17%	27%	7%	20%	15%	15%	20%	17%	15%	18%
No difference	64%	66%	40%	75%	64%	64%	67%	63%	63%	70%	59%

APPENDICES

Q11. If you were a defendant in a criminal case, would you want the trial to be televised, not want it to be televised, or would it not make any difference to you?

	Total	Race		Watch Trials on TV		Age				Gender	
		White	Black	Yes	No	18–30	31–44	45–60	Over 60	Men	Women
Want it televised	6%	5%	13%	8%	4%	7%	5%	7%	5%	8%	4%
Not want it televised	69%	75%	31%	43%	86%	59%	70%	76%	69%	63%	75%
No difference	25%	20%	56%	49%	10%	34%	25%	17%	26%	29%	21%

Q12. If you were a crime victim, would you want the trial to be televised, not want it to be televised, or would it not make any difference to you?

	Total	Race		Watch Trials on TV		Age				Gender	
		White	Black	Yes	No	18–30	31–44	45–60	Over 60	Men	Women
Want it televised	13%	12%	13%	25%	8%	9%	13%	19%	10%	16%	10%
Not want it televised	68%	71%	59%	48%	78%	71%	63%	67%	77%	60%	76%
No difference	19%	17%	28%	27%	14%	20%	24%	14%	13%	24%	14%

Q13. If there were television cameras in the courtroom, would you be more willing to testify as a witness to a crime, less willing, or would the cameras not make any difference to you?

	Total	Race		Watch Trials on TV		Age				Gender	
		White	Black	Yes	No	18–30	31–44	45–60	Over 60	Men	Women
More willing	4%	4%	0%	8%	3%	5%	4%	4%	2%	5%	3%
Less willing	54%	55%	45%	41%	60%	59%	54%	53%	53%	42%	64%
No difference	42%	41%	55%	51%	37%	36%	42%	43%	45%	53%	33%

Q14. If your image was blurred so that viewers could not see your face on television, would you be more willing to testify as a witness to a crime, less willing, or would the blurred image not make any difference to you? (Asked only of those who in the previous question responded that they were less willing to testify as a witness to a crime if there were television cameras in the courtroom.)

	Total	Race		Watch Trials on TV		Age				Gender	
		White	Black	Yes	No	18–30	31–44	45–60	Over 60	Men	Women
More willing	38%	35%	47%	49%	32%	46%	42%	35%	29%	41%	36%
Less willing	34%	34%	31%	26%	35%	12%	38%	40%	38%	36%	33%
No difference	28%	31%	22%	25%	33%	42%	20%	25%	33%	23%	31%

Q15. If there were only newspaper reporters, no cameras, in the courtroom, would you be willing to testify as a witness to a crime, not willing, or would the presence of newspaper reporters not make any difference on your willingness to testify?

	Total	Race		Watch Trials on TV		Age				Gender	
		White	Black	Yes	No	18–30	31–44	45–60	Over 60	Men	Women
Willing	18%	17%	10%	20%	16%	18%	21%	14%	17%	14%	21%
Not willing	20%	21%	16%	20%	21%	20%	14%	26%	23%	16%	23%
No difference	62%	62%	74%	60%	63%	62%	65%	60%	60%	70%	56%

Appendix C
Judiciary Law, Section 218

1. Authorization. Notwithstanding the provisions of section fifty-two of the civil rights law and subject to the provisions of this section, the chief judge of the state or his designee may authorize an experimental program in which presiding trial judges, in their discretion, may permit audio-visual coverage of civil and criminal court proceedings, including trials.

2. Definitions. For purposes of this section:

(a) "Administrative judge" shall mean the administrative judge of each judicial district; the administrative judge of Nassau county or of Suffolk county; the administrative judge of the civil court of the city of New York or of the criminal court of the city of New York; or the presiding judge of the court of claims.

(b) "Audio-visual coverage" shall mean the electronic broadcasting or other transmission to the public of radio or television signals from the courtroom, the recording of sound or light in the courtroom for later transmission or reproduction, or the taking of still or motion pictures in the courtroom by the news media.

(c) "News media" shall mean any news reporting or news gathering agency and any employee or agent associated with such agency, including television, radio, radio and television networks, news services, newspapers, magazines, trade papers, in-house publications, professional journals or any other news reporting or news gathering agency, the function of which is to inform the public, or some segment thereof.

(d) "Presiding trial judge" shall mean the justice or judge presiding over proceedings at which audio-visual coverage is authorized pursuant to this section.

(e) "Covert or undercover capacity" shall mean law enforcement activity involving criminal investigation by peace or police officers who usually and customarily wear no uniform, badge, or other official identification in public view.

(f) "Arraignment" shall have the same meaning as such term is defined in subdivision nine of section 1.20 of the criminal procedure law.

(g) "Suppression hearing" shall mean a hearing on a motion made pursuant to the provisions of section 710.20 of the criminal procedure law; a hearing on a motion to determine the admissibility of any prior criminal, vicious or immoral acts of a defendant and any other hearing held to determine the admissibility of evidence.

(h) "Nonparty witness" shall mean any witness in a criminal trial proceeding who is not a party to such proceeding; except an expert or professional witness, a peace or police officer who acted in the course of his or her duties and was not acting in a covert or undercover capacity in connection with the instant court proceeding, or any government official acting in an official capacity, shall not be deemed to be a "nonparty witness".

(i) "Visually obscured" shall mean that the face of a participant in a criminal trial proceeding shall either not be shown or shall be rendered visually unrecognizable to the viewer of such proceeding by means of special editing by the news media.

3. Requests for coverage of proceedings; administrative review.

(a) Prior to the commencement of the proceedings, any news media interested in providing audio-visual coverage of court proceedings shall file a request with the presiding trial judge, if assigned, or if no assignment has been made, to the judge responsible for making such assignment. Requests for audio-visual coverage shall be made in writing and not less than seven days before the commencement of the judicial proceeding, and shall refer to the individual proceeding with sufficient identification to assist the presiding trial judge in considering the request. Where circumstances are such that an applicant cannot reasonably apply seven or more days before the commencement of the proceeding, the presiding trial judge may shorten the time period for requests.

(b) Permission for news media coverage shall be at the discretion of the presiding trial judge. An order granting or denying a request for audio-visual coverage of a proceeding shall be in writing and shall be included in the record of such proceeding. Such order shall contain any restrictions imposed by the judge on the audio-visual coverage and shall contain a statement advising the parties that any violation of the order is punishable by contempt pursuant to article nineteen of this chapter. Such order for initial access shall be subject only to review by the appropriate administrative judge; there shall be no further judicial review of such order or determination during the pendency of such proceeding before such trial judge. No order allowing audio-visual coverage of a proceeding shall be sealed.

(c) Subject to the provisions of subdivision seven of this section, upon a request for audio-visual coverage of court proceedings, the presiding trial judge shall, at a minimum, take into account the following factors: (i) the type of case involved; (ii) whether such coverage would cause harm to any participant in the case or otherwise interfere with the fair administration of justice, the advancement of a fair trial or the rights of the parties; (iii) whether any order directing the exclusion of witnesses from the courtroom prior to their testimony could be rendered substantially ineffective by allowing audio-visual coverage that could be viewed by such witnesses to the detriment of any party; (iv) whether such coverage would interfere with any law enforcement activity; or (v) involve lewd or scandalous matters.

(d) A request for audio-visual coverage made after the commencement of a trial proceeding in which a jury is sitting shall not be granted unless, (i) counsel for all parties to the proceeding consent to such coverage, or (ii) the request is for coverage of the verdict and/or sentencing in such proceeding.

4. Supervision of audio-visual coverage; mandatory pretrial conference; judicial discretion.

(a) Audio-visual coverage of a court proceeding shall be subject to the supervision of the presiding trial judge. In supervising audio-visual coverage of court proceedings, in particular any which involve lewd or scandalous matters, a presiding trial judge shall, where necessary for the protection of any participant or to preserve the welfare of a minor, prohibit all or any part of the audio-visual coverage of such participant, minor or exhibit.

(b) A pretrial conference shall be held in each case in which audio-visual coverage of a proceeding has been approved. At such conference the presiding trial judge shall review, with counsel and the news media who will participate in the audio-visual coverage, the restrictions to be imposed. Counsel shall convey to the court any concerns of prospective witnesses with respect to audio-visual coverage.

(c) There shall be no limitation on the exercise of discretion under this subdivision except as provided by law. The presiding trial judge may at any time modify or reverse any prior order or determination.

5. Consent. (a) Audio-visual coverage of judicial proceedings, except for arraignments and suppression hearings, shall not be limited by the objection of counsel, parties, or jurors, except for a finding by the presiding trial judge of good or legal cause.

(b) Audio-visual coverage of arraignments and suppression hearings shall be permitted only with the consent of all parties to the proceeding; provided, however, where a party is not yet represented by counsel consent may not be given unless the party has been advised of his or her right to the aid of counsel pursuant to subdivision four of section 170.10 or 180.10 of the criminal procedure law and the party has affirmatively elected to proceed without counsel at such proceeding.

(c) Counsel to each party in a criminal trial proceeding shall advise each nonparty witness that he or she has the right to request that his or her image be visually obscured during said witness' testimony, and upon such request the presiding trial judge shall order the news media to visually obscure the visual image of the witness in any and all audio-visual coverage of the judicial proceeding.

6. Restrictions relating to equipment and personnel; sound and light criteria. Where audio-visual coverage of court proceedings is authorized pursuant to this section, the following restrictions shall be observed:

(a) Equipment and personnel:

(i) No more than two electronic or motion picture cameras and two camera operators shall be permitted in any proceeding.

(ii) No more than one photographer to operate two still cameras with not more than two lenses for each camera shall be permitted in any proceeding.

(iii) No more than one audio system for broadcast purposes shall be permitted in any proceeding. Audio pickup for all media purposes shall be effectuated through existing audio systems in the court facility. If no technically suitable audio system is available, microphones and related wiring essential for media purposes shall be supplied by those persons providing audio-visual coverage. Any microphones and sound wiring shall be unobtrusive and located in places designated by the presiding trial judge.

(iv) Notwithstanding the provisions of subparagraphs (i), (ii) and (iii) of this paragraph, the presiding trial judge may modify his original order to increase or decrease the amount of equipment that will be permitted into a courtroom on a finding of special circumstances so long as it will not impair the dignity of the court or the judicial process.

(v) Notwithstanding the provisions of subparagraphs (i), (ii) and (iii) of this paragraph, the equipment authorized therein shall not be admitted into a court proceeding unless all persons interested in providing audio-visual coverage of such proceedings shall have entered into pooling arrangements for their respective groups. Furthermore, a pool operator for the electronic and motion picture media and a pool operator for the still photography media shall be selected, and procedures for cost sharing and dissemination of audio-visual material established. The court shall not be called upon to mediate or resolve any dispute as to such arrangements. In making pooling arrangements, consideration shall be given to educational users' needs for full coverage of entire proceedings.

(b) Sound and light criteria:

(i) Only electronic and motion picture cameras, audio equipment and still camera equipment which do not produce distracting sound or light shall be employed to cover judicial proceedings. The chief administrator of the courts shall promulgate a list of acceptable equipment models.

(ii) No motorized drives shall be permitted, and no moving lights, flash attachments, or sudden lighting changes shall be permitted during judicial proceedings.

(iii) No light or signal visible or audible to trial participants shall be used on any equipment during audio-visual coverage to indicate whether it is operating.

(iv) It shall be the affirmative duty of any person desiring to use equipment other than that authorized by the chief administrator to demonstrate to the presiding trial judge, adequately in advance of any proceeding, that the equipment sought to be utilized meets acceptable sound and light criteria. A failure to obtain advance judicial approval for equipment shall preclude its use in any proceeding.

(v) With the concurrence of the presiding trial judge modifications and additions may be made to light sources existing in the facility, provided such modification or additions are installed and maintained at the expense of the news media who are providing audio-visual coverage and provided they are not distracting or otherwise offensive.

(c) Location of equipment and personnel. Cameras, equipment and personnel shall be positioned in locations designated by the presiding trial judge.

(i) All audio-visual coverage operators shall assume their assigned, fixed position within the designated area and once established in such position, shall act in a manner so as not to call attention to their activities.

(ii) The areas so designated shall provide reasonable access to coverage with the least possible interference with court proceedings. Equipment that is not necessary for audio-visual coverage from inside the courtroom shall be located in an area outside the courtroom.

(d) Movement of equipment during proceedings. Equipment shall not be placed in, moved about or removed from the courtroom, and related personnel shall not move about the courtroom, except prior to commencement or after adjournment of proceedings each day, or during a recess. Camera film and lenses shall be changed only during a recess in proceedings.

7. **Restrictions on audio-visual coverage.** Notwithstanding the initial approval of a request for audio-visual coverage of any court proceeding, the presiding trial judge shall have discretion throughout the proceeding to revoke such approval or limit such coverage, and may where appropriate exercise such discretion to limit, restrict or prohibit audio or video broadcast or photography of any part of the proceeding in the courtroom, or of the name or features of any participant therein. In any case, audio-visual coverage shall be limited as follows:

(a) no audio pickup or audio broadcast of conferences which occur in a court facility between attorneys and their clients, between co-counsel of a client, or between counsel and the presiding trial judge, shall be permitted without the prior express consent of all participants in the conference;

(b) no conference in chambers shall be subject to audio-visual coverage;

(c) no audio-visual coverage of the selection of the prospective jury during voir dire shall be permitted;

(d) no audio-visual coverage of the jury, or of any juror or alternate juror, while in the jury box, in the courtroom, in the jury deliberation room during recess, or while going to or from the deliberation room at any time shall be permitted; provided, however, that, upon consent of the foreperson of a jury, the presiding trial judge may, in his or her discretion, permit audio coverage of such foreperson delivering a verdict;

(e) no audio-visual coverage shall be permitted of a witness, who as a peace or police officer acted in a covert or undercover capacity in connection with the instant court proceeding, without the prior written consent of such witness;

(f) no audio-visual coverage shall be permitted of a witness, who as a peace or police officer is currently engaged in a covert or undercover capacity, without the prior written consent of such witness;

(g) no audio-visual coverage shall be permitted of the victim in a prosecution for rape, sodomy, sexual abuse or other sex offense under article one hundred thirty or section 255.25 of the penal law; notwithstanding the initial approval of a request for audio-visual coverage of such a proceeding, the presiding trial judge shall have discretion throughout the proceeding to limit any coverage which would identify the victim, except that said victim can request of the presiding trial judge that audio-visual coverage be permitted of his or her testimony, or in the alternative the victim can request that coverage of his or her testimony be permitted but that his or her image shall be visually obscured by the news media, and the presiding trial judge in his or her discretion shall grant the request of the victim for the coverage specified;

(h) no audio-visual coverage of any arraignment or suppression hearing shall be permitted without the prior consent of all parties to the proceeding; provided, however, where a party is not yet represented by counsel consent may not be given unless the party has been advised of his or her right to the aid of counsel pursuant to subdivision four of section 170.10 or 180.10 of the criminal procedure law and the party has affirmatively elected to proceed without counsel at such proceeding;

(i) no judicial proceeding shall be scheduled, delayed, reenacted or continued at the request of, or for the convenience of the news media;

(j) no audio-visual coverage of any participant shall be permitted if the presiding trial judge finds that such coverage is liable to endanger the safety of any person;

(k) no audio-visual coverage of any judicial proceedings which are by law closed to the public, or which may be closed to the public and which have been closed by the presiding trial judge shall be permitted; and

(l) no audio-visual coverage shall be permitted which focuses on or features a family member of a victim or a party in the trial of a criminal case, except while such family member is testifying. Audio-visual coverage operators shall make all reasonable efforts to determine the identity of such persons, so that such coverage shall not occur.

8. Violations. Any violation of an order or determination issued under this section shall be punishable as a contempt pursuant to article nineteen of this chapter.

9. Review committee. (a) There shall be created a committee to review audio-visual coverage of court proceedings. The committee shall consist of twelve members, three to be appointed by the governor, three to be appointed by the chief judge of the courts, two to be appointed by the majority leader of the senate, two to be appointed by the speaker of the assembly, one to be appointed by the minority leader of the senate and one to be appointed by minority leader of the assembly. The chair of the committee shall be appointed by the chief judge of the courts. At least one member of the committee and no more than two members of the committee shall be a representative of the broadcast media, be employed by the broadcast media, or receive compensation from the broadcast media. At least two members of the committee shall be members of the bar, engaged in the practice of law, and regularly conduct trials and/or appellate arguments; and at least one member of the committee shall by professional training and expertise be qualified to evaluate and analyze research methodology relevant to analyzing the impact and effect of audio-visual coverage of judicial proceedings. No one who has served on an earlier committee established by law to review audio-visual coverage of judicial proceedings in New York state may be appointed to such committee. No member or employee of the executive, legislative, or judicial branches of the state government may be appointed to such committee.

(b) The members of the committee shall serve without compensation for their services as members of the committee, except that each of the nonpublic members of the committee may be allowed the necessary and actual travel, meals and lodging expenses which he or she shall incur in the performance of his or her duties under this section. Any expenses incurred pursuant to this section shall be a charge against the office of court administration.

(c) The committee shall have the power, duty and responsibility to evaluate, analyze, and monitor the provisions of this section. The office of court administration and all participants in proceedings where audio-visual coverage was permitted, including judges, attorneys and jurors, shall cooperate with the committee in connection with the review of the impact of audio-visual coverage on such proceedings. The committee shall request participation and assistance from the New York state bar association and other bar associations. The committee shall issue a report to the legislature, the governor, and the chief judge evaluating the efficacy of the program and whether any public benefits accrue from the program, any abuses that occurred during the program, and the extent to which and in what way the conduct of participants in court proceedings changes when audio-visual coverage is present. The committee shall expressly and specifically analyze and evaluate the degree of compliance by trial judges and the media with the provisions of this section and the effect of audio-visual coverage on the conduct of trial judges both inside and outside the courtroom. Such report shall be submitted to the legislature, the governor and the chief judge by January thirty-first, nineteen hundred ninety-seven.

10. **Rules and regulations.** The chief administrator shall promulgate appropriate rules and regulations for the implementation of the provisions of this section after affording all interested persons, agencies and institutions an opportunity to review and comment thereon. Such rules and regulations shall include provisions to ensure that audio-visual coverage of trial proceedings shall not interfere with the decorum and dignity of courtrooms and court facilities.

11. **Duration.** The provisions of this section shall be of no force and effect after June thirtieth, nineteen hundred ninety-seven.

(Added L.1992, c. 187, § 1; amended L.1992, c. 274, § 1; L.1993, c. 348, § 1; L.1995, c. 8, § 1.)

Historical and Statutory Notes

1995 Amendments. Subd. 9, par. (a). L.1995, c. 8, § 1, eff. Jan. 31, 1995, substituted reference to chief judge for reference to chief administrator in 2 places; substituted provisions requiring 1 or 2 committee members be representatives of, employed by, or paid by broadcast media, for provisions requiring at least 1 committee member be representative of broadcast news media; and added provisions requiring 2 practicing litigators and 1 qualified research analyst on committee, and prohibiting appointment of former committee members and members or employees of state government.

Subd. 9, par. (c). L.1995, c. 8, § 1, eff. Jan. 31, 1995, made request of bar assistance mandatory; substituted provisions regarding report evaluating program's efficacy, public benefits, abuses, and effect on participants, for provisions regarding recommendations as to efficacy of program and desirability of its continuation; required express and specific analysis and evaluation of compliance and effect on judges' conduct; and substituted due date of Jan. 31, 1997 for due date of Nov. 30, 1994.

Subd. 11. L.1995, c. 8, § 1, eff. Jan. 31, 1995, delayed expiration until June 30, 1997 from Jan. 31, 1995.

1993 Amendments. Subd. 3, par. (b). L.1993, c. 348, § 1, prohibited the sealing of orders allowing audio-visual coverage. For effective date, see note below.

1992 Amendments. Subd. 7, par. (h). L.1992, c. 274, § 1, eff. June 23, 1992, omitted exception authorizing victim to request judge to permit audio-visual coverage of his or her testimony, either with or without obscuring of victim's image, in court's discretion.

Effective Date of Amendment by L.1993, c. 348; Application; Expiration Unaffected. L.1993, c. 348, § 2, eff. July 21, 1993, provided: "This act [amending this section] shall take effect immediately [July 21, 1993] and shall apply to all proceedings commenced on and after such effective date; provided, however that the amendment to section 218 of the judiciary law made by section one of this act shall not affect the expiration of such section 218 and shall be deemed to expire therewith."

Effective Date. Section effective June 23, 1992, pursuant to L.1992, c. 187, § 1.

Derivation. Former § 218, added L.1987, c. 113, § 2; amended L.1989, c. 115, §§ 1 to 8; repealed L.1992, c. 187, § 1.

Short Title. This section is popularly known as the "cameras in the courtroom law".

New York Codes, Rules and Regulations

Audio-visual coverage of judicial proceedings, see 22 NYCRR 131.1 et seq., set out in McKinney's New York Rules of Court Pamphlet [N.Y.Ct.Rules 131.1 et seq.].

Electronic Recording and audio-visual coverage of court proceedings, see 22 NYCRR 29.1 et seq., set out in McKinney's New York Rules of Court Pamphlet [N.Y.Ct. Rules 29.1 et seq.].

Videotape recording of civil depositions—
  Court of claims, see 22 NYCRR 206.11, set out in McKinney's New York Rules of Court Pamphlet [N.Y.Ct.Rules 206.11].
  Supreme court and county court, see 22 NYCRR 202.15, set out in McKinney's New York Rules of Court Pamphlet [N.Y.Ct.Rules 202.15].

Appendix D
Rules of the Chief Administrative Judge

PART 131
AUDIO-VISUAL COVERAGE OF JUDICIAL PROCEEDINGS
(Statutory authority: Judiciary Law, § 218)

Sec.
131.1   Purpose, provisions
131.2   Definitions
131.3   Application for audio-visual coverage
131.4   Determination of the application
131.5   Review
131.6   Mandatory pretrial conference
131.7   Use and deployment of equipment and personnel by the news media
131.8   Additional restrictions on coverage
131.9   Supervision of audio-visual coverage
131.10 Cooperation with committee
131.11 Appellate courts
131.12 Forms
131.13 Acceptable equipment

Historical Note
Part (§ 131.1) filed July 14, 1986; renum. Part 133, new (§§ 131.1–131.13) filed Dec. 2, 1987 eff. Dec. 1, 1987.

§ 131.1 Purpose; general provisions.
(a) These rules are promulgated to comport with the legislative finding that an enhanced public understanding of the judicial system is important in maintaining a high level of public confidence in the Judiciary, and with the legislative concern that cameras in the courts be compatible with the fair administration of justice.

(b) These rules shall be effective for any period when audio-visual coverage in the trial courts is authorized by law and shall apply in all counties in the State.

(c) Nothing in these rules is intended to restrict any preexisting right of the news media to appear at and to report on judicial proceedings in accordance with law.

(d) Nothing in these rules is intended to restrict the power and discretion of the presiding trial judge to control the conduct of judicial proceedings.

(e) No judicial proceeding shall be scheduled, delayed, reenacted or continued at the request of, or for the convenience of, the news media.

(f) In addition to their specific responsibilities as provided in these rules, all presiding trial judges and all administrative judges shall take whatever steps are necessary to insure that audio-visual coverage is conducted without disruption of court activities, without detracting from or interfering with the dignity or decorum of the court, courtrooms and court facilities, without compromise of the safety of persons having business before the court, and without adversely affecting the administration of justice.

Historical Note

Sec. filed July 14, 1986; renum. 133.1, new filed Dec. 2, 1987; amds. filed: Oct. 17, 1989; Nov. 12, 1992; March 23, 1995 eff. March 23, 1995. Amended (b).

§ 131.2 Definitions.

For purposes of this Part:

(a) *Administrative judge* shall mean the administrative judge of each judicial district; the administrative judge of Nassau County or of Suffolk County; the administrative judge of the Civil Court of the City of New York, the Criminal Court of the City of New York or the Family Court of the City of New York; or the presiding judge of the Court of Claims.

(b) *Audio-visual coverage* or *coverage* shall mean the electronic broadcasting or other transmission to the public of radio or television signals from the courtroom, the recording of sound or light in the courtroom for later transmission or reproduction, or the taking of still or motion pictures in the courtroom by the news media.

(c) *News media* shall mean any news-reporting or news-gathering agency and any employee or agent associated with such agency, including television, radio, radio and television networks, news services, newspapers, magazines, trade papers, in-house publications, professional journals, or any other news-reporting or news-gathering agency, the function of which is to inform the public or some segment thereof.

(d) *Presiding trial judge* shall mean the justice or judge presiding over judicial proceedings at which audio-visual coverage is authorized pursuant to this Part.

(e) *Covert or undercover capacity* shall mean law enforcement activity involving criminal investigation by peace officers or police officers who usually and customarily wear no uniform, badge or other official identification in public view.

(f) *Judicial proceedings* shall mean the proceedings of a court or a judge thereof conducted in a courtroom or any other facility being used as a courtroom.

(g) *Child* shall mean a person who has not attained the age of 16 years.

(h) *Arraignment* shall have the same meaning as such term is defined in subdivision nine of section 1.20 of the Criminal Procedure Law.

(i) *Suppression hearing* shall mean a hearing on a motion made pursuant to the provisions of section 710.20 of the Criminal Procedure Law; a hearing on a motion to determine the admissibility of any prior criminal, vicious or immoral acts of a defendant; and any other hearing held to determine the admissibility of evidence.

(j) *Nonparty witness* shall mean any witness in a criminal trial proceeding who is not a party to such proceeding; except an expert or professional witness, a peace or police officer who acted in the course of his or her duties and was not acting in a covert or undercover capacity in connection with the instant court proceedings, or any government official acting in an official capacity, shall not be deemed to be a nonparty witness.

(k) *Visually obscured* shall mean that the face of a participant in a criminal trial proceeding shall either not be shown or shall be rendered visually unrecognizable to the viewer of such proceeding by means of special editing by the news media.

Historical Note
Sec. filed Dec. 2, 1987; amds. filed: Oct. 17, 1989; Nov. 12, 1992 eff. Nov. 5, 1992. Amended (i); added (j)-(k).

§ 131.3 Application for audio-visual coverage.

(a) Coverage of judicial proceedings shall be permitted only upon order of the presiding trial judge approving an application made by a representative of the news media for permission to conduct such coverage.

(b) (1) Except as provided in paragraph (2) of this subdivision, an application for permission to conduct coverage of a judicial proceeding shall be made to the presiding trial judge not less than seven days before the scheduled commencement of that proceeding. Where circumstances are such that an applicant cannot reasonably apply more than seven days before commencement of the proceeding, the presiding trial judge may shorten the time period. The application shall be in writing and shall specify such proceeding with sufficient particularity to assist the presiding trial judge in considering the application, and shall set forth which of the types of coverage described in section 131.2(b) of this Part is sought, including whether live coverage is sought. Upon receipt of any application, the presiding trial judge shall cause all parties to the proceeding to be notified thereof.

(2) An application for permission to conduct coverage of an arraignment in a criminal case or of any other proceeding after it has commenced may be made to the presiding trial judge at any time and shall be otherwise subject to the provisions of paragraph (1) of this subdivision.

(3) Each application shall relate to one case or proceeding only, unless the presiding trial judge permits otherwise.

(c) Where more than one representative of the news media makes an application for coverage of the same judicial proceeding, such applications shall be consolidated and treated as one.

Historical Note
Sec. filed Dec. 2, 1987 eff. Dec. 1, 1987.

§ 131.4 Determination of the application.

(a) Upon receipt of an application pursuant to section 131.3 of this Part, the presiding trial judge shall conduct such review as may be appropriate, including:

(1) consultation with the news media applicant;

(2) consultation with counsel to all parties to the proceeding of which coverage is sought, who shall be responsible for identifying any concerns or objections of the parties, prospective witnesses, and victims, if any, with respect to the proposed coverage, and advising the court thereof; and

(3) review of all statements or affidavits presented to the presiding trial judge concerning the proposed coverage.

Where the proceedings of which coverage is sought involve a child, a victim, a prospective witness, or a party, any of whom object to such coverage, and in any other appropriate instance, the presiding trial judge may hold such conferences and conduct any direct inquiry as may be fitting.

(b) (l) Except as otherwise provided in paragraphs (2) and (3) of this subdivision or section 131.8 of this Part, consent of the parties, prospective witnesses, victims or other participants in judicial proceedings of which coverage is sought is not required for approval of an application for such coverage.

(2) An application for audio-visual coverage of a trial proceeding in which a jury is sitting, made after commencement of such proceeding, shall not be approved unless counsel to all parties to such proceeding consent to such coverage; provided, however, this paragraph shall not apply where coverage is sought only of the verdict or sentencing, or both, in such proceeding.

(3) Counsel to each party in a criminal trial proceeding shall advise each nonparty witness that he or she has the right to request that his or her image be visually obscured during said witness' testimony, and upon such request the presiding trial judge shall order the news media to visually obscure the visual image of the witness in any and all audio-visual coverage of the judicial proceeding.

(c) In determining an application for coverage, the presiding trial judge shall consider all relevant factors, including but not limited to:

(l) the type of case involved;

(2) whether the coverage would cause harm to any participant;

(3) whether the coverage would interfere with the fair administration of justice, the advancement of a fair trial, or the rights of the parties;

(4) whether any order directing the exclusion of witnesses from the courtroom prior to their testimony could be rendered substantially ineffective by allowing audio-visual coverage that could be viewed by such witnesses to the detriment of any party;.

(5) whether the coverage would interfere with any law enforcement activity;

(6) whether the proceedings would involve lewd or scandalous matters;

(7) the objections of any of the parties, prospective witnesses, victims or other participants in the proceeding of which coverage is sought;

(8) the physical structure of the courtroom and the likelihood that any equipment required to conduct coverage of proceedings can be installed and operated without disturbance to those proceedings or any other proceedings in the courthouse; and

(9) the extent to which the coverage would be barred by law in the judicial proceeding of which coverage is sought.

The presiding trial judge also shall consider and give great weight to the fact that any party, prospective witness, victim, or other participant in the proceeding is a child.

(d) Following review of an application for coverage of a judicial proceeding, the presiding trial judge, as soon as practicable, shall issue an order, in writing, approving such application, in whole or in part, or denying it. Such order shall contain any restrictions imposed by the judge on the audio-visual coverage and shall contain a statement advising the parties that any violation of the order is punishable by contempt pursuant to article 19 of the Judiciary Law. Such order shall be included in the record of such proceedings and, unless it wholly approves the application and no party, victim or prospective witness objected to coverage, it shall state the basis for its determination.

(e) Before denying an application for coverage, the presiding trial judge shall consider whether such coverage properly could be approved with the imposition of special limitations, including but not limited to:

(1) delayed broadcast of the proceedings subject to coverage; provided, however, where delayed broadcast is directed, it shall be only for the purpose of assisting the news media to comply with the restrictions on coverage provided by law or by the presiding trial judge;

(2) modification or prohibition of audio-visual coverage of individual parties, witnesses, or other trial participants, or portions of the proceedings; or

(3) modification or prohibition of video coverage of individual parties, witnesses, or other trial participants, or portions of the proceedings.

Historical Note
Sec. filed Dec. 2, 1987; amds. filed: Oct. 17, 1989; Nov. 12, 1992 eff.Nov. 5, 1992. Amended (b)-(d).

§ 131.5 Review.

(a) Any order determining an application for permission to provide coverage, rendered pursuant to section 131.4(d) of this Part, shall be subject to review by the administrative judge in such form, including telephone conference, as he or she may determine, upon the request of a person who is aggrieved thereby and who is either:

(1) a news media applicant; or

(2) a party, victim, or prospective witness who objected to coverage.

(b) Upon review of a presiding trial judge's order determining an application for permission to provide coverage, the administrative judge shall uphold such order unless it is found that the order reflects an abuse of discretion by the presiding trial judge, in which event the administrative judge may direct such modification of the presiding trial judge's order as may be deemed appropriate. Any order directing a modification or overruling a presiding trial judge's order determining an application for coverage shall be in writing.

(c) No judicial proceeding shall be delayed or continued to allow for review by an administrative judge of an order denying coverage in whole or in part.

(d) This section shall authorize review by the administrative judge only of a presiding trial judge's order pursuant to paragraph 3(b) of section 218 of the Judiciary Law, determining an application for permission to provide coverage of judicial proceedings and shall not authorize review of any other orders or decisions of the presiding trial judge relating to such coverage.

Historical Note
Sec. filed Dec. 2, 1987; amds. filed: Oct. 17, 1989; Nov. 12, 1992 eff. Nov. 5, 1992. Amended (b)-(d).

§ 131.6 Mandatory pretrial conference.

(a) Where a presiding trial judge has approved, in whole or in part, an application for coverage of any judicial proceeding, the judge, before any such coverage is to begin, shall conduct a pre-trial conference for the purpose of reviewing, with counsel to all parties to the proceeding and with representatives of the news media who will provide such coverage, any objections to coverage that have been raised, the scope of coverage to be permitted, the nature and extent of the technical equipment and personnel to be deployed, and the restrictions on coverage to be observed. The court may include in the conference any other person whom it deems appropriate, including prospective witnesses and their representatives. In an appropriate case, the presiding trial judge may conduct the pretrial conference concurrently with any consultations or conferences authorized by section 131.4(a) of this Part.

(b) Where two or more representatives of the news media are parties to an approved application for coverage, no such coverage may begin until all such representatives have agreed upon a pooling arrangement for their respective news media prior to the pretrial conference. Such pooling arrangement shall include the designation of pool operators and replacement pool operators for the electronic and motion picture media and for the still photography media, as appropriate. It also shall include procedures for the cost-sharing and dissemination of audio-visual material and shall make due provision for educational users' needs for full coverage of entire proceedings. The presiding trial judge shall not be called upon to mediate or resolve any dispute as to such arrangement. Nothing herein shall prohibit a person or organization that was not party to an approved application for coverage from making appropriate arrangements with the pool operator to be given access to the audio-visual material produced by the pool.

(c) In determining the scope of coverage to be permitted, the presiding trial judge shall be guided by a consideration of all relevant factors, including those prescribed in section 131.4(c) of this Part. Wherever necessary or appropriate, the presiding trial judge shall, at any time before or during the proceeding, proscribe coverage or modify, expand, impose or remove special limitations on coverage, such as those prescribed in section 131.4(e) of this Part.

Historical Note
Sec. filed Dec. 2, 1987 eff. Dec. 1, 1987.

§ 131.7 Use and deployment of equipment and personnel by the news media.

(a) *Limitations upon use of equipment and personnel in the courtroom.*

(1) No more than two electronic or motion picture cam-

eras and two camera operators shall be permitted in any proceeding.

(2) No more than one photographer to operate two still cameras, with not more than two lenses for each camera, shall be permitted in any proceeding.

(3) No more than one audio system for broadcast purposes shall be permitted in any proceeding. Audio pickup for all news media purposes shall be effectuated through existing audio systems in the court facility. If no technically suitable audio system is available, microphones and related wiring essential for media purposes shall be supplied by those persons providing coverage. Any microphones and sound wiring shall be unobtrusive and placed where designated by the presiding trial judge.

(4) Notwithstanding the provisions of paragraphs (1)-(3) of this subdivision, the presiding trial judge on a finding of special circumstances may modify any restriction on the amount of equipment or number of operating personnel in the courtroom, compatible with the dignity of the court or the judicial process.

(b) *Sound and light criteria.* (1) Only electronic and motion picture cameras, audio equipment and still camera equipment that do not produce distracting sound or light may be employed to cover judicial proceedings. The equipment designated in section 131.13 of this Part shall be deemed acceptable.

(2) Use of equipment other than that authorized in section 131.13 of this Part may be permitted by the presiding trial judge provided the judge is satisfied that the equipment sought to be utilized meets the sound and light criteria specified in paragraph (1) of this subdivision. A failure to obtain advance approval shall preclude use of such equipment in the coverage of the judicial proceeding.

(3) No motorized drives, moving lights, flash attachments, or sudden lighting changes shall be permitted during coverage of judicial proceedings.

(4) No light or signal visible or audible to trial participants shall be used on any equipment during coverage to indicate whether it is operating.

(5) With the concurrence of the presiding trial judge and the administrative judge, modifications and additions may be made in light sources existing in the court facility, provided such modifications or additions are installed and maintained at media expense and are not distracting or otherwise offensive.

(c) *Location of equipment and personnel.* Electronic and motion picture cameras, still cameras, and personnel shall be positioned in such locations as shall be designated by the presiding trial judge. The areas designated shall provide the news media with reasonable access to the persons they wish to cover while causing the least possible interference with court proceedings. Equipment that is not necessary for audio-visual coverage from inside the courtroom shall be located in an area outside the courtroom.

(d) *Movement of equipment and media personnel.* During the proceedings, operating personnel shall not move about, nor shall there be placement, movement or removal of equipment, or the changing of film, film magazines or lenses. All such activities shall take place each day before the proceeding begins, after it ends, or during a recess.

(e) *Identifying insignia.* Identifying marks, call letters, words, and symbols shall be concealed on all equipment. Persons operating such equipment shall not display any identifying insignia on their clothing.

(f) *Other restrictions.* The presiding trial judge may impose any other restriction on the use and deployment of equipment and personnel as may be appropriate.

Historical Note
Sec. filed Dec. 2, 1987; amd. filed Nov. 12, 1992 eff. Nov. 5, 1992. Amended (f).

§ 131.8 Additional restrictions on coverage.
(a) No audio pickup or audio broadcast of conferences that occur in a court facility between attorneys and their clients, between co-counsel of a client, or between counsel and the presiding trial judge, shall be permitted without the prior express consent of all participants in the conference.

(b) No conference in chambers shall be subject to coverage.

(c) No coverage of the selection of the prospective jury during *voir dire* shall be permitted.

(d) No coverage of the jury, or of any juror or alternate juror, while in the jury box, in the courtroom, in the jury deliberation room, or during recess, or while going to or from the deliberation room at any time, shall be permitted provided, however, that, upon consent of the foreperson of a jury, the presiding trial judge may, in his or her discretion, permit audio coverage of such foreperson delivering a verdict.

(e) No coverage shall be permitted of a witness, who as a peace officer or police officer acted in a covert or undercover capacity in connection with the proceedings being covered, without the prior written consent of such witness.

(f) No coverage shall be permitted of a witness, who as a peace officer or police officer is currently engaged in a covert or undercover capacity, without the prior written consent of such witness.

(g) No coverage shall be permitted of the victim in a prosecution for rape, sodomy, sexual abuse, or other sex offense under article 130 or section 255.25 of the Penal Law; notwithstanding the initial approval of a request for audio-visual coverage of such a proceeding, the presiding trial judge shall have discretion throughout the proceeding to limit any coverage that would identify the victim, except that said victim can request of the presiding trial judge that audio-visual coverage be permitted of his or her testimony, or in the alternative the victim can request that coverage of his or her testimony be permitted but that his or her image shall be visually obscured by the news media, and the presiding trial judge in his or her discretion shall grant the request of the victim for the coverage specified.

(h) No coverage of any participant shall be permitted if the presiding trial judge finds that such coverage is liable to endanger the safety of any person.

(i) No coverage of any judicial proceedings that are by law closed to the public, or that may be closed to the public and that have been closed by the presiding trial judge, shall be permitted.

(j) No coverage of any arraignment or suppression hearing shall be permitted without the prior consent of all parties to the proceeding; provided, however, where a party is not yet represented by counsel, consent may not be given unless the party has been advised of his or her right to the aid of counsel pursuant to subdivision 4 of section 170.10 or 180.10 of the Criminal Procedure Law and the party has affirmatively elected to proceed without counsel at such proceeding.

(k) No audio-visual coverage shall be permitted which focuses on or features a family member of a victim or a party in the trial of a criminal case, except while such family member is testifying. Audio-visual coverage operators shall make all reasonable efforts to determine the identity of such persons, so that such coverage shall not occur. The restrictions specified in subdivisions (a) through (k) of this section may not be waived or modified except as provided therein.

Historical Note
Sec. filed Dec. 2, 1987; amds. filed: Oct. 17. 1989; Nov. 12, 1992 eff. Nov. 5, 1992. Amended (d), (g), (j); added (k).

§ 131.9 Supervision of audio-visual coverage.

(a) Coverage of judicial proceedings shall be subject to the continuing supervision of the presiding trial judge. No coverage shall take place within the courtroom, whether during recesses or at any other time, when the presiding trial judge is not present and presiding.

(b) Notwithstanding the approval of an application for permission to provide coverage of judicial proceedings, the presiding trial judge shall have discretion throughout such proceedings to revoke such approval or to limit the coverage authorized in any way. In the exercise of this discretion, the presiding trial judge shall be especially sensitive and responsive to the needs and concerns of all parties, victims, witnesses, and other participants in such proceedings, particularly where the proceedings unnecessarily threaten the privacy or sensibilities of victims, or where they involve children or sex offenses or other matters that may be lewd or scandalous. The presiding trial judge shall be under a continuing obligation to order the discontinuation or modification of coverage where necessary to shield the identity or otherwise insure the protection of any such person, party, witness, or victim, or in order to preserve the welfare of a child.

(c) Counsel to each party in a trial proceeding that is subject to coverage shall inquire of each witness that he or she intends to call regarding any concerns or objections such witness might have with respect to coverage. Where counsel thereby is advised that a witness objects to coverage, counsel shall so notify the presiding trial judge.

Historical Note
Sec. filed Dec. 2, 1987; amd. filed Oct. 17, 1989 eff. Oct. 11, 1989. Added (c).

§ 131.10 Cooperation with committee.

(a) All officers and employees of the Unified Court System, and all participants in proceedings where audio-visual coverage was permitted, including judges, attorneys and jurors, shall cooperate with the committee to review audio-visual coverage of court proceedings in connection with the committee's review of the impact of audio-visual coverage on such proceedings.

Historical Note
Sec. filed Dec. 2, 1987; amds. filed: Jan. 25, 1988; Oct. 17, 1989; repealed, new filed Nov. 12, 1992 eff. Nov.5, 1992.

§ 1 31.11 Appellate courts.
These rules shall not apply to coverage of proceedings in appellate courts or affect the rules governing such coverage contained in Part 29 of the Rules of the Chief Judge (22 NYCRR Part 29).

Historical Note
Sec. filed Dec. 2, 1987 eff. Dec. 1, 1987.

§ 1 31.12 Forms.
The Chief Administrator will promulgate and make available forms for applications pursuant to section 131.3 and for judicial orders pursuant to section 131.4 of this Part.

Historical Note
Sec. filed Dec.2, 1987; amds. filed: Oct. 17, 1989; Nov. 12, 1992 eff. Nov.5, 1992.

§ 131.13 Acceptable equipment.
The following equipment shall be deemed acceptable for use in audio-visual coverage of trial court proceedings pursuant to this Part:

(a) *Video cameras.*

Sony:

BVP-3, BVP-3A, BVP-3U, BVP-5, BVP-30, BVP-33Am, BVP-50J, BVP-110, BVP-150, BVP-250, BVP-300, BVU-300, BVV-1, BVV-5, DXC-3000, M-3

Ikegami:

HL-79, HL-79D, HL-79E, HL-83, HL-95, ITC-170, SP-3A, 75-D, 79-E, 95, 730, 730a, 730ap

JVC:

KY-1900, KY-2000, KY-2700, BY-110

RCA:

TK-76

Thompson:

501, 601

NEC:

SP-3A

Sharp:

XC-800

Panasonic:

X-100 (the recam system in a camera/recorder combination)

Ampex:

Betacam

(b) *Still cameras.*

Leica:

M

Nikon:

FE, F-3, FM-2, 2000

Canon:

F-1, T-90

(c) Any other audio or video equipment may be used with the permission of the presiding trial judge.

Historical Note
Sec. filed Dec. 2, 1987 eff. Dec. 1, 1987.

EXHIBIT 1

APPLICATION FOR PERMISSION TO CONDUCT AUDIO-VISUAL COVERAGE

_____ Court, _____ County
_____x
In the Matter of an Application to
Conduct Audio-Visual Coverage of

           Index No. _____
           Indictment No. _____
           Calendar No. _____
           (Complete as applicable, if known)

v.

           Judge assigned (if known):
           _____

_____x

TO THE COURT:
1. The undersigned hereby applies for permission to conduct audio-visual coverage of the above judicial proceeding as follows (check as appropriate):

 ____ televise live   ____ audio (radio) broadcast live

 ____ videotape for later broadcast   ____ audiotape for later broadcast

 ____ film   ____ use still photography

 ____ tape record   ____ other (specify)

2. The scope of coverage requested is (check as appropriate):
 ____ throughout the above proceeding

 ____ during only the following portion(s) of such proceeding (specify):
 _____

           _____
           (Signature)

           _____
           (Name)

           (Media organization)
           _____

           _____
           (Address)
Dated: _____   ( )_____
           (Telephone number)

EXHIBIT 2

ORDER DETERMINING APPLICATION FOR AUDIO-VISUAL COVERAGE

_____ Court, _____ County
———————————————x

In the Matter of an Application to Conduct Audio-Visual Coverage of

ORDER DETERMINING APPLI-
CATION FOR AUDIO-VISUAL
COVERAGE

v.

(Index) (Indictment) (Calendar) No. __

———————————————x

PRESENT: Hon. _____

An application having been made to this Court on _____, 19____, pursuant to section 131.3 of the Rules of the Chief Administrative Judge by _____ (news media applicant), requesting permission to (specify type of coverage) _____ the above judicial proceeding; and

The Court having reviewed this application and the attached statements and affidavits presented to the Court concerning the proposed coverage; and

The Court having consulted with the news media applicant and counsel to all parties to the above-named proceeding (and with (specify others—*e.g.*, victims, witnesses, etc.—as appropriate) _____);

NOW, upon consideration of all relevant factors, including those specified in section 131.1(c) of the Rules of the Chief Administrative Judge, it is hereby

ORDERED that the application is (approved) (denied) (approved with the following special limitations: _____) (strike out inapplicable language).

The basis for the determination is (to be completed unless the application is approved without special limitations *and* no party, victim or prospective witness objects to coverage):

_____
_____
_____
_____

_____
(Justice) (Judge)

Dated:

Appendix E
California Rule of Court 980

[NOTE: *The Judicial Council has adopted the following amendments to rule 980 effective January 1, 1997.*]

Rule 980. **Photographing, recording, and broadcasting in the court** [*Amendments effective January 1, 1997.*]

(a) **[Introduction] The judiciary is** responsible for ensuring the fair and equal administration of justice. The judiciary adjudicates controversies, both civil and criminal, in accordance with established legal procedures in the calmness and solemnity of the courtroom. Photographing, recording, and broadcasting of courtroom proceedings may be permitted as circumscribed in this rule if executed in a manner that ensures that the fairness and dignity of the proceedings are not adversely affected. This rule does not create a presumption for or against granting permission to photograph, record, or broadcast court proceedings. [*Adopted effective Jan. 1, 1997.*]

(b) **[Definitions]** For the purposes of this rule,

(1) "Media coverage" means any photographing, recording, or broadcasting of court proceedings by the media using television, radio, photographic, or recording equipment;

(2) "Media" or "media agency" means any person or organization engaging in news gathering or reporting and includes any newspaper, radio or television station or network, news service, magazine, trade paper, in-house publication, professional journal, or other news-reporting or news-gathering agency;

(3) "Court" means the courtroom at issue, the courthouse, and its entrances and exits;

(4) "Judge" means the judicial officer or officers assigned to or presiding at the proceeding, except as provided in subdivision

(e)(l) if no judge has been assigned. [*Amended and relettered effective Jan. 1, 1997.*]

(c) [Photographing, recording, and broadcasting prohibited] Except as provided in this rule, court proceedings shall not be photographed, recorded, or broadcast. This rule does not prohibit courts from photographing or videotaping sessions for judicial education or publications and is not intended to apply to closed-circuit television broadcasts solely within the courthouse or between court facilities if the broadcasts are controlled by the court and court personnel. [*Adopted effective Jan. 1, 1997.*]

(d) [Personal recording devices] The judge may permit inconspicuous personal recording devices to be used by persons in a courtroom to make sound recordings as personal notes of the proceedings. A person proposing to use a recording device shall obtain permission from the judge in advance. The recordings shall not be used for any purpose other than as personal notes. [*Amended and unlettered effective Jan. 1, 1997.*]

(e) [Media coverage] Media coverage shall be permitted only on written order of the judge as provided in this subdivision. The judge in his or her discretion may permit, refuse, limit, or terminate media coverage. This rule does not otherwise limit or restrict the right of the media to cover and report court proceedings.

(1) (Request for order) The media may request an order permitting media coverage on a form approved by the Judicial Council. The form shall be filed at least five court days before the portion of the proceeding to be covered unless good cause is shown. A completed, proposed order on a form approved by the Judicial Council shall be filed with the request. The judge assigned to the proceeding shall rule upon the request. If no judge has been assigned, the request shall be submitted to the judge supervising the calendar department, and thereafter be ruled upon by the judge assigned to the proceeding. The clerk shall promptly notify the parties that a request has been filed.

(2) (Hearing) The judge may hold a hearing on the request or rule on the request without a hearing.

(3) (Factors to be considered by the judge) In ruling on the request, the judge shall consider the following factors:

(i) Importance of maintaining public trust and confidence in the judicial system;

(ii) Importance of promoting public access to the judicial system;

(iii) Parties' support of or opposition to the request;

(iv) Nature of the case;

(v) Privacy rights of all participants in the proceeding, including witnesses, jurors, and victims;

(vi) Effect on any minor who is a party, prospective witness, victim, or other participant in the proceeding;

(vii) Effect on the parties' ability to select a fair and unbiased jury;

(viii) Effect on any ongoing law enforcement activity in the case;

(ix) Effect on any unresolved identification issues;

(x) Effect on any subsequent proceedings in the case;

(xi) Effect of coverage on the willingness of witnesses to cooperate, including the risk that coverage will engender threats to the health or safety of any witness;

(xii) Effect on excluded witnesses who would have access to the televised testimony of prior witnesses;

(xiii) Scope of the coverage and whether partial coverage might unfairly influence or distract the jury;

(xiv) Difficulty of jury selection if a mistrial is declared;

(xv) Security and dignity of the court;

(xvi) Undue administrative or financial burden to the court or participants;

(xvii) Interference with neighboring courtrooms;

(xviii) Maintaining orderly conduct of the proceeding;

(xix) Any other factor the judge deems relevant.

(4) (Order permitting media coverage) The judge ruling on the request to permit media coverage is not required to make findings or a statement of decision. The order may incorporate any local rule or order of the presiding or supervising judge regulating media activity outside of the courtroom. The judge may condition the order permitting media coverage on the media agency's agreement to pay any increased court-incurred costs resulting from the permitted media coverage (for example, for additional court security or utility service). Each media agency shall be responsible for ensuring that all its media personnel who cover the court proceeding know and follow the provisions of the court order and this rule.

(5) (Modified order) The order permitting media coverage may be modified or terminated on the judge's own motion or upon application to the judge without the necessity of a prior hearing or written findings. Notice of the application and any modification or termination ordered pursuant to the application shall be given to the parties and each media agency permitted by the previous order to cover the proceeding.

(6) (Prohibited coverage) The judge shall not permit media coverage of the following:

(i) Proceedings held in chambers;

(ii) Proceedings closed to the public;

(iii) Jury selection;

(iv) Jurors or spectators; and

(v) Conferences between an attorney and a client, witness, or aide, between attorneys, or between counsel and the judge at the bench.

(7) (equipment and personnel) The judge may require media agencies to demonstrate that proposed personnel and equipment comply with this rule. The judge may specify the placement of media personnel and equipment to permit reasonable media coverage without disruption of the proceedings.

Unless the Judge in his or her discretion and for good cause orders otherwise, the following rules shall apply:

(i) One television camera and one still photographer shall be permitted.

(ii) The equipment used shall not produce distracting sound or light. Signal lights or devices to show when equipment is operating shall not be visible.

(iii) An order permitting or requiring modification of existing sound or lighting systems is deemed to require that the modifications be installed, maintained, and removed without public expense or disruption of proceedings. Microphones and wiring shall be unobtrusively located in places approved by the judge and shall be operated by one person.

(iv) Operators shall not move equipment or enter or leave the courtroom while the court is in session, or otherwise cause a distraction.

(v) Equipment or clothing shall not bear the insignia or marking of a media agency.

(8) (Media pooling) If two or more media agencies of the same type request media coverage of a proceeding, they shall file a statement of agreed arrangements. If they are unable to agree, the judge may deny media coverage by that type of media agency.

[*Amended and relettered effective Jan. 1, 1997.*]

(f) [Sanctions] Any violation of this rule or an order made under this rule is an unlawful interference with the proceedings of the court and may be the basis for an order terminating media coverage, a citation for contempt of court, or an order imposing monetary or other sanctions as provided by law. [*Amended and relettered effective Jan. 1, 1997.*]

MEDIA AGENCY *(name)* CHANNEL/FREQUENCY NO PERSON SUBMITTING REQUEST *(name)* ADDRESS TELEPHONE NO	FOR COURT USE ONLY
Insert name of court and name of judicial district and branch court if any	
TITLE OF CASE	
NAME OF JUDGE	
MEDIA REQUEST TO PHOTOGRAPH, RECORD, OR BROADCAST	CASE NUMBER

1 PORTION OF THE PROCEEDINGS TO BE COVERED *(e g , particular witnesses at trial, the sentencing hearing, etc)*

2 DATE OF PROPOSED COVERAGE *(specify)*   *(File this form at least five court days before the proposed coverage date If not feasible, explain good cause for noncompliance)*

3 TYPE OF COVERAGE
   a ☐ TV camera and recorder   d ☐ Audio
   b ☐ Still camera   e ☐ Other *(specify)*
   c ☐ Motion picture camera

4 ☐ SPECIAL REQUESTS OR ANTICIPATED PROBLEMS *(specify)*

5 ☐ INCREASED COSTS This agency acknowledges that it will be responsible for increased court-incurred costs, if any, resulting from this media coverage *(estimate)* $
      ☐ Amount unknown

6 PROPOSED ORDER A completed, proposed order on Judicial Council form MC-510 is attached *(required by Cal Rules of Court, rule 980(e)(1))*

CERTIFICATION

I certify that if the court permits media coverage in this case, all participating personnel in this media agency will be informed of and will abide by the provisions of California Rules of Court, rule 980, the provisions of the court order, and any additional restrictions imposed by the court

Date

▶

(TYPE OR PRINT NAME)   (SIGNATURE)

Telephone No
                                                        (SUPERVISORY POSITION IN MEDIA AGENCY)

NOTICE OF HEARING *(A hearing is optional.)*

A HEARING will be held as follows

Date Address of the court	Time	Dept /Div	Room

                                       Clerk, by _____, Deputy

Form Adopted by the Judicial Council of California
MC 500 [Rev. January 1 1995]

MEDIA REQUEST TO PHOTOGRAPH, RECORD, OR BROADCAST

Cal Rules of Court
rule 980(e)(1)

APPENDICES 155

MEDIA AGENCY (name)	FOR COURT USE ONLY
CHANNEL/FREQUENCY NO	
PERSON SUBMITTING REQUEST (name)	
ADDRESS	
TELEPHONE NO	

Insert name of court and name of judicial district and branch court, if any

TITLE OF CASE.

NAME OF JUDGE.

ORDER ON MEDIA REQUEST TO PERMIT COVERAGE | CASE NUMBER

AGENCY MAKING REQUEST (name)

1. a ☐ No hearing was held.
   b. ☐ Date of hearing   Time   Dept /Div.   Room
2. The court considered all the relevant factors listed in subdivision (e)(3) of California Rules of Court, rule 980 (see reverse)
3. ☐ THE COURT FINDS (findings or a statement of decision are optional) ☐ Attached ☐ As follows

THE COURT ORDERS

4. The request to photograph, record, or broadcast is
   a ☐ denied
   b ☐ granted subject to the conditions in rule 980, California Rules of Court, AND the following
       (1) ☐ The local rules of this court regulating media activity outside the courtroom (copy attached)
       (2) ☐ The order of the presiding or supervising judge regulating media activity outside the courtroom (copy attached)
       (3) ☐ Payment to the clerk of increased court-incurred costs of (specify) $ ☐ to be determined
       (4) ☐ The media agency shall demonstrate to the court that the proposed personnel and equipment comply with California Rules of Court, rule 980, and any local rule or order
       (5) ☐ Personnel and equipment shall be placed ☐ as directed ☐ as indicated in the attachment ☐ as follows (specify)

       (6) (i) ☐ The attached statement of agreed pooling arrangements is approved
           (ii) ☐ A statement of agreed pooling arrangements satisfactory to the court shall be filed before coverage begins
       (7) ☐ This order
           (i) ☐ shall not apply to allow coverage of proceedings that are continued
           (ii) ☐ shall apply to allow coverage of proceedings that are continued
       (8) ☐ Other (specify)

5. Coverage granted in item 4b is permitted in the following proceedings
   a. ☐ All proceedings *except* those prohibited by California Rules of Court, rule 980, and those proceedings prohibited by further court order
   b ☐ Only the following proceedings (specify type or date or both)

6 ☐ The order made on (date)   is ☐ terminated ☐ modified as follows (specify)

7 ☐ Number of pages attached

Date.
_____
(See reverse for additional information)   JUDGE

Form Adopted by the
Judicial Council of California
MC-510 [New January 1, 1997]   **ORDER ON MEDIA REQUEST TO PERMIT COVERAGE**   Cal. Rules of Court
rule 980(e)(4)

156 APPENDICES

CASE NAME	CASE NUMBER

FACTORS CONSIDERED BY THE JUDGE IN MAKING THIS ORDER (Rule 980(e)(3))

1. Importance of maintaining public trust and confidence in the judicial system
2. Importance of promoting public access to the judicial system
3. Parties' support of or opposition to the request
4. Nature of the case
5. Privacy rights of all participants in the proceeding, including witnesses, jurors, and victims
6. Effect on any minor who is a party, prospective witness, victim, or other participant in the proceeding
7. Effect on the parties' ability to select a fair and unbiased jury
8. Effect on any ongoing law enforcement activity in the case
9. Effect on any unresolved identification issues
10. Effect on any subsequent proceedings in the case
11. Effect of coverage on the willingness of witnesses to cooperate, including the risk that coverage will engender threats to the health or safety of any witness
12. Effect on excluded witnesses who would have access to the televised testimony of prior witnesses
13. Scope of the coverage and whether partial coverage might unfairly influence or distract the jury
14. Difficulty of jury selection if a mistrial is declared
15. Security and dignity of the court
16. Undue administrative or financial burden to the court or participants
17. Interference with neighboring courtrooms
18. Maintaining orderly conduct of the proceeding
19. Any other factor the judge deems relevant

PROHIBITED COVERAGE (Rule 980(e)(6))

This order does *not* permit photographing, recording, or broadcasting of the following in the court

1. The jury or the spectators
2. Jury selection
3. A conference between an attorney and a client, witness, or aide
4. A conference between attorneys
5. A conference between counsel and the judge at the bench ("sidebars")
6. A proceeding closed to the public
7. A proceeding held in chambers

MEDIA PERSONNEL AND EQUIPMENT (Rule 980(e)(7))

NOTE These requirements apply unless the judge orders otherwise Refer to the order for additional requirements

1. No more than one television camera
2. No more than one still photographer
3. No more than one microphone operator and no obtrusive microphones or wiring
4. No operator entry or exit or other distraction when the court is in session
5. No moving equipment when the court is in session
6. No distracting sounds or lights
7. No visible signal light or device that shows when equipment is operating
8. No disruption of proceedings, nor public expense, to install, operate, or remove modifications to existing sound and lighting systems
9. No media agency insignia or marking on equipment or clothing

SANCTIONS FOR VIOLATING THIS ORDER (Rule 980(f))

Any violation of this order or rule 980 is an unlawful interference with the proceedings of the court The violation may result in an order terminating media coverage, a citation for contempt of court, or an order imposing monetary or other sanctions

MC-510 [New January 1 1997] **ORDER ON MEDIA REQUEST TO PERMIT COVERAGE** Page two

Appendix F
Overview of Camera Coverage Laws in the Fifty States[1]

---

[1] The following table is reprinted with the permission of Gregory C. Read, Esq., of Sedgwick, Detert, Moran & Arnold, San Francisco, California. Prepared with the assistance of Ann J. Reavis, Esq. and Fey Epling, the following table was included as part of a presentation on Cameras in the Courtroom at the first annual meeting of the Defense Research Institute in Chicago, Illinois on October 6–13, 1996.

TABLE OF STATUTES/RULES BY STATE GOVERNING USE OF CAMERAS IN COURTROOM[115]

State	Rule(s)/Statute(s)	Effective Date	Civil	Crim	Proceedings Partially or Totally Excluded from Coverage	Court	Party	Witness	Counsel	Notice
							Consent Required			
Alabama	Canon 3A(7), 3A(7A), and 3A(7B), Alabama Canons of Judicial Ethics, Ala. Code, Vol. 24A (Rules of Alabama Supreme Court).	P 2/1/76	T/A	T/A	Juvenile	Y	Y	Y	Y	
Alaska	Rule 50, Rules Governing the Administration of All Courts, Alaska Rules of Court (West).	*8/24/78* P 1/15/90	T/A	T/A	Family, Juvenile	Y	Y[116]	Y	N	1-D*
Arizona	Rule 122, Rules of the Arizona Supreme Court, Ariz. Rev. Stat., Vol. 17a.	*5/31/79* P 7/1/83	T/A	T/A	Adoption, Juvenile	Y	N	N	N	1-D+ (S)
Arkansas	Administrative Order Number 6, Rules of Civil Procedure - Appendix, Arkansas Code of 1987 Annotated (Court Rules).	*1/1/81* P 3/8/82	T/A	T/A	Family, Adoption, Juvenile, Witness Protection, Sex Crimes, In Camera	N	Y	Y	Y	N

[115] This table was created using information from the following sources: *News Media Coverage and Judicial Proceedings with Cameras and Microphones: A Survey of the States January 1996*, Radio–Television News Directors Association. "Summary of TV Cameras in the State Courts," January 1, 1996, Rev. 3/4/96, Information Service of the National Center for State Courts.

[116] All parties' consent is required for domestic violence and family proceedings.

KEY: T = Trial; A = Appellate; S = Superior; E = Experimental; P = Permanent; Italicized dates indicate the initial adoption of experimental rules no longer in effect; D = Day
★Waivable Time Requirement
+ "Reasonable Time" Requirement

State	Rule(s)/Statute(s)	Effective Date	Civil	Crim	Proceedings Partially or Totally Excluded from Coverage	Consent Required				Notice
						Court	Party	Witness	Counsel	
California	Cal. Misc. R. 980, California Rules of Court, Vol. 23 (West).	6/1/80 P 7/1/84	T/A	T/A	None	Y	N	N	N	+
Colorado	Canon 3(A)(8), Colorado Code of Judicial Conduct, Colo. Rev. Stat., Vol. 7A (Court Rules), Appendix to Chapter 24.	P 2/27/56	T/A	T/A	In Camera, Voir Dire	Y	N	N	N	1-D*
Connecticut	§§ 4116, 4116A, 4116B, Rules of Appellate Procedure; §§ 7A, 7B, and 7C, Rules for the Superior Court, Connecticut Rules of Court (West).	1982 P 10/1/84	T/A	T/A	Adoption, Family, Sex Crimes, Trade Secrets, Voir Dire	Y	N	N	N	13D-A 3D-T
Delaware	Canon 3A(7), Delaware Judges' Code of Judicial Conduct, adopted by Rule 84, Rules of the Delaware Supreme Court, Del. Code, Vol. 16; Rule 53, Delaware Family Court, Criminal Rules, Del. Code, Vol. 16; Rule 53, Delaware Superior Court Criminal Rules, Del. Code, Vol. 17; Rule 31, Delaware Courts of Justices of the peace, Criminal Rules, Del. Code, Vol. 16. See also Rule 169, Rules of the Delaware Court of Chancery, Del. Code, Vol. 17 (as modified by above-referenced orders).	E 5/1/82 (no term. date)	A	A	None	N	N	n/a	N	Y

KEY: T = Trial; A = Appellate; S = Superior; E = Experimental; P = Permanent; Italicized dates indicate the initial adoption of experimental rules no longer in effect; D = Day
*Waivable Time Requirement
+ "Reasonable Time" Requirement

State	Rule(s)/Statute(s)	Effective Date	Civil	Crim	Proceedings Partially or Totally Excluded from Coverage	Consent Required: Court	Consent Required: Party	Consent Required: Witness	Consent Required: Counsel	Notice
District of Columbia	District of Columbia Courts, Annual Report, 1973, pp. 3 and 8. Rule 53(b) of the Superior Court Rules of Criminal Procedure, Rule 203(b) of the Superior Court Rules of Civil Procedure, Superior Court Neglect Proceedings Rule 24(b), Superior Court Juvenile Proceedings Rule 53(b), and Superior Court Domestic Relations Rule 203(b); D.C. Code Ann. (Court Rules-D.C. Courts).									
Florida	Rule 2.170, Rules of Judicial Administration, Florida Rules of Court.	7/5/77 P 5/1/79	T/A	T/A	None	N	N	N	N	N
Georgia	Rules 75-91, Supreme Court Rules; Rule 22, Superior Court Rules; Rules 3.8, 26.1 and 26.2, Juvenile Court Rules; Rule 18, Probate Court Rules; Rule 11, Magistrate Court Rules, Georgia Rules of Court Annotated (Michie).	P 5/12/77	T/A	T/A	Juvenile	Y-T/A N-S	N	N	N	7D-A
Hawaii	Canon 3A(7), Hawaii Code of Judicial Conduct, modified by Rules 5.1, 5.2, Rules of the Supreme Court of the State of Hawaii (Supreme Court of Hawaii).	1/1/84 P 12/7/87	T/A	T/A	In Camera, Voir Dire, Witness Protection, Sex Crimes, Motion to Suppress, Trade Secrets	N-A Y-T	N	N	N	N-A T+

KEY: T = Trial; A = Appellate; S = Superior; E = Experimental; P = Permanent; Italicized dates indicate the initial adoption of experimental rules no longer in effect; D = Day
*Waivable Time Requirement
+ "Reasonable Time" Requirement

APPENDICES

State	Rule(s)/Statute(s)	Effective Date	Civil	Crim	Proceedings Partially or Totally Excluded from Coverage	Consent Required — Court	Consent Required — Party	Consent Required — Witness	Consent Required — Counsel	Notice
Idaho	Canon 3A(7), Idaho Code of Judicial Conduct, Idaho State Bar Desk Book (as modified by above-referenced orders).	E 1/4/82 E 2/15/95-96 P 8/27/79 P 10/1/80	A T S-Boise S-Circ.	A T	Adoption, Juvenile, Grand Jury	N-A Y-T	N	N	N	N-A
Illinois	Rule 63(A)(7), Rules of the Illinois Supreme Court, Ill. Rev. Stat. Chapter 110A; Ill. Rev. Stat. Chapter 51, § 57 (as modified by above-referenced orders).	1/1/84 P 1/22/85	A	A	None	N	N	N/A	N	5-D
Indiana	Canon 3B(13), Indiana Code of Judicial Conduct, Ind. Code Ann. (Court Rules, Book 2) (Burns).				No coverage allowed					
Iowa	Canon 3A(7), Iowa Code of Judicial Conduct, Iowa Rules of Court (West).	1/1/80 P 1/1/82	T/A	T/A	Voir Dire, Juvenile, Family, Adoption, Trade Secret	Y	N[117]	N	N	

[117] Except in certain family law and juvenile matters and trade secret cases.

KEY: T = Trial; A = Appellate; S = Superior; E = Experimental; P = Permanent; Italicized dates indicate the initial adoption of experimental rules no longer in effect; D = Day
*Waivable Time Requirement
+ "Reasonable Time" Requirement

State	Rule(s)/Statute(s)	Effective Date	Civil	Crim	Proceedings Partially or Totally Excluded from Coverage	Court	Party	Witness	Counsel	Notice
Kansas	Canon 3A(7), Kansas Code of Judicial Conduct, adopted by Rule 601, Rules of Kansas Supreme Court, Kan. Stat. § 20-176; Rule 1001, Rules of the Kansas Supreme Court, Kan. Court Rules Annot. 357 (1988) (repealing Kansas Supreme Court Rule 1.07).	*9/14/81* P 9/1/88	T/A	T/A	None	Y	Y[118]	Y	N	7D
Kentucky	Canon 3A(7), Kentucky Code of Judicial Conduct, Rule 4.300, Rules of the Kentucky Supreme Court, Ky. Rev. Stat. Ann.	P 7/1/81	T/A	T/A	None	Y	N	N	N	
Louisiana	Canon 3A(7), Louisiana Code of Judicial Conduct, La. Rev. Stat. Ann., Vol. 8 (Appendix); La. Rev. Stat. Ann. § 13-4164 (as modified by the above-referenced order).	P 4/30/85	A	A	None	N	N	N/A	N	20D
Maine	Administrative Order In re Photographic and Electronic Coverage of the Courts (August 7, 1991), Maine Rules of Court (West) (as modified by above-reference orders); and P.L. 1985 Ch. 515.	*4/2/82* P 8/1/94	T/A	T/A[119]	Adoption, Family, Juvenile, Sex Crimes, Trade Secrets, All Testimonial Criminal Proceedings	Y	N	N	N	

[118] However, participants may bar coverage by objection in certain evidentiary, family & trade secret proceedings.
[119] Non-testimonial proceedings only.

KEY: T = Trial; A = Appellate; S = Superior; E = Experimental; P = Permanent; Italicized dates indicate the initial adoption of experimental rules no longer in effect; D = Day
★Waivable Time Requirement
+"Reasonable Time" Requirement

APPENDICES 163

State	Rule(s)/Statute(s)	Effective Date	Civil	Crim	Proceedings Partially or Totally Excluded from Coverage	Consent Required				Notice
						Court	Party	Witness	Counsel	
Maryland	Rule 1209, Maryland Rules of Procedure, Annotated Code of Maryland, Maryland Rules, Volume 2.	*1/1/81* P 7/1/84	T/A	A	Adoption, Family, Juvenile, Motion to Suppress, Trade Secrets	Y	Y-T N-A	Y[120]	N-A Y-Civil	5D*
Massachusetts	Canon 3(A)(7), Massachusetts Code of Judicial Conduct, adopted by Rule 3:09, Rules of Massachusetts Supreme Judicial Court, Massachusetts Rules of Court, Desk Copy.	*4/1/80(A)* *6/1/80(T)* P 1/1/83	T/A	T/A	Motion to Suppress, Probable Cause, Motion to Dismiss, Voir Dire	N	N	N	N	+
Michigan	Canon 3A(7), Michigan Code of Judicial Conduct, Michigan rules of Court 1986 (as modified by the above-referenced order).	*2/1/88* P 1/13/89	T/A	T/A	Sex Crimes, Witness ID Protection	Y	N	N	N	3D*

[120] Only required from victims.

KEY: T = Trial; A = Appellate; S = Superior; E = Experimental; P = Permanent; Italicized dates indicate the initial adoption of experimental rules no longer in effect; D = Day
*Waivable Time Requirement
+ "Reasonable Time" Requirement

State	Rule(s)/Statute(s)	Effective Date	Civil	Crim	Proceedings Partially or Totally Excluded from Coverage	Court	Party	Witness	Counsel	Notice
Minnesota	Canon 3A(7), Minnesota Code of Judicial Conduct, Minn. Stat. Ann. vol. 52 (West); Rule 2.7, Court of Appeals Internal Rules, Minn Stat Ann. vol. 51 (West).	E 4/18/83- 1/1/94[121]	T	T	Family, Juvenile, Suppress, Witness ID, Sex Crimes, Motion to Dismiss, Voir Dire, Trade Secrets, Motion for Directed Verdict, Motions in Limine, Evidentiary Hearings	N-A Y-T	N-A Y-T	Y	N	1D★
		1/27/78 P 4/20/83	A	A						
Mississippi	Canon 3A(7), Code of Judicial Conduct of Mississippi Judges, Code of Professional Responsibility, Code of Judicial Conduct, Ethics Opinions (Mississippi State Bar), Rule 1 04, Uniform Rules of Circuit and County Court, Mississippi Rules of Court.				No coverage allowed.					
Missouri	Administrative Rule 16, Missouri Supreme Court Rules, Mo. Ann. Stat. vol. 1 (Vernon).	*10/1/92*	T/A	T/A	Adoption, Family, Juvenile	Y	N	Y	N	5D
		P 10/1/94	A	A						
		P 7/1/95	T	T						
Montana	Canon 35, Montana Canons of Judicial Ethics, 176 Mont. xxiii, 6 Media L. Rep. (BNA) 1543 (1980).	*4/1/78* P 4/18/80	T/A	T/A	None	N	N	N	N	Y

[121] Term of experiment has expired, and coverage is on a case-by-case basis.

KEY: T = Trial; A = Appellate; S = Superior; E = Experimental; P = Permanent; Italicized dates indicate the initial adoption of experimental rules no longer in effect; D = Day
★Waivable Time Requirement
+"Reasonable Time" Requirement

APPENDICES 165

State	Rule(s)/Statute(s)	Effective Date	Civil	Crim	Proceedings Partially or Totally Excluded from Coverage	Consent Required				Notice
						Court	Party	Witness	Counsel	
Nebraska	Canon 3A(7), Nebraska Code of Judicial Conduct, Nebraska Supreme Court Rules 8.1-.3 (1986) (as modified by above-referenced order).	E 10/1/82 P 1/18/85	A[122]	A[122]	None	N	N[124]	N[125]	N	N
Nevada	Canon 3A(7), Nevada Code of Judicial Conduct, Nev. Rev. Stat. vol. 1, Supreme Court Rules, Parts IV and VI. In Re Rules Setting Forth the Standards of Conduct and Technology Governing Electronic Media and Still Photo Coverage of Judicial Proceedings, ADK T 38.	4/1/80 P 4/29/88	T/A	T/A	None	Y	N	N	N	3D*
New Hampshire	Rules 19 and 38, New Hampshire Supreme Court Rules (Equity); Rule 78(A), New Hampshire Superior Court Rules and Directory (Equity); Rule 1.4, New Hampshire District and Municipal Court Rules. See also N.H. Rev. Stat. Ann. § 502-A: 27-d (District Courts).	P 1/1/78	T/A	T/A	None	Y	N	N	N	
New Jersey	Canon 3A(9), New Jersey Code of Judicial Conduct; rule 1:14, Rules of General Application to the Courts of New Jersey, New Jersey Rules of Court (West).	5/1/79	T/A	T/A	Family, Juvenile, Sex Crimes,	Y	N	N	N	+
		P 10/8/80	A	A	Trade Secrets					
		P 6/9/81	T	T						

[122] Audio coverage allowed under experimental rules or open court proceedings of non-jury matters.
[123] Experimental rules allow only audio coverage, and only sentencing proceedings may be covered.
[124] Any party in a civil proceeding may bar coverage of the proceeding by objecting.
[125] Any alleged sex crime victim in a criminal proceeding or any prospective witness in civil proceeding may bar coverage by objecting.

KEY: T = Trial; A = Appellate; S = Superior; E = Experimental; P = Permanent; Italicized dates indicate the initial adoption of experimental rules no longer in effect; D = Day
★Waivable Time Requirement
+ "Reasonable Time" Requirement

State	Rule(s)/Statute(s)	Effective Date	Civil	Crim	Proceedings Partially or Totally Excluded from Coverage	Consent Required				Notice
						Court	Party	Witness	Counsel	
New Mexico	Canon 21-300(A)(8); Rule 23-104; Rule 23-107, Supreme Court General Rules, N.M. Stat. Ann. (Judicial Volume).	7/1/80 P 1/1/83	T/A	T/A	Witness ID, Sex Crimes, Voir Dire	N	N	N	N	ID*
New York	Canon 3A(7), New York Code of Judicial Conduct, as modified by N.Y. JUDICIARY LAW, § 218 (McKinney 1988); 22 NYCRR Part 131 (Dec. 31, 1987) and 22 NYCRR § 29.3 (Dec. 31, 1987) (trial court rules) (expired May 31, 1991); 22 NYCRR §§ 29.1-29.2 (Dec. 31, 1986) (appellate court rules), as modified by the Laws of 1992, Chapter 18 (effective July 1, 1992, as amended January 30, 1995).	E 6/23/92 to 6/30/97 P 1/1/81	T A	T A	Motion to Suppress, Voir Dire, Arraignments, Sex Crimes	Y	Y[126]	Y	Y[127]	7D-T*
North Carolina	Canon 3A(7), North Carolina Code of Judicial Conduct, N.C. Gen. Stat., vol. 4A (Appendix VII-A); Rule 15, General Rules of Practice for the Superior and District Courts of North Carolina, N.C. Gen. Stat., vol 4A (Appendix I(5)).	10/18/92 P 7/25/90 +	T/A	T/A	Adoption, Family, Juvenile, Motion to Suppress, Witness ID, Sex Crimes, In Camera Probable Cause, Voir Dire, Trade Secrets	N	N	N	N	N

[126] Party's consent required only in arraignment and suppression hearings.
[127] Counsel must consent to coverage of jury trials in progress.

KEY: T = Trial; A = Appellate; S = Superior; E = Experimental; P = Permanent; Italicized dates indicate the initial adoption of experimental rules no longer in effect; D = Day
*Waivable Time Requirement
+ "Reasonable Time" Requirement

APPENDICES 167

State	Rule(s)/Statue(s)	Effective Date	Civil	Crim	Proceedings Partially or Totally Excluded from Coverage	Consent Required			Notice
						Court	Party	Witness	Counsel	
North Dakota	Administrative Rule 21; Rule 53, North Dakota Rules of Criminal Procedure; Rule 10.1, North Dakota Rules of Court (North Dakota Court Rules).	2/1/79 P 7/1/80 9/1/88 P 7/1/95	A T	A T	Sex Crimes	Y	N	Y	N	3D-A 7D-T
Ohio	Canon 3A(7), Ohio Code of Judicial Conduct; Rule 11, Rules of Superintendence for Courts of Common Pleas; Rule 9, Rules of Superintendence for Municipal and County Courts; Rule XV, Rules of Practice of the Supreme Court. All rules cited in this paragraph are contained in Ohio Rev. Code Ann. (Rules Governing the Courts of Ohio).	6/1/79 P 1/1/82	T/A	T/A	None	Y	N	Y	N	1D-S
Oklahoma	Title 5, Oklahoma Statutes, Chapter 1, Appendix 4, Canon 3A(7).	1/1/79 P 2/22/82	T/A	T/A	None	Y	Y[128]	Y	N	2D-A
Oregon	Rule 8.35, Rules of Appellate Procedure; Rule 3.180 Uniform Trial Court Rules, Oregon Rules of Court-State (West).	2/15/89 P 8/1/92	T/A	T/A	Adoption, Family, Juvenile, Sex Crimes, Voir Dire, Trade Secrets	N-A Y-T	N	Y	N	N-A

[128] Consent required of criminal defendant.

KEY: T = Trial; A = Appellate; S = Superior; E = Experimental; P = Permanent; Italicized dates indicate the initial adoption of experimental rules no longer in effect; D = Day
★Waivable Time Requirement
+ "Reasonable Time" Requirement

168   APPENDICES

State	Rule(s)/Statue(s)	Effective Date	Civil	Crim	Proceedings Partially or Totally Excluded from Coverage	Consent Required				Notice
						Court	Party	Witness	Counsel	
Pennsylvania	In Re WTAE-TV, No. 51 (W.D. Misc. Docket 1978). Rules 27 and 328 of the Pennsylvania Rules of Criminal Procedure and Rule 7 of the Rules of Conduct, Office Standards and Civil Procedure for District Justices. Pennsylvania Rules of Court, Desk Copy (West 1980).	E 10/1/79	T[129]		Family	Y	N	Y	N	
Rhode Island	Article VII, Rhode Island Supreme Court Rules, Rhode Island Court Rules Annotated (Michie).	10/1/81 P 3/8/93	T/A	T/A	Adoption, Family, Juvenile, Motion to Suppress, Motion to Dismiss, Voir Dire	N	N	Y	N	N
South Carolina	Rule 605, South Carolina Appellate Court Rules, South Carolina Rules of Court (West).	10/1/92 P 9/21/93	T/A	T/A		Y	N	N	N	Y
South Dakota	Canon 3B(12), South Dakota Code of Judicial Conduct, S.D. Codified Laws, § 16-2 (Appendix).									
Tennessee	Rule 30; Canon 3A(7), Tennessee Code of Judicial Conduct, adopted by Rule 10 (formerly Rule 43), Rules of the Tennessee Supreme Court, Tenn. Code Ann., Vol. 5A (Court Rules).	E 1/1/96 97 P 2/27/79	T/A	T/A	Juvenile	Y	Y[130]	N	N	2D*

[129] Non-jury trials only.
[130] Consent is required of criminal defendants, civil parties and juveniles.

KEY: T = Trial; A = Appellate; S = Superior; E = Experimental; P = Permanent; Italicized dates indicate the initial adoption of experimental rules no longer in effect; D = Day
*Waivable Time Requirement
+"Reasonable Time" Requirement

State	Rule(s)/Statute(s)	Effective Date	Civil	Crim	Proceedings Partially or Totally Excluded from Coverage	Consent Required				Notice
						Court	Party	Witness	Counsel	
Texas	Tex. R. Civ. P. Ann. r. 18c (Vernon); Tex. R. App. P. Ann. r. 21 (Vernon).	P 1/1/90	T/A	T/A	None	Y	Y	Y	Y	
Utah	Canon 3A(7), 3A(8), Utah Code of Judicial Conduct, Utah State Bar Desk Book (Utah State Bar), as modified by 816 P.2d 1222 (1991).	1/1/88 P 8/30/91	T[131] A	T[132] A	None	N-T Y-A	Y	Y	N	2D-A
Vermont	Canon 3A(7), Vermont Code of Judicial Conduct, Vt. Stat. Ann. Title 12, Appendix VIII; Rule 35, Vermont Rules of Appellate Procedure; Rule 53, Vermont Rules of Criminal Procedure; Rule 79.2, Vermont Rules of Civil Procedure; Rule 79.3, District Court Civil Rules; and 79.2, Rules of Probate Procedure.	7/1/84 P 3/12/92	T/A	T/A	None	N	N	N	N	N
Virginia	Va. Code Ann. § 19.2-266 (1992).	7/1/87 P 7/1/92	T/A	T/A	Adoption, Family, Juvenile, Motion to Suppress, Witness ID, Sex Crimes, In Camera, Trade Secrets	N	N	N	N	N
Washington	Rule 16, General Rules, Washington Court Rules-State (West).	P 9/20/76	T/A	T/A	None	Y	N	N	N	

[131] Still photography only.
[132] Still photography only.

KEY: T = Trial; A = Appellate; S = Superior; E = Experimental; P = Permanent; Italicized dates indicate the initial adoption of experimental rules no longer in effect; D = Day
*Waivable Time Requirement
+ "Reasonable Time" Requirement

State	Rule(s)/Statute(s)	Effective Date	Civil	Crim	Proceedings Partially or Totally Excluded from Coverage	Consent Required - Court	Consent Required - Party	Consent Required - Witness	Consent Required - Counsel	Notice
West Virginia	Canon 3B(12), West Virginia Code of Judicial Conduct, Rules Governing Camera Coverage of Courtroom Proceedings, West Virginia Code Annotated (Court Rules).	*1/1/79* P 5/28/81	T/A	T/A	N	Y	N	N	N	
Wisconsin	Chapter 61, Wisconsin Supreme Court Rules.	*4/1/78* P 7/1/79	T/A	T/A	N	Y	N	N	N	
Wyoming	Canon 3A(7), Wyoming Code of Judicial Conduct, Rule 53, Wyoming Rules of Criminal Procedure, Wyoming Court Rules Annotated (Michie).	*8/14/81* P 12/27/91	T/A	T/A	Motion to Suppress, Witness ID	N-A Y-T	N	N	N	N-A 1D-T

KEY: T = Trial; A = Appellate; S = Superior; E = Experimental; P = Permanent; Italicized dates indicate the initial adoption of experimental rules no longer in effect; D = Day
★Waivable Time Requirement
+"Reasonable Time" Requirement

Appendix G
Jury Consultant Interviews

MEMORANDUM

To: New York State Committee to Review Audio-Visual Coverage of Court Proceedings
From: Professor Beth Schwartz
Re:: Informal Survey of Experts in Field of Jury Analysis
Date: January 17, 1996

On November 8, 1996, I wrote to eleven trial consultants, to solicit their opinions and comments regarding the impact, if any, of televised coverage of court proceedings. The people to whom I wrote were presumed to be individuals with expertise in jury analysis. (A sample of the letters which were sent to each of the experts is attached to this memo.)

I spoke with only three of the individuals to whom I had written. None of the consultants had done much research into the issues which I raised in my letter. None had conducted, or was familiar with, any empirical research into the issue of the impact of audio-visual coverage of court proceedings on jurors. Each offered me her personal view about the nature and degree of the impact on jurors of television coverage of judicial proceedings, based upon her personal experiences.

The first expert with whom I spoke was Denise de la Rue, who is based in Atlanta, Georgia. Ms. de la Rue is a private consultant, and has worked on both civil and criminal trials. Approximately 60% of her work is for criminal defendants. With respect to the issue of the impact of television coverage of judicial proceedings on jurors, it was Ms. de la Rue's opinion that the presence of cameras in the courtroom exaggerates the importance of a case, and that this exaggeration might turn out to be either "good" or "bad" for any particular party, depending upon whether the case is civil or criminal, whether the party is a plaintiff or a defendant, and other factors.

Ms. de la Rue described her experience in one particular civil case, in which she was a consultant for the plaintiff and which was covered by television; Ms. de la Rue expressed that the jury's verdict was at the high end of what was anticipated. Her opinion was that the presence of cameras in the courtroom helped the plaintiff in that case. In most cases, however, Ms. de la Rue believes that clients are hurt by the presence of cameras in the courtroom, rather than benefited.

Ms. de la Rue was a consultant for Susan Smith, who had requested the removal of television cameras, which were present during the pre-trial proceedings. Smith made a motion for the removal of the cameras, on the ground that some witnesses would be less forthcoming if cameras were present. Some of these witnesses would testify about Smith's history of sexual abuse. The judge was persuaded by this argument, and ordered the cameras removed. One additional consequence of the removal of the cameras was the impact on the length of the trial. Ms. de la Rue believes that the trial would have taken about three times longer than it did if cameras had been present.

Ms. de la Rue believes that most attorneys and judges involved in televised proceedings inevitably "play" to the camera, and become overly concerned about how television reporters and commentators are characterizing the events of a trial. Ms. de la Rue favors giving "veto" power to all parties, i.e., limiting televised coverage of trials to those cases where the parties, attorneys, and judge all agree that cameras ought to be present.

I also spoke with Elissa Krauss, who works in New York City for the National Jury Project. She stated that the National Jury Project has had limited experience with televised coverage of court proceedings. Ms. Krauss's opinion was that jurors are not significantly affected by the presence of television cameras in the courtroom during the trial itself. She does have concerns, however, about members of the public who are potential jurors, and who have watched televised coverage of trials and who may be misled, i.e., they may be led to make certain incorrect assumptions about the judicial system based upon their observations of televised trials and the commentaries which many television stations provide. Ms. Krauss indicated that she has been involved in cases in which jurors have expressed concern about whether they would be televised if the trial were televised. She knows of only one state that permits the televising of jurors—Florida.

Ms. Krauss also expressed her belief that the public, in general, has less respect for the judicial process after having viewed televised trials. She believes that this comes, in part, from misleading and inaccurate representations of court proceedings. Ms. Krauss favors providing the option of television coverage of trials, but with the proviso that any party should be permitted to "veto" such coverage in any particular case.

The third expert with whom I spoke was Marjorie Fargo, who works for Jury Services, Inc., in Alexandria, Virginia. Ms. Fargo has not systematically interviewed jurors on the issue of televised coverage of court proceedings. She believes that one important factor which affects how much of an impact the televising of judicial proceedings might have is the positioning of the cameras. It is her opinion that there is not much impact where there is only one camera in a courtroom, and it is focused on the witness. She has observed that during some of the televised trials in which she has been present, the jurors appear to pay little or no attention to the cameras. Ms. Fargo indicated that it seems possible that some jurors might be concerned that if there is televised coverage of a trial, they may be asked to account for their verdict. As mentioned previously, however, Ms. Fargo did not have any empirical evidence to support this hypothesis.

(212) 636-6821
November 8, 1996

Dear:

I am writing to you on behalf of John Feerick, the Dean of Fordham Law School and the Chair of the New York State Committee to Review Audio Visual Coverage of Court Proceedings. Because of your expertise in the field of jury analysis, the Committee would be interested in hearing from you about your opinions and experiences regarding the impact, if any, of audio visual coverage of court proceedings on the selection and behavior of juries, as well as the behavior of other trial participants insofar as it relates to juries.

I hope that you are able to take some time to respond to the questions which are posed below, either in writing or in a telephone conversation with me which can be held at your convenience. I would also welcome any other information, materials, opinions, or thoughts which you believe might be relevant to the Committee's undertaking.

Specifically, the Committee would be interested in receiving responses to the following questions:

1. Have you observed trials in which television cameras were present?
   If so, how many such trials have you observed? What were some of the types of cases (e.g. civil or criminal) of the televised proceedings which you have observed?
2. Have you observed televised trials in both jury and non-jury proceedings? If so, approximately how many of each type of proceeding have you observed?
3. Have you conducted any post-verdict interviews with individuals who have served as jurors in trials which were televised?
4. Based upon your observations and experiences, in your opinion, does the presence of cameras in the courtroom affect an individual's willingness to serve as a juror?
5. Based upon your observations and experiences, in your opinion, does the presence of cameras in the courtroom affect the jury selection process in any other manner?
6. Based upon your observations and experiences, in your opinion, does the presence of cameras in the courtroom have any impact on the jury deliberation process?
7. In your experience, has the presence of cameras appear to ever have affected a jury's verdict?
8. Based upon your observations and experiences, in your opinion, does the presence of cameras in the courtroom have any significant impact on trial participants other than jurors, *i.e*, parties, non-party witnesses, lawyers and judges?
9. If you have knowledge that a trial is likely to be televised, does it affect your opinion about what type of individual would be an "ideal" juror?

I appreciate your time and consideration, and I look forward to receiving your responses to these questions. I can be reached at (212) 636-6821. Thank you.

Sincerely yours,

Beth G. Schwartz
Associate Clinical Professor of Law

Appendix H
Office of Court Administration Data on News Media Applications for Audio-Visual Coverage of Court Proceedings

MEMORANDUM
March 26, 1997

TO: NEW YORK STATE COMMITTEE TO REVIEW AUDIO-VISUAL COVERAGE OF COURT PROCEEDINGS

FROM: JOSEPH GUGLIELMELLI, ESQ.

RE: STATISTICAL DATA COMPILED BY THE OFFICE OF COURT ADMINISTRATION REGARDING APPLICATIONS FOR *AUDIO-VISUAL COVERAGE OF JUDICIAL PROCEEDINGS*

According to data compiled by the New York State Office of Court Administration ("OCA"), there were at least 540 applications requesting audio-visual coverage of judicial proceedings, either in whole or in part, during the period January 31, 1995 through September 1, 1996. (See Table 1 attached). Based on their discussions with court personnel throughout the state, the OCA staff have advised the Committee that the total number of applications for this nineteen month period is greater. However, because there is no regulatory or statutory requirement that the judicial districts forward applications for audio-visual coverage to a central location,[1] there is no practical means of ascertaining how many more applications for audio-visual coverage were actually made. (A sample application for audio-visual coverage of a judicial proceeding is attached at Exhibit 1.)

A. General Information

The following shows the number of applications for audio-visual coverage in each of New York's judicial districts made during the period of the OCA study (*See also* Table 2):

Judicial districts	Applications
1, 2, 11 & 12 [New York City]	136
3rd [Albany]	10
4th [Saratoga]	67
5th [Syracuse]	18
6th [Binghampton]	N/A
7th [Rochester]	154
8th [Buffalo]	92
9th [White Plains]	17
10th [Nassau]	44
11th [Suffolk]	2

Far more applications for audio-visual coverage were granted than denied during this period. (See Table 1). OCA found 451 orders granting audio-visual coverage, approximately 84% of the total 540 applications. However, 233 applications were granted with limitations on coverage specified in the order, more than had of the overall orders granting coverage during the nineteen month period. The remaining 217 orders granting audio-visual coverage did so with the limitations already contained in NY Judiciary Law Section 218.[2]

---

[1] It is precisely for this reason that any data from the Sixth Judicial District in the Binghampton area is unavailable. Court officials from the Sixth Judicial District were aware that applications for audio-visual coverage were made during the nineteen month period but could not estimate the number of such applications.

[2] A total of 89 aplications for audio-visual coverage were denied. (*See* Table 1). Reasons for denial of the applications include, among other things, defense objections (51), untimely nature of media application (4), disruptiveness due to nature of proceeding (8) and/or the age of a party or witness (4). On 21 occasions applications were denied without any explanation. (*See* Table 6.)

More than half of the total applications were for videotape coverage for later broadcast—262 applications for videotape only with an additional 81 applications for videotape combined with audio and/or still photography. During the nineteen month period, there were only 24 applications to cover a judicial proceeding live either on television or radio. (See Table 4.)

B. Coverage of Criminal Cases

The OCA data demonstrate that the media was primarily interested in covering criminal cases. Whereas 29 applications, or approximately 5% of the 540 total, were made to cover civil proceedings, 507 applications, or 94% of overall, were to cover criminal ones. (*See* Table 5A.) The single application for audio-visual coverage of Family Court (*see* Table 3) was not to cover any specific proceeding but rather for footage of a Family Court judge in Rockland County as he went through a typical day on the bench. The footage was to be used for a general report on the Family Court system in that area of New York State.

Because the applications contain minimal information (see Exhibit 1), OCA used follow-up questionnaires to ascertain the nature of the criminal cases for which audio-visual coverage was sought and the dispositions of those applications. Through this method, OCA was able to receive information on 183 criminal proceedings, including arraignments.[3] The nature of these criminal proceedings can be broken down as follows:

- Of the 108 applications for violent (but not sex related) crimes such as murder, 78 orders granting audio-visual coverage were entered.
- Of the 62 applications for non-violent crimes such as fraud, 49 orders granting audio-visual coverage were entered.

---

[3] Several reasons exist for the discrepancy between the number of applications for audio-visual coverage of criminal proceedings (507) and the number of criminal cases for which OCA was able to ascertain further information (183). First, OCA could not further investigate applications that did not identify a specific criminal such as applications that sought permission to film "for the day." Moreover, OCA could not ascertain the subsequent history of criminal cases where it did not receive a response to its follow-up questionnaire. Finally, a single criminal case may be the subject of multiple applications. For example, one criminal case was the subject of eleven different applications for coverage at different stages of that proceeding.

- Of the 13 applications for sex related offenses such as rape, 11 orders granting audio-visual coverage were entered. (*See* Table 5B.)

Of the 70 applications for audio-visual coverage of arraignments, 40 orders granting audio-visual coverage were entered. Twenty-five (25) denials of applications to cover arraignments were the result of defense objections.[4] (See Table 5C.)

No similiar breakdown is available for the 29 civil proceedings where applications for audio-visual coverage were submitted.

C. Limitations on Audio-Visual Coverage

Despite an examination of orders determining applications for audio-visual coverage and OCA use of follow-up questionnaires, it was still extremely difficult in many cases to ascertain whether or not objections to camera coverage were raised; the nature of any such objections; the identity of the party, witness or other person raising them; the rationale for the court's rejection or acceptance of the objections; and/or the nature of specifically tailored limitations imposed in a particular case.[5] This is partly due to the fact that many judges use the form order found at NY Court Rules, Part 131 to rule on audio-visual applications and frequently fill in the blank specifying grant or denial without explanation. The "fill in the blanks" approach was taken in 213 orders examined by OCA. (A sample order is attached at Exhibit 2.)

Nevertheless, the following general data with respect to limitations imposed on audio-visual coverage was supplied by OCA:
- Regarding *defendants*, courts ordered that a defendant's name could not be revealed on 22 occasions and that a defendant's face could not be shown on 36 occasions;

---

[4] To identify applications for audio-visual coverage of arraignments, OCA not only relied on the express text of the applications and their corresponding orders but also made rinferences where the judge/part set forth on the applications were known to be an arraignment judge/part.

[5] For example, an order may grant coverage "except movant may not show Ms. Jones' face." From the face of the order, a reader cannot tell whether Mrs. Jones is a witness, a victim, or possibly even a defendant, whose attorney raised the objection, the nature of the objections and, most importantly, the rationale for this limitation. OCA examined at least 145 orders of this type.

- Regarding *victims,* courts ordered that a victim's name could not be revealed on 1 occasion, that a victim's face could not be shown on 7 occasions and that victim must remain completely anonymous (neither the face shown nor the name disclosed) on 13 occasions.
- Regarding *witnesses,* courts ordered that a witness' face could not be shown on 7 occasions and that a witness must remain completely anonymous (neither the face shown nor the name disclosed) on 6 occasions.
- Twenty (20) orders precluded showing any of the trial's spectators. Approximately 85 orders imposed limitations on the media's placement and use of video and audio equipment in the courtroom. (*See* Table 8.)

INDEX OF TABLES AND EXHIBITS

Table	Number
Application and Orders for Audio-Visual Coverage of Judicial Proceedings	1
Application and Orders for Audio-Visual Coverage of Judicial Proceedings by Judicial District	2
Application and Orders for Audio-Visual Coverage of Judicial Proceedings by Type of Court	3
Type of Audio-Visual Coverage Requested by the Media and Percent Granted Coverage	4
Requests for Audio-Visual Coverage of Judicial Proceedings by Type of Case	5A
Breakdown of Criminal Cases	5B
Arraignment Cases Only	5C
Reasons for Denial of Audio-Visual Coverage of Judicial Proceedings	6
Applications and Orders for Audio-Visual Coverage of Judicial Proceedings by Type of Proceeding	7
Applications and Orders for Audio-Visual Coverage Limits Imposed by Court	8

Exhibit	Number
Sample Application for Audio-Visual Coverage of Judicial Proceedings	1
Sample Order Determining Application for Audio-Visual Coverage	2

Table 1

Applications and Orders for Audio-Visual Coverage of Judicial Proceedings

Study Period	1/31/95–9/1/96
Duration (Months)	19 Months
Applications Received	540
Orders Granting Coverage*	451 (83.5%)
Orders Denying Coverage	89 (16.5%)
Pending Cases	–
Proceedings With a Witness Image Obscured**	1

*Includes 233 orders granting coverage with special limitations.
**Based upon the responses to cameras in the Court Follow-up Questionnaire in which there was an order granting coverage and where image was actually obscured.

TABLE 2

Applications and Orders for Audio-Visual Coverage of Judicial Proceedings by Judicial District

Judicial District	Total Applications	Orders Granting Coverage	% Approved
New York City			
J. D. (1, 2, 11, 12)	136	104	76.5%
Long Island			
10th J. D. (Nassau)	44	36	81.8%
10th J. D. (Suffolk)	2	2	100%
Upstate			
3rd J.D.	10	10	100%
4th J.D.	67	61	91.0%
5th J.D.	18	18	100%
6th J.D.	—		
7th J.D.	154	136	88.3%
8th J.D.	92	67	72.8%
9th J.D.	17	17	100%

TABLE 3

Applications for Audio Visual Coverage of Judicial Proceeding by Type of Court

Type of Court	Number	Relative %
Supreme	87	16.1%
County	238	44.0%
Family	1	.2%
District	2	.4%
NYC Criminal	114	21.1%
City	96	17.7%
Town/Village	3	.6%
Total Applications	541	

TABLE 4

Type of Audio-Visual Coverage Requested by the* Media and Percent Granted Coverage

	Applications	Relative % of Total	Percent Coverage	Granted (Orders)
Multiple Audio-Visual Coverage (Videotape, Audiotape, and Still Photography)	81	15.0%	82.7%	(67)
Videotape ONLY	262	48.4%	82.4%	(216)
Still Photography ONLY	165	30.5%	84.8%	(140)
Audiotape ONLY	8	1.5%	75%	(6)
Other*	24*	4.6%	91.7%	(22)
Total Applications	540			

*There were 24 cases where there was a request for coverage other than for video, still, or audiotape. They included requests to televise live, film, tape record or audio (radio) broadcast live.

TABLE 5A

Requests for Audio-Visual Coverage of Judicial Proceedings By Type of Case

Type of Case	Applications	Relative % of Total	Orders Granting Coverage	% Granting Coverage
Criminal	507	94%	418	82%
Civil	29	5%	29	100%
Family	1	1%	1	100%
Total Applications	537*			

*Four cases where the "type of case" was not available.

TABLE 5B
Breakdown of Criminal Cases*

	Applications	Relative % of Total	Orders Granting Coverage	% Granting Coverage
Violent Crime (Excludes sex related offenses	108	59%	78	72%
Non-violent crime	62	34%	49	79%
Sex related offenses	13	7%	11	85%
Overall**	183			

Based on 183 responses to Cameras in the Court Follow-up Questionnaire completed by courts throughout the state.

**Overall number does not equal number of criminal applications because questionnaires were not sent in cases where there were either multiple applications for same defendant or cases where no specific defendant was named (i.e. filming "for the day").

TABLE 5C
Arraignment Cases Only*

Number	Granted**	Relative % of Total	Denied	Relative % of Total
70	40	57	30	43

Reasons for Denial

Defense objection	25
Other	1
Not specified	4

*Arraignment cases were categorized as such based on information identified on either: 1) the application, 2) the order or 3) where a particular judge/part were known to be an arraignment part.

TABLE 6

Reasons for Denial of Audio-Visual Coverage of Judicial Proceedings*

	Number of Total Cases	Relative %	Number of Cases Excluding Arraignments	%
Defense Objected (No Consent)	51	50%	26	36%
Untimately Application	4	4%	4	6%
Interfere with Defendant's Right to Fair Trial	—			
No Defense Counsel to Consult	—			
Mental/Emotional Harm or Disruptive due to Nature of Proceeding	8	8%	8	11%
Age/Youthful Offender	4	4%	4	6%
Other	15	14%	14	19%
Reason Not Given	21	20%	16	22%
Total*	103		72	

*Sum of reasons exceeds the sum of orders denying coverage because given orders were denied based on multiple reasons.

TABLE 7

Applications and Orders for Audio-Visual Coverage Requests by Type of Proceeding

	Number
Throughout the Proceeding	406
For the Day	3
Arraignment	70
Bail Hearing	1
Suppression Hearing	—
Other Pre-trial Motion	7
Trial	10
Verdict	8
Sentencing	37
Plea	7
Other	26

*Total number of categories exceed total number of applications because multiple categories could be checked off for a given application.

TABLE 8

Applications and Orders for Audio-Visual Coverage Limits Imposed by Court*

• No faces shown	5
• Defendant's name may not be revealed	22
• Defendant's face may not be photographed or filmed	36
• No faces of people on the bench	3
• Victims name **(1)** face **(7)** both **(13)** may not be identified	
• Witness name **(0)** face **(7)** both **(6)** may not be identified	
• No attorney fees	1
• No coverage if attorney objects	9
• No cameras in the well	1
• Cameras on tripod only	1
• No flashes	15
• No spectators shown	20
• Media equipment limitation	68
• Other (see orders)	145
• No limitations	213

*Multiple reasons may be given for any application.

ORDER DETERMINING APPLICATION
FOR AUDIO-VISUAL COVERAGE

_____ Court, _____ County
_____x
In the Matter of an Application to
Conduct Audio-Visual Coverage of

                              ORDER DETERMINING APPLI-
                              CATION FOR AUDIO-VISUAL
                                    COVERAGE

v.   (Index) (Indictment) (Calendar) No. __

_____x

PRESENT: Hon. _____

    An application having been made to this Court on _____,
19____, pursuant to section 131.3 of the Rules of the Chief Administrative Judge by _____ (news media applicant), requesting permission to (specify type of coverage) _____ the above judicial proceeding; and

    The Court having reviewed this application and the attached statements and affidavits presented to the Court concerning the proposed coverage; and

    The Court having consulted with the news media applicant and counsel to all parties to the above-named proceeding (and with (specify others—*e.g.*, victims, witnesses, etc.—as appropriate) _____
_____);

    NOW, upon consideration of all relevant factors, including those specified in section 131.1(c) of the Rules of the Chief Administrative Judge, it is hereby

    ORDERED that the application is (approved) (denied) (approved with the following special limitations: _____
_____) (strike out inapplicable language).

    The basis for the determination is (to be completed unless the application is approved without special limitations *and* no party, victim or prospective witness objects to coverage):

_____
_____
_____
_____

                                         _____
                                           (Justice) (Judge)

Dated:

APPLICATION FOR PERMISSION TO CONDUCT AUDIO-VISUAL COVERAGE

_____ Court, _____ County

_____x

In the Matter of an Application to
Conduct Audio-Visual Coverage of

v.

_____x

Index No. _____
Indictment No. _____
Calendar No. _____
(Complete as applicable, if known)

Judge assigned (if known):
_____

TO THE COURT:
1. The undersigned hereby applies for permission to conduct audio-visual coverage of the above judicial proceeding as follows (check as appropriate):

    ___ televise live   ___ audio (radio) broadcast live

    ___ videotape for later broadcast   ___ audiotape for later broadcast

    ___ film   ___ use still photography

    ___ tape record   ___ other (specify)

2. The scope of coverage requested is (check as appropriate):
    ___ throughout the above proceeding
    ___ during only the following portion(s) of such proceeding (specify):
    _____

_____
(Signature)

_____
(Name)

_____
(Media organization)

_____
(Address)

Dated: _____   ( )_____
                                   (Telephone number)

Appendix I
Sample Monitoring Instrument for Camera-Experienced Lawyers

CAMERAS IN THE COURTROOM

ATTORNEY SURVEY

THIS QUESTIONNAIRE IS TO BE COMPLETED ONLY BY LAWYERS WHO HAVE HAD EXPERIENCE WITH CAMERAS IN THE COURTS OF NEW YORK STATE OR WITH PROCEEDINGS IN WHICH PERMISSION FOR CAMERA COVERAGE WAS SOUGHT

A. Background

1. Which side do you typically represent

   Criminal   **Civil**

   Prosecution [ ]   Plaintiff [ ]
   Defendant   [ ]   Defendant [ ]

2. In the case in which you participated where television camera coverage was sought, which side did you represent

   Criminal   **Civil**

   Prosecution [ ]   Plaintiff [ ]
   Defendant   [ ]   Defendant [ ]

B. Decisions about Camera Coverage

3. When you learned that the proceeding you were involved in was one in which the media had applied for permission of the court to allow television cameras to be present, did you (please circle the appropriate response for each question)

                                                    Yes   No

   3a Have an adequate opportunity   1   2
       to notify your <u>client</u> of
       the prospect of camera coverage?

3b Have an adequate opportunity   1   2
    to notify your <u>witnesses</u> of
    the prospect of camera coverage?

3c Have an opportunity to register   1   2
    an objection to camera coverage
    of the proceeding?

3d. Object to camera coverage?   1   2

4 If you objected to camera coverage, please explain the basis for your objection

5 If you objected to camera coverage, did you (please circle the appropriate response for each question):

	Yes	No
5a Have an adequate opportunity to brief your objection?	1	2
5b Have an adequate opportunity to argue your objection?	1	2
5c Have an adequate opportunity to present evidence in support of your object?	1	2

6 (a) Have you ever had an objection to camera coverage which you did not raise?
           Yes [1]   No [2]

   (b) If the answer to 6(a) is yes, why did you elect not to
       raise your objection?

7 In determining whether to allow television camera
   coverage, do you think that the court gave adequate
   consideration to the views of (please circle the appropriate response for each question)

	Yes	No
7a Attorneys?	1	2
7b Witnesses?	1	2
7c Parties?	1	2
7d Jurors?	1	2
7e. Defendant (in a criminal case)?	1	2
7f Crime victim (or victim's family members) in a criminal case?	1	2

8 If your client were to have been given an absolute right to refuse camera coverage of the proceeding, would your client have done so?

    Yes 1 [ ]
    No 2 [ ]
    I don't know 3 [ ]

9 a Did any of your witnesses decline to testify because of the prospect of television camera coverage?

    Yes 1 [ ]
    No 2 [ ]
    I don't recall 3 [ ]

b Did any of your witnesses inform you that they were reluctant to testify because of the prospect of television camera coverage?

    Yes 1 [ ]
    No 2 [ ]
    I can't recall 3 [ ]

c Did any of your witnesses request that their face not be shown or be visually obscured?

    Yes 1 [ ]
    No 2 [ ]
    I don't recall 3 [ ]

C. Experiences with Camera Coverage in New York State

10 The following is a list of questions regarding possible effects of cameras in the court
For each question, please use circle the answer that best reflects your experience, using the following codes

> Strongly agree   1
> Somewhat agree   2
> Somewhat disagree   3
> Strongly disagree   4
> No effect   5
> No opinion   6

Cameras in the courtroom in your case

a motivated witnesses to be
   more truthful than they
   otherwise would be   1 2 3 4 5 6

b distracted witnesses   1 2 3 4 5 6

c made witnesses more
   nervous than they otherwise
   would be   1 2 3 4 5 6

d. deterred witnesses from   1 2 3 4 5 6
   testifying

e violated witnesses' privacy   1 2 3 4 5 6

f increased juror
   attentiveness   1 2 3 4 5 6

g distracted jurors   1 2 3 4 5 6

h motivated lawyers to
   come to court better
   prepared   1 2 3 4 5 6

i caused trial participants to   1 2 3 4 5 6
   be sensitive to how the day's events
   would "play" on the evening news

j distracted attorneys	1 2 3 4 5 6	
k prompted attorneys to be more courteous	1 2 3 4 5 6	
l increased the judge's attentiveness	1 2 3 4 5 6	
m prompted the judge to be more courteous	1 2 3 4 5 6	
n caused judges to rule differently than they might otherwise have ruled	1 2 3 4 5 6	
o disrupted the courtroom proceedings	1 2 3 4 5 6	
p affected the outcome of the case	1 2 3 4 5 6	
q fostered public scrutiny of court proceedings	1 2 3 4 5 6	
r served as a deterrent against injustice	1 2 3 4 5 6	
s increased the accuracy of news accounts of the proceeding	1 2 3 4 5 6	

11 Compared to similar cases covered only by the print media, did your opposing counsel make more or fewer attempts to offer unnecessary (check all that apply)

	More	Fewer	About the same
a Motions	1 [ ]	2 [ ]	3 [ ]
b Evidence	1 [ ]	2 [ ]	3 [ ]
c Witnesses	1 [ ]	2 [ ]	3 [ ]
d Objections	1 [ ]	2 [ ]	3 [ ]
e Argument	1 [ ]	2 [ ]	3 [ ]

12a In what way, if any, did cameras in the courtroom affect the fairness of the proceeding?

[ ] 1 It had no effect on the fairness of the proceeding
[ ] 2 It increased the fairness of the proceeding
[ ] 3 It decreased the fairness of the proceeding

12b In your view, was this due to the fact that cameras were present in the courtroom, or would print media coverage (without camera access) have had similar effects?

[ ] 1 Print media coverage would have had similar effects

[ ] 2 Print media coverage would have had a less detrimental effect on the fairness of the proceedings

[ ] 3 Print media coverage would have had a more detrimental effect on the fairness of the proceedings

12c If you wish, please comment on the effects of television camera coverage on the fairness of the proceeding

13 (a) Are you aware of any violations of section 218 of the Judiciary Law (which governs cameras in the court)?

Yes 1 [ ]
No 2 [ ]

(b) If yes, describe (including case caption, index, indictment or calendar number, date, court, presiding judge, and type of proceeding)

D. Views About Television Camera Coverage of New York State Court Proceedings

14 How do you feel overall about cameras in the courts in *criminal* trials in New York?

[ ] 1 I strongly favor coverage
[ ] 2 I somewhat favor coverage
[ ] 3 I somewhat oppose coverage
[ ] 4 I strongly oppose coverage
[ ] 5 I have no opinion on coverage

15. How do you feel overall about cameras in the courts in *civil* trials in New York?

      [ ] 1 I strongly favor coverage
      [ ] 2 I somewhat favor coverage
      [ ] 3 I somewhat oppose coverage
      [ ] 4 I strongly oppose coverage
      [ ] 5 I have no opinion on coverage

16. How do you feel overall about cameras in the courts in *criminal* pre-trial proceedings in New York?

      [ ] 1 I strongly favor coverage
      [ ] 2 I somewhat favor coverage
      [ ] 3 I somewhat oppose coverage
      [ ] 4 I strongly oppose coverage
      [ ] 5 I have no opinion on coverage

17. How do you feel overall about cameras in the courts in *civil* pre-trial proceedings in New York?

      [ ] 1 I strongly favor coverage
      [ ] 2 I somewhat favor coverage
      [ ] 3 I somewhat oppose coverage
      [ ] 4 I strongly oppose coverage
      [ ] 5 I have no opinion on coverage

18. Please use the space below if you wish to provide any additional comments

Optional:

    Name:
    Address:
    Telephone:

    Thank you for your assistance.

Appendix J
Judicial Training Program Outline

I. Course on Cameras in the Courts
   A. Introduction
      1. Historical, constitutional and statutory background
      2. Overview of the results of the 1997 judicial survey conducted by New York State Committee to Review Audio-visual Coverage of Court Proceedings
   B. Section 218 of the Judiciary Law and Part 131 of the New York Rules of Court (Audio-Visual Coverage of Court Proceedings)
      1. Authorization
      2. Definitions
      3. Time frame for filing requests for camera coverage
      4. Consent requirement (arraignments, suppression hearings, requests filed after commencement of proceedings)
      5. Exercise of judicial discretion
         a. consultation with counsel to all parties
         b. consideration of objections of parties, prospective witnesses, crime victims and others
         c. review of statutory and regulatory factors to be considered in the exercise of judicial discretion
         d. no presumption for or against camera access
      6. Circumstances when an evidentiary hearing should be held
      7. Special considerations in rape, death penalty and child custody cases
      8. Safeguards for witnesses' safety and privacy
         a. criminal proceedings
         b. civil proceedings
      9. Pre-trial conference
      10. Instructions and safeguards for jurors
      11. Supervision of audio-visual coverage throughout

the proceedings; revocation of judicial consent; imposition of additional limits and restrictions
12. Violations and sanctions
13. Judicial review
14. Questions and answers

II. Assigned Readings
  1. Section 218 of the Judiciary Law
  2. N.Y. Ct. Rules, Part 131
  3. 1997 Report of the New York State Committee to Review Audio-Visual Coverage of Court Proceedings
  4. Selected cases (*Estes, Chandler, Richmond Newspapers,* etc.)
  5. Selected readings from law review and psychosocial literature on cameras in the courts (*see e.g.,* bibliography appended to the 1997 Report of the New York State Committee to Review Audio-Visual Coverage of Court Proceedings)

III. Discussion of hypotheticals presenting issues calling for the exercise of judicial discretion

IV. Case studies of abuses and violations of section 218

V. A simulated hearing on an application for audio-visual coverage in a criminal trial where the defendant objects to camera coverage

VI. Faculty
  1. Chief Administrative Judge or representative
  2. Panels of camera-experienced judges, lawyers, witnesses, jurors, journalists and media scholars

Appendix K
Selected Bibliography

The following bibliography includes a partial listing of the hundreds of articles and other materials published on the subject of cameras in the courtroom. Similarly, the organizations listed here represent only a portion of those who helped the Committee gather background information about camera coverage laws in other states.

It is the Committee's hope that the books, articles and resource organizations listed here will lead the interested reader to other sources.

Books

Susanna Barber, *News Cameras in the Courtroom: A Free Press-Fair Trial Debate* (1987).

M. Ethan Katsh, *The Electronic Media and the Transformation of Law* (Oxford University Press, 1989).

Paul Thaler, *The Watchful Eye: American Justice in the Age of the Television Trial* (Praeger, 1994).

Paul Thaler, *The Spectacle: Media and the Making of the O.J. Simpson Story* (Praeger, forthcoming August 1997).

Articles

30th Anniversary Special Report, Cameras in the Courtroom, *Quill* (October 1996).

Eugene Borgida, Kenneth G. DeBono & Lee A. Buckman, Cameras in the Courtroom: The Effects of Media Coverage on Witness Testimony and Juror Perceptions, 14 *Law and Human Behavior* 489 (1990).

Steven Brill, That's Entertainment! The Continuing Debate Over Cameras in the Courtroom, 42 *Federal Lawyer* 28 (July 1995).

Steven Brill, The Eye That Educates, *The New York Times* (July 15, 1994).

Lincoln Caplan, "Why Play-by-Play Coverage Strikes Out for Lawyers," 82 Jan. ABA J. 62 (1996).

Columbia University, Graduate School of Journalism, Annual DuPont Forum Symposium, "America Through The T.V. Looking Glass" (1995).

Gail Diane Cox, Lights! Camera! Justice?, *National Law Journal*, p. 1 (January 29, 1996).

Don J. DeBenedictis, The National Verdict: Most Americans Think They Know More About the Law from Watching and Reading About the O. J. Simpson Case, But Do They Trust the Lawyers and Media Who Set the Tone for Trials Throughout the Nation?, 80 Oct. ABA. J. 52 (Oct. 1994).

Max Frankel, I Am Not a Camera, *The New York Times Magazine*, p. 28 (October 16, 1994).

Max Frankel, Out of Focus, *The New York Times Magazine* (November 5, 1995).

George Gerbner, Cameras on Trial: The "O.J. Show" Turns the Tide, 39 *Journal of Broadcasting & Electronic Media* 562 (1995).

Matthew Goldstein, "Televising Trials Still a Hot Issue," *New York Law Journal* (Oct. 30, 1996).

James C. Goodale, "Cameras, the Courts and the Missing 'Simpson' Backlash," *New York Law Journal*, (Aug. 2, 1996).

Erwin N. Griswold, The Standards of the Legal Profession: Canon 35 Should Not Be Surrendered, 48 *American Bar Association Journal* 615 (July 1962).

Valerie Hans & Juliet L. Dee, Media Coverage of the Law: Its Impact on Juries and the Public, 35 *Behavioral Scientist* 136 (1991).

Susan Harding, Cameras and the Need for Unrestricted Electronic Media Access to Federal Courtrooms, 69 *Southern California Law Review* 827 (1996)

David A. Harris, The Appearance of Justice: Court TV, Conventional Television, and Public Understanding of the Criminal Justice System, 35 *Arizona Law Review* 785 (1993).

William J. Harte, Why Make Justice a Circus? The O.J. Simpson, Dahmer and Kennedy–Smith Debacles Make the Case Against Cameras in the Courtroom, 39 *Trial Law. Guide* 379 (Winter 1996).

Richard Heffner, Cameras in the Courtroom: A Bad Idea Whose Time Has Come, *New York Law Journal* (1989).

Rikke J. Klieman and Jack T. Litman, "Dialogue: Cameras in the Courtroom?" *The Champion* (Jan./Fete. 1996).

Kathleen M. Krygier, The Thirteenth Juror: Electronic Media's Struggle to Enter State and Federal Courtrooms, 3 *CommLaw Conspectus* 71 (Institute for Communications Law Studies, Columbus School of Law, Catholic University of America) (1995).

Christo Lassiter, Put the Lens Cap Back on Cameras in the Courtroom: A Fair Trial Is at Stake, 67 *N.Y. State Bar J.* 6 (Jan. 1995).

Christo Lassiter, TV or Not TV: That Is the Question, 86 *Journal of Criminal Law & Criminology* 928 (1996).

M. David Lepofsky, Cameras in the Courtroom: Not Without My Consent, 6 *National Journal of Constitutional Law* 161 (1996).

Rory K. Little, That's Entertainment: The Continuing Debate Over Cameras in the Courtroom, 42 *Federal Lawyer* 28 (July 1995).

Roger J. Miner, Eye on Justice, 67 *New York State Bar Journal* 8 (February 1995).

Francis T. Murphy, Opposing Televising of Criminal Trials, *New York Law Journal* (Nov. 4, 1996).

Francis T. Murphy, The Case Against Cameras in the Courtroom, 211 *New York Law Journal* 2 (June 30, 1994).

Stephen A. Metz, Justice Through the Eyes of a Camera: Cameras in the Courtrooms in the United States, Canada, England and Scotland, 14 *Dickinson Journal of International Law* 673 (1996).

Honorable John F. Onion, Jr., Mass Media's Impact on Litigation: A Judge's Perspective, 14 *Rev. Litig.* 585 (Summer 1995).

Carolyn E. Riemer, Television Coverage of Trials: Constitutional Protection Against Absolute Denial of Access in the Absence of a Compelling Interest, 30 *Villanova L. Rev.* 1267 (1985).

Gregory C. Read, Fade to Black: A Defense Perspective on Cameras in the Courtroom, Defense Research Institute, *The American Jury System: Worth Preserving.* Special Issue, Vol. 1996, No. 4.

Burton B. Roberts, Cameras in the Courtroom: A Rebuttal, *New York Law Journal* (July 13, 1994).

Nadja S. Sodos, The Ethical Considerations of Televising Federal Courtroom Proceedings, 4 *Georgetown Journal of Legal Ethics* 915 (Spring 1992).

Ruth Ann Strickland & Richter H. Moore, Cameras in State Courts: A Historical Perspective, 78 *Judicature* 128 (Nov/Dec 1994).

Nadine Strossen, Free Press and Fair Trial: Implications of the O.J. Simpson Case, 26 *University of Toledo Law Review* 647 (Spring 1995).

Paul Thaler, On Trial, *Forbes Media Critic* (Fall 1994).

Anton R. Valukas, William A. Von Hoene, Jr., & Liza M. Murphy, Cameras in the Courtroom: An Overview, 13 *Communications Lawyer* 1 (Fall 1995).

Frances Kahn Zemans, Public Access: The Ultimate Guardian of Fairness in our Justice System, 79 Judicature 173 (Jan./Fete. 1996).

State and Federal Reports

Administrative Office of the Courts, Taskforce on Photographing, Recording and Broadcasting in the Courtroom (California 1996).

Administrative Office of the Courts, Report on Cameras in the Courtroom Surveys (Tennessee 1996).

Daniel Amundson & S. Robert Lichter, Cameras in the Courtroom: A Content Analysis of the Use of Courtroom Footage in Television Newscasts, A Report to the Federal Judicial Center (Center for Media and Public Affairs, September 30, 1993).

Crosson, Matthew T., Report of the Chief Administrator to the New York State Legislature, the Governor and the Chief Judge on the Effect of Audio-Visual Coverage on the Conduct of Judicial Proceedings (1991).

Crosson, Matthew T., Memorandum to all Judges and Justices, Cameras in the Courts, June 16, 1992.

Federal Judicial Center, Electronic Media Coverage of Federal Civil Proceedings: An Evaluation of the Pilot Program in Six District Courts and Two Courts of Appeal (1994).

Report of the New York State Advisory Committee on Audio-Visual Coverage of Judicial Proceedings, June 4, 1990.

Report of the New York State Committee on Audiovisual Coverage of Court Proceedings (May 1994) and Minority Report of the Committee on Audiovisual Coverage of Court Proceedings (December 1994).

Rosenblatt, Albert M., Report of the Chief Administrative Judge to the New York State Legislature, the Governor and the Chief Judge on the Effect of Audio-Visual Coverage on the Conduct of Judicial Proceedings (1989).

Ernest H. Short & Associates, Evaluation of California's Experiment with Extended Media Coverage of Courts (September 1991).

Unpublished Materials

William J. Bowers & Margaret Vandiver, "Cameras in the Courtroom Make New Yorkers Reluctant to Testify," Executive Summary of a New York State Survey Conducted March 1–4, 1991 (Northeastern University, College of Criminal Justice, 1991).

Steven Brill, "Facts and Opinions about Cameras in the Courtroom" (Court TV July 1995).

Roberta Entner, Encoding the Image of the American Judiciary Institution: A Semiotic Analysis of the Broadcast Trials to Ascertain Its Definition of the Court System (PhD thesis, New York University 1993).

New York State Defenders Association: The Intrusion of Cameras in New York's Criminal Courts: A Report by the Public Defense Backup Center (May 12, 1989)

Radio–Television News Directors Association, News Media Coverage of Judicial Proceedings With Cameras and Microphones: A Survey of the States (January 1997)

Ann J. Reavis, Fey Epling & Gregory Read, "Cameras in the Courtroom" (Defense Research Institute) (October 1996).

Times Mirror Center for People and the Press, TV Trials Captivate Public (February 4, 1994).

David Weiner, "The Courtroom Camera," Opening Statement, Litigation Section, American Bar Association (Winter 1995).

Videotapes

"Cameras in the Courtroom: A Structured Dialogue," Dec. 5, 1995, Educational Forum at McGeorge School of Law.

Defense Research Institute, National Forum on Cameras in the Courtroom, Chicago, Illinois (Oct. 9, 1996).

Cameras in the Criminal Courts, OCA Videotape Excerpts compiled by New York State Defenders Association in May 1989.

Organizations

Administrative Office of Illinois Courts (312) 793-7869

Administrative Office of the United States Courts, Washington, D.C. (202) 273-4153

California Judicial Council (415) 396-9111

Courtroom Television Network, 600 Third Avenue, New York, NY 10016 (212) 973-2800

Defense Research Institute, 750 Lake Shore Drive, Suite 500, Chicago, IL 60611 (312) 944-0575

Paulette Holahan, Deputy Judicial Administrator, 301 Loyola Avenue, Room 109, New Orleans, LA 70112-1887 (504) 568-5747

National Association of Criminal Defense Lawyers, 1627 K Street, N.W. Suite 1200, Washington, D.C. 2006 (202) 872-8688

National Center for State Courts, 300 Newport Ave., P.O. Box 8798, Williamsburg, VA 23187 (757) 253-2000.

National Jury Project, 285 West Broadway, Suite 200, New York, NY 10013 (212) 219-8962

New York Fair Trial/Free Press Conference, Professor Jay B. Wright, Executive Director, S.I. Newhouse Communications Center, Syracuse University, Syracuse, NY 13244-2100 (315) 443-2381

New York State Association of Criminal Defense Lawyers (212) 532-4434

New York State Bar Association, One Elk Street, Albany, NY 12207 (518) 463-3200

New York State Defenders Association, 11 North Pearl Street, 18th floor, Albany, NY (518) 465-3524

New York Broadcasters Courtroom Pool (718) 488-7646

New York County Lawyers Association, 14 Vesey Street, New York, NY 10007 (212) 267-6646.

Radio and Television News Directors Association (202) 659-6510.

Times Mirror Center for People and the Press, 1875 Eye Street, N.W., Suite 1110, Washington, DC 20006 (202) 293-3126.

MINORITY REPORT
Leonard E. Noisette

CONTENTS

The Minority Recommendation   211

I. Introduction   211

II. The Committee Majority Report recommendation to make Section 218 of the Judiciary Law permanent is not supported by the extensive record it developed   212
  - A. The Report's arguments as to "openness" and a need for public scrutiny of our courts do not meet the required showing of public benefits flowing from television coverage of court proceedings   213
    - (1) Public Education   213
    - (2) Public Scrutiny and Judicial Accountability   214
    - (3) Compliance with Statute by Judges and the Media   214
    - (4) Adverse Effect on Trial Participants   214

III. The experiment has failed to prove that TV cameras in the courts provide a public benefit, significantly enhance public understanding of the judicial process, or help to maintain a high level of public confidence in the judiciary   215
  - A. Camera proponents have not demonstrated the public benefit goals that were the legislative basis for the experimental removal of the bar to cameras in the court   216
  - B. Televised court proceedings, done for entertainment, not education, have a seriously detrimental effect on the integrity of the judicial system   219
  - C. The O. J. Simpson experience, the ultimate in TV coverage of courtroom proceedings, was a TV media dream come true, and, for New York, a wake-up call   221
  - D. The intrusion of cameras in our courts undermines the independent integrity and dignity of our judicial process and courtrooms   223

	E. "Open Courtrooms" should not relinquish the dispensing of justice to the TV Court of Public Opinion	225
	F. If there is a need for greater education of New York citizens as to the workings of New York's judicial system, it should be dealt with directly by the State and the courts, without turning the educational task over to commercial TV	226
IV.	The "openness" and "no instance of prejudice" arguments of camera proponents are diversionary and do not deal with the realities of televised coverage of courtroom proceedings and TV's usurpation of individual rights and privacy interests	227
	A. Our New York courts are open, as they were before 1987 and have continued to be	228
	B. Televised coverage does affect court proceedings, subordinating the rights and privacy interests of participants to the rights of the TV camera	230
	(1) The Adverse Effects on Defendants in Criminal Trials	231
	(2) Effect on Trial Participants	233
	(3) The testimony of media experts confirms the adverse effect of television on court proceedings	235
V.	The Committee Majority Recommendation and its rejection of additional modest Section 218 "safeguards" reflects an incorrect assumption that TV camera rights should be superior to individual rights and privacy interests	236
	A. The Committee's recommended permanence of Section 218 with all existing safeguards will quickly be eroded	239
VI.	Conclusion	240

THE MINORITY RECOMMENDATION

I respectfully dissent from the Committee Majority Report's recommendation that Judiciary Law Section 218 be made permanent, giving trial judges discretion to allow audiovisual coverage of New York State civil and criminal court proceedings in accordance with the provisions of that statute as previously applied on an experimental basis.

Recommendation. I submit the following as a Committee Minority Report in support of the recommendation that:

> the Judiciary Law Section 218 experiment be ended and that the statute be allowed to expire on June 30, 1997, so that, as was true from 1952 to 1987, there shall be no audio-visual coverage of New York State court proceedings.

I. INTRODUCTION

In 1952, the New York State Legislature enacted section 52 of the Civil Rights Law, banning audio-visual coverage of public proceedings, including court proceedings, "in which the testimony of witnesses by subpoena or other compulsory process is or may be taken. . . ." The statute was established in response to the Legislature's concerns about the detrimental effect audio-visual coverage would have on participants involved in such proceedings.

When, in 1987, after an unsuccessful attempt in 1982, media advocates sought to have cameras allowed in New York's courtrooms, Section 218 of the Judiciary Law was enacted. The statute allowed cameras in the courtroom on an experimental basis to determine whether there was a public benefit in televising courtroom proceedings that would outweigh the concerns which were the basis for the presumption against cameras in our courts.

The 1987 legislative findings describe the public benefits that the legislature hoped could result from the televising of court proceedings: "an enhanced public understanding of the judicial system [which] is important in maintaining a high level of public confidence in the judiciary." From the wording of the mandate in Section 218 (9) as enacted by the legislature in 1995, and from the legislative history, the primary evaluation to be made by this Committee is whether public benefits have accrued from the televising of court proceedings in New York State.

The Committee, its chair, and its staff are to be commended for the development of a record which will be helpful to the Legislature when it again considers how to deal with the mtter of television cameras in our courts—a record that includes independent surveys and the unpaid, disinterested testimony of media experts and professionals with extensive experience in courtrooms. The record establishes that after ten years and four experimental periods, camera proponents are still unable to provide any study or empirical evidence that television coverage of court proceedings has met the statutory goals of the experiment. To the contrary, the Committee's most important contributions—its survey of the judiciary of this state and its New York voters survey—indicate that the experiment has been a failure in this regard.

The question before the Legislature is: given this lack of evidence of any benefits from the intrusion of cameras into our courts, should New York remove its 45-year-old presumption against cameras in our courts under Section 52 of the Civil Rights Law, and permit audio-visual coverage to become a permanent component of its court proceedings? For the reasons more fully set out below, I respectfully submit that the answer to this question is no.

II. THE COMMITTEE MAJORITY REPORT RECOMMENDATION TO MAKE SECTION 218 OF THE JUDICIARY LAW PERMANENT IS NOT SUPPORTED BY THE EXTENSIVE RECORD IT DEVELOPED.

The Committee Majority Report provides a helpful review of the work of the Committee in conscientiously performing its job in open hearings and open meetings; of the testimony and other evidence that it compiled; and of arguments on both sides of various issues that the Committee considered.

The overarching problem with the Majority's assessment of the record is that it presumes that the burden is on those opposed to cameras in our courts to prove the harm they cause, instead of recognizing that camera proponents should be required to demonstrate the benefits that accrue for allowing such access. As such, the conclusions the Majority reaches after its assessment of the record are not consistent with a fair reading of the record or with the statutory history and legislative intent of the experiment.

A. THE REPORT'S ARGUMENTS AS TO "OPENNESS" AND A NEED FOR PUBLIC SCRUTINY OF OUR COURTS DO NOT MEET THE REQUIRED SHOWING OF PUBLIC BENEFITS FLOWING FROM TELEVISION COVERAGE OF COURT PROCEEDINGS

On the broad policy issues, including those bearing on "the efficacy of the program and whether any public benefits accrue from the [cameras-in-the-court] program," the Majority Report has very little to offer.

There is no Committee finding that our judicial system needs TV coverage of court proceedings.

There is no suggestion as to how our New York system of justice was deficient prior to 1987 when there was no TV coverage of court proceedings.

There is no suggestion as to how our New York system of justice would be deficient in the future if there were no TV coverage of court proceedings.

1. Public Education

The Committee asserts that allowing cameras in our courts enhances public understanding of our judicial system, but a careful review of the record reveals that meaningful public education is an aspirational goal, at best, and that claims that it currently exists are largely made by media representatives with vested interests.

Such a benefit might be the result of regular, meaningful coverage of court proceedings. As the Majority concedes, however, the record makes clear that the overwhelming majority of footage of court proceedings actually consists of short features—snippets, which shed little light on the complexity of court proceedings. Significantly, the responses of deans of New York's law schools indicated that, other than public television coverage of Court of Appeals arguments and the rare extensive coverage of trial proceedings, there was little educational value to or use of television footage.

2. Public Scrutiny and Judicial Accountability

The primary public benefit that the Committee finds is that TV coverage is good because "openness" and "public access" are fundamental aspects of our democratic society. Such openness, according to the Majority, fosters the goal of "judicial scrutiny" and heightened judicial accountability. (It is not clear why the Committee believes our courts are in particular need of heightened accountability.)

But if it were thought that the "openness" of having cameras in the courtroom were *per se* the primary public benefit to be achieved then there would have been no need for an experimental period. The legislature hoped for something more.

The finding that cameras in our courts significantly foster the goals of judicial scrutiny is still another conclusion unsupported by the record. Such scrutiny presumes a degree of coverage of judicial conduct that does not in fact exist.

Most important, the Committee's openness and access conclusions fail to deal with the nature of television and the difference between the experience of actually being in a courtroom and that of viewing selective and filtered TV tube images. The report also inadequately acknowledges that the presence of cameras effects the fact-finding and deliberation process occurring inside the courtroom.

3. Compliance with Statute by Judges and the Media

Although instances of significant abuses were brought to the Committee's attention, they were fewer in number than in past experimental periods and the Committee found that judges and the media generally complied with the provisions of the statute. This modest success between the last experimental phase and the current one is little consolation, however.

4. Adverse Effect on Trial Participants

With respect to the extent to which the conduct of participants in court proceedings changes when audio-visual coverage is present, the Committee's findings were more equivocal.

The Majority acknowledged the views expressed by a range of witnesses regarding the deterrent effect on witnesses—sex crime and domestic violence victims' advocates; prosecutors; defense attorneys; judges. The Committee also noted that the U.S. Judicial Conference terminated its "cameras in the court" pilot project because "the intimidating effect of cameras on some witnesses and jurors was cause for concern" and that some members of the Judicial Conference, which voted by a 2-1 margin to disapprove the request to permit cameras in the Federal courts in civil proceedings, "believed that *any* negative impact on witnesses or jurors could be a threat to the fair administration of justice."

Similarly, there was a substantial degree of concern about the effect on lawyers, judges, and jurors of cameras being in the courtroom. Though they understood possible problems, the Committee Majority dismissed "the fears regarding the impact of cameras on trial participants" on the narrow grounds that there was "no demonstrable evidence" of any instances in which such fears have been realized in New York.

The Committee reached this conclusion minimizing cameras' effect on court proceeding participants despite their Marist survey results which indicated that the majority of voters would not want trials to be televised if they were criminal defendants, civil parties, witnesses, or victims (Marist Survey [hereinafter "MS"], Questions 7, 8, 12, and 13). And the Committee's conclusion was in the face of the response of 37% of the New York judges to their Judicial Survey who agreed that the presence of television cameras in the courtroom tends to cause judges to issue ruling they otherwise might not issue (Judicial Survey [hereinafter "JS"], Question 4(g)), and the observation of 40% of judges that witnesses appeared more nervous when cameras were present (JS, Q. 22(f)).

The Committee Majority Report recommendation that Judiciary Law section 218 be made permanent is not consistent with the voluminous record before it, that the televising of court proceedings has an adverse impact on trial participants and the conducting of a fair trial.

III. THE EXPERIMENT HAS FAILED TO PROVE THAT TV CAMERAS IN THE COURTS PROVIDE A PUBLIC BENEFIT, SIGNIFICANTLY ENHANCE PUBLIC UNDERSTANDING OF THE JUDICIAL PROCESS, OR HELP TO MAINTAIN A HIGH LEVEL OF PUBLIC CONFIDENCE IN THE JUDICIARY

When, in 1987, the Legislature first decided to allow cameras in our courts on an experimental basis, it was with the hope that granting such access would have a public benefit. The 1987 legislative findings describe the public benefits which the Legislature hoped could result from the televising of court proceedings: "an enhanced public understanding of the judicial system [which] is important in maintaining a high level of public confidence in the judiciary."

Section 218 (9), as enacted by the Legislature in 1995, makes clear that an assessment of the public benefits that accrue from allowing cameras in our courts is still the primary legislative concern.

A. CAMERA PROPONENTS HAVE NOT DEMONSTRATED THE PUBLIC BENEFIT GOALS THAT WERE THE LEGISLATIVE BASIS FOR THE EXPERIMENTAL REMOVAL OF THE BAR TO CAMERAS IN THE COURT

There has been no study and no empirical evidence that television coverage of court proceedings has met the goals of enhancing public understanding of New York's judicial system or helping to maintain a high level of confidence in the judiciary. The responses of the judges to the Committee's Judicial survey (App. A to the Committee Report) and of the voters to the December 1996 survey of the Marist Institute for Public Opinion (App. B to the Committee Report) support the contrary conclusion.

The Committee's two surveys are a major contribution to the information base available to the legislature for its consideration of the extent to which the law should restrict television coverage of proceedings in New York courts. The surveys were well designed and professionally carried out to produce statistically reliable results.

The Marist Institute for Public Opinion is one of the nation's most respected organizations in its field. Its report (App. B, at pp. 1-4) spells out the meticulous attention given to assure that the survey produced accurate and usable information. Similarly credible is the Judicial Survey designed with the assistance of Committee member James Tien, an expert in the field, and the impressively credentialed Professor Edmund Mantell of Pace University.

Overall, a substantial majority of the responses of the judges and voters surveyed indicate a lack of public benefits from television coverage of New York court proceedings and show adverse effects of such coverage.

The Judges' Responses. Directly on point here are the judges' response to the question of whether television coverage "has enhanced public understanding of New York's judicial system" (JS Q. 4(b)): 25% of the judges strongly disagreed, while 26% somewhat disagreed. Only 10% of the judges strongly agreed with the statement.

Even more telling are the judges' responses to the next question, whether television coverage "is more likely to serve as a source of entertainment than education for the viewing public" (JS Q. (c)): 41% of the judges strongly agreed, and 39% somewhat agreed.

The Voters' Responses. The judges' high level of skepticism as to the putative educational value of courtroom television coverage parallels that of a substantial part of the general public as reflected in the Marist voter survey: 61% believed that televised courtroom trials were a bad idea; and 61% believed that television in the courtroom was more a source of entertainment than something that would increase the public's understanding of the justice system. (MS Q1 and Q3).

Even the responses of the 22% of the voters who "watch trials on TV" . . . "always or sometimes" demonstrate the lack of public education benefits. While 51% of that minority of surveyed voters believed that the presence of cameras increased the public's understanding of the justice system, some 43% candidly responded that it was more a source of entertainment (MS Q. 3), and 43% felt cameras served more to sensationalize a trial than increase the accuracy of news coverage (MS Q.2).

These statistics resoundingly rebut the bald assertions of self-interested journalists, and they are a dose of reality for those hopeful, disinterested witnesses regarding the educational benefits of cameras in our courts. They are the voice of New Yorkers voting for sunset of this law.

Moreover, these findings are supported by expert testimony as well. In untranscribed remarks, Richard D. Heffner, Dowling Professor of Communications and Public Policy at Rutgers University, repeated to this Committee points he had made before the 1994 Committee; his conclusions about the educational value of courtroom television were like those of the surveyed voters and judges.

> That television has had more grist for its nightly news goes without saying. But "an enhanced public understanding" of the judicial sys-

tem was the Legislature's intent, not just enhanced television audiences. And while media ratings have been hyped, there is no evidence whatsoever that public education has been . . . except as the media wish becomes father to reality, or in typical media fashion, the claim becomes confused with the fact, the more so frequently trumpeted (cited at p. 52 of the 1994 Minority Report).

One of the techniques the media uses in advancing their arguments about the educational value of TV coverage is to give primary attention to continuous gavel-to-gavel coverage as though that is what is mainly involved. For example, in trying to put the case for cameras-in-the-courts in the best educational light, Steven Brill, of Court TV, submitted to the Committee a newspaper article describing an instance of classroom use of Court TV videotapes of various kinds of trials and proceedings.

Such extensive coverage of a court action is what others are thinking of when they speak expansively of TV's educational value in this area. And, indeed, an argument could be made for allowing consented-to videotaping of different kinds of trials and proceedings with the tape being shown in law school and other classrooms or on commercial TV—*after* the case had been decided by the judge or jury.

But that is not the kind of coverage that TV wants or typically shows. The nature of television, and particularly television driven by bottom line commercial needs, is to emphasize emotional responses rather than logical studied understanding. In a word, that is what sells; sound bites are the rule; and McNeil/Lehrer indepth reports are the noncommercial exception.

While New York has never done any significant content analysis of court footage during its experimental period, the Federal Judicial Center did so as part of its evaluation of its pilot program. Its findings are instructive. On average, actual courtroom footage made up only 56 seconds of a TV news story, and occupied 59% of total air time. The Judicial Center concluded from its analysis that the visual information was typically used to reinforce a verbal presentation rather than to add new and different material to the report, and that the coverage did a poor job of providing information to viewers about the legal process. *Electronic Media Coverage of Federal Civil Proceedings*, the Federal Judicial Center Evaluation, 1994, pp 32-36.

In sum, the media have not achieved the educational goals they promoted as a justification for the cameras-in-the-court experiment.

B. TELEVISED COURT PROCEEDINGS, DONE FOR ENTERTAINMENT, NOT EDUCATION, HAVE A SERIOUSLY DETRIMENTAL EFFECT ON THE INTEGRITY OF THE JUDICIAL SYSTEM

Not only have televisions in our courts not led to greater public education, but the focus on the coverage for entertainment purposes has also had a detrimental effect on the integrity of the judicial system. The Committee has done an excellent job of compiling information for the Legislature that establishes what judges, trial lawyers, and ordinary citizens believe is the case: that television coverage is more about entertainment than about education; that it adversely affects the integrity of our judicial system; and that, if anything, it lowers, rather than raises, public confidence in the judicial system.

These conclusions are supported by the Committee's judicial survey and opinion poll efforts, and by disinterested testimony (i.e., non-media testimony) before the Committee, including that by uncontroverted media scholars. For example, to the question of whether television coverage "transforms sensational criminal trials into mass-marketed commercial products" (JS Q. 4 (f)), an overwhelming 87% of the judges agreed, 56% strongly and 31% somewhat. Similarly, 61% of voters believe that television in the courtroom is more a source of entertainment than something that would increase the public's understanding of the justice system (MS Q3).

Unhappily, this assessment of television coverage of court proceedings accords with our general experience with the role of television in our culture. In the ten years since the experiments began, the TV media has done nothing which would raise our expectations about its interest in educating rather than entertaining or about its interest in maintaining a high level of confidence in the judiciary or any governmental institution.

If anything, the American experience since 1987 lowers our expectations as to possible public benefits flowing from the TV media. Walter Cronkite decries the continuing lowering of the quality of television news—it is entertainment, not education. There is minimal coverage of foreign affairs. News analyses are supplanted by pictures, emotional scenes, scandal-mongering, and gossip about celebrities. Local crime stories get heavy emphasis (significantly, the Committee's OCA study shows that 94% of the applications for courtroom TV coverage are for criminal proceedings). Every four years TV's Presidential campaign sound bites get shorter and shorter. Every year commercials get longer and longer. And for education about our courts we get the Joey Buttofuocco and John Wayne Bobbit stories.

Even Steven Brill, the former Court TV impresario and the industry's most articulate defender of cameras in the courtroom, admits to the low state of commercial television in general. In an Op-Ed piece submitted to the Committee, he defended the televising of the first O. J. Simpson trial on the grounds, among others, that at least that trial was better than the "freak of the day" and other "garbage" which his viewers would otherwise have been watching.

Interestingly, the media now candidly admits that it is not in the education business and is not in the business of praising flawed governmental institutions. The idea is that the media just gives the public the facts and holds up a mirror to reality. But of course, the media's mirror is not reality; the facts are filtered and selected to give the public a picture story, the primary purpose of which is entertainment.

In the end, the business of commercial TV media is business. It's about making money, and as such that's not a bad thing. But the business of our courts and our judicial system is the administration of justice. Real people in real courtrooms try hard to do their best to serve that ideal, with judges and juries giving careful attention to the rights of the parties before them and making decisions after careful deliberations based on the evidence presented in the courtroom and uninfluenced by outside pressures.

To make the serious and important proceedings in our New York courtrooms grist for today's television mills is to give away a vital part of our heritage. We should today be as sensitive to the incursion of television on the individual rights of New York citizens as was Governor Dewey when he said, in 1952, in approving the ban on television cameras in the courts, as enacted in Civil Rights Law Section 52, a part of Article 5—The Right of Privacy:

> It is basic to our concept of justice that a witnesses compelled to testify have a fair opportunity to present his testimony. No right is

more fundamental to our traditional liberties. The use of television, motion pictures and radios at such proceedings impairs this basic right (Governor's Memorandum of Bills Approved, Civil Rights Law, New York State Legislative Annual [1952], p. 366).

Allowing Section 218 of the Judiciary Law to expire on June 30, 1997, would reinstate the provisions of Section 52 which stood the State of New York in good stead for thirty-five years, banning cameras from our courts.

C. THE O. J. SIMPSON EXPERIENCE, THE ULTIMATE IN TV COVERAGE OF COURTROOM PROCEEDINGS, WAS A TV MEDIA DREAM COME TRUE, AND, FOR NEW YORK, A WAKE-UP CALL

Why are the surveyed judges and voters as negative as they are to the idea of televised courtroom proceedings? Is it the O. J. Simpson trial? Mistrust of the media? Or is it both and also something deeper, something which relates to the real experience of courtroom proceedings?

Even if the O. J. Simpson trial influenced the respondents, that is to be expected. The trial was conducted by a judge who was reputed to be one California's best trial judges and, though one might disapprove of his failure to reign in high powered attorneys who sought to put in every conceivable bit of evidence which would help their client's case, Judge Ito was guilty of no misconduct and made no irrational rulings. Objectively, Judge Ito did nothing to bring the judicial system of California into disrepute.

As Max Frankel, one of the Committee's witnesses, said, the television coverage caused the problem of low public esteem for the whole process. For the viewer who believed that Mr. Simpson was innocent, the system is wrong in publicly convicting him through television (and setting the scene for a second trial). For the viewer who believed that Mr. Simpson was guilty, the system is wrong for failing to convict him. (October 29, 1996 Hearing, Tr. 191).

Camera proponents, concerned about how the televising of the Simpson case will impact on the legislature's deliberations, dismiss its significance to this debate. Thus, Steven Brill can say that his Court TV coverage of the O. J. Simpson trial had some educational value and can ask us to disregard the "irresponsible" coverage by talk shows and his competitors, like Geraldo Rivera and company. According to Mr. Brill, all that bad stuff happened outside the courtroom and he shouldn't be blamed for it.

But what happened outside the O. J. Simpson courtroom was born of the pictures generated by the cameras inside. That will be true in the future of any big case of the kind the TV media thrives on. Once the TV courtroom images are available, they will be used. The mass audience which, like most of us, works during the day, will see selected interesting, controversial, and entertaining sound bite images of policemen, experts, a crying sister, a groupie flake, flamboyant and angry attorneys, and a judge in some less than impressive moments.

Even that selective nighttime TV presentation to the majority of the audience who are not gavel-to-gavel viewers will be an invitation to them to judge the credibility and character of the faces which appear on their TV tubes. In the end, as I believe happened in the Simpson case, they may be asked to call a 900 number and register their vote on the guilt or innocence of the defendant, or they may get to give their vote to a pollster. In the TV Court of Public Opinion, the appeal is to the emotions, with hearsay, gossip, and other inadmissible evidence tossed in. There is none of the kind of attentive, focused deliberation which we strive for in our courts.

The O. J. Simpson trial was exactly the kind of trial the television corporations want.

Significantly, under New York law, the television people are the ones who decide what kind of show they want to have televised. Criminal trials are more interesting and entertaining than civil cases; and that is why 94% of the applications for television coverage relate to criminal proceedings. The educational value of the Marla Maples shoe fetish case may have been zero; but the ratings were good, and products were sold. Nightly snippets of Colin Ferguson's murder defense provided little that would add to a high level of respect for the judicial system, but the bizarre behavior of a mentally ill man became entertainment during bedtime snacks.

The surveyed judges and voters probably do distrust the television media with responsibly portraying the important work of our courts, and not without good reason. They know that televisors are not interested in educating citizens (a key word in the 1987 legislation), except incidentally; what they are necessarily interested in is consumers who will buy products.

The Committee Majority Report includes a cursory discussion of the Simpson case. It accepts the arguments of camera proponents that "the television coverage of that case made an important contribution to the public's understanding of the judicial process" and dismisses concerns it heard by characterizing them simply as assertions that Simpson's televising "personifies the evils of cameras in the courts . . . [and] in the eyes of some observers, brought the American legal system into disrepute."

But the Committee Majority offers no assurance that the Simpson trial experience and problems will not occur and reoccur in New York in the future, despite the "safeguards" in Section 218. Nor does the Committee Majority attempt to deal with the obvious question of whether the second Simpson case, without courtroom cameras, wasn't the better way to proceed—in the true interests of the public and the public's judicial system.

The Committee Majority Report refers to the Committee's review of voluminous materials made available to it by the California task force that was re-evaluating camera courtroom coverage law in California. The Report also notes that the Committee heard the testimony of the judge who headed that task force, as well as the testimony of "one of the criminal defense lawyers who played a pivotal role in [the Simpson case]" (the lawyer, Barry Scheck, had a number of negative reactions to the effect that televising trials causes).

In the end, with respect to the Simpson case experience and problems, the Committee Majority decided to follow California's lead and to do what California did: overlook legitimate concerns and recommend to do nothing.

D. The intrusion of cameras in our courts undermines the independent integrity and dignity of our judicial process and courtrooms

As the legislature recognized in the 1987 statute: ". . . court proceedings are complex, often involving human factors that are difficult to measure. There may be inherent problems in any court proceeding which could possibly be complicated by audiovisual coverage."

In 1987, legislators expressed concern about possible interference with "the dignity and decorum of the courtroom." They gave particular attention to the distractions that could be caused by the television equipment and its operators. Apparently, such problems have largely been reduced by technology and conscientious operators; but as Committee witnesses testified, the cameras and cameramen can still be a distraction.

The media have tried to confine this issue to whether the physical cameras and camera operators are intrusive. Of course, after a while, in trials that last more than a week, those in the courtroom would likely "get used to" the cameras; and, where coverage is not continuous, they can get used to the comings and goings of the camera operators (something which is, however, not without its effects in indicating to jurors what testimony or witnesses would be important to the public).

But although someone in the courtroom may get used to the presence of cameras, there is also the palpable presence of the masses of viewers for whom the camera is, according to TV media proponents, a "surrogate" presence. These viewers, who will see images on the TV tube without having the full experience of being in the courtroom, will, given the TV image illusion of reality, feel free to make judgments as to judicial and attorney competence and witness credibility and to second-guess the juror's findings of liability, guilt, and innocence.

However inconspicuously placed the cameras are, their presence and the surrogate presence of thousands of viewers, is an unwarranted and unneeded intrusion on the dignity and decorum of the courtroom; and to so facilitate trials in the court of public opinion is to threaten the integrity of our judicial system. Indeed, 45% of respondents to the Judicial Survey believed that the presence of cameras in courts poses a threat to judicial independence (JS 4(h)).

The real-life sense of decorum in a courtroom is of great importance. It is not unrealistic to believe that the average law-abiding citizen who does have experience in a courtroom sees it as a solemn—in a way, sacred—place where we stand when the judge enters; where the judge may wear robes; where oaths are taken—and taken seriously; where attentive quiet pervades; and where jurors listen carefully to a judge's instructions, fear that they may unfairly convict a defendant, and deliberate with respect for fellow jurors, the judge, and the parties before them.

But that true "firsthand" experience of a trial is altogether different from the experience of the TV viewer in his living room or a barroom. It is respectfully submitted that the citizens who were surveyed by Marist knew the difference. Thus, 62% of the voters surveyed in the Marist study thought television cameras in the courtroom get in the way of a fair trial; and only 20% thought cameras in the courtroom have a positive effect, while 52% thought they had a negative effect (MS Q4 and Q5).

It is hoped that the Legislators will note the responses of the judges and voters and will find that this commercial use of our courts does not fit with the dignity and respect American citizens have accorded their courts, State as well as Federal.

E. "OPEN COURTROOMS" SHOULD NOT RELINQUISH THE DISPENSING OF JUSTICE TO THE TV COURT OF PUBLIC OPINION

The TV media are basically unconcerned about the extent to which justice in the courtroom is held hostage to the TV Court of Public Opinion. This can be seen in a number of revealing arguments by proponents of cameras in the court.

For example, they support their case by citing the testimony of a defense attorney in Wyoming County who said that he wants cameras in the courtroom because before all white juries he has to defend Black men accused of committing crimes in Attica and other prisons in his area, and he wants the all-white juries to know that they are being observed and will be judged by TV viewers from a broad area.

As a criminal defense attorney, most of whose clients are persons of color, I am sympathetic to the approach of the Wyoming County public defender. As would any advocate, he seeks to use everything at his disposal to best represent his clients. But what does his story tell us? For him cameras in the courtroom represent not a neutral presence, but something to be assessed in terms of how they will affect the proceedings. For camera-in-the-court proponents to endorse that kind of thinking is to wholly discredit their cause.

In addition, it is a deeply troubling notion that cameras are necessary in courtrooms to protect a clients' rights. The need to pressure a jury pool presumed to be permeated by racial bias by trying a case in the TV Court of Public Opinion does little to address the underlying issue which would exist in the vast majority of cases for which no cameras are present. In the long run, we should be able to depend on the independence and integrity of our courts, trial and appellate, for assurance of fairness, and not on TV.

A similar argument exists with respect to the claim that cameras positively affect the conduct of judges. The Majority Report had to acknowledge the overwhelming evidence that judges are affected by cameras, including the admission of 37% of respondents to the judicial survey that cameras led judges to render rulings they otherwise might not issue. The conclusion the Majority ultimately reaches is telling. On the one hand, in rejecting testimony that the presence of cameras could adversely affect a judge's ruling, the Majority deems it inappropriate "to presume that judges will not faithfully discharge their responsibilities" if cameras are allowed in courtrooms. Yet, the Majority's report then goes on to presume that the affect on judicial decisions that 37% of judges admit to must have been a positive one, as they are probably on their best behavior when they know they are being watched by the public.

The record demonstrates that the presence of the camera is not neutral, that is has an effect on judges. And, because our judges are fallible human beings like the rest of us, it is unrealistic to presume that the effect of the TV Court of Public Opinion is always a positive one—particularly given the current trend to hold members of the judiciary up to public scrutiny regarding how tough they are on crime. As acknowledged by the 45% of the respondents to the judicial survey who expressed the concern that cameras affected judicial independence, this concern is a real one.

F. IF THERE IS A NEED FOR GREATER EDUCATION OF NEW YORK CITIZENS AS TO THE WORKINGS OF NEW YORK'S JUDICIAL SYSTEM, IT SHOULD BE DEALT WITH DIRECTLY BY THE STATE AND THE COURTS, WITHOUT TURNING THE EDUCATIONAL TASK OVER TO COMMERCIAL TV

If the Legislature believes that New York citizens need more information about the workings of the judicial system so that a high level of confidence in the judiciary may be sustained, it can deal with the matter directly, asking for the assistance of the State's lawyers and judges rather than asking commercial television interests to assume that educational responsibility. Our courts should be the concern of citizens and we ought not to turn them over to those who use the courtroom "performances" of unconsenting real people to entertain consumers.

Without doubt the greatest way to educate our citizens about our judicial process is to get them to serve as jurors. That is a real experience of active participation, not passive viewing, and that experience, shared with fellow citizens, can be truly rewarding. It can also be reassuring, providing a high level of confidence in the system and a respect for the citizens who make it go—as contrasted with the viewer who feels free to second-guess those who are actively involved.

The best way to enhance public understanding and to maintain high public regard for the judicial system is to do the kind of thing that the Legislature did when it recently eliminated exemptions from jury duty. Improving court conditions for jurors and litigants also serves those goals. Thus New York should give Chief Judge Kaye all the financial and other support needed to renovate courthouses, to carry out the program of improving the lot of jurors and making the jury experience as fulfilling as possible, and to improve the way divorces are dealt with in the courts. To maintain high regard for our courts, the Legislature should ensure that adequate legal assistance for the poor is provided in civil and criminal cases.

To the extent it is believed that televised courtroom proceedings could help to educate the public beneficially, the law should be changed so that the decisions as to what proceedings would best fulfill that goal will not be made by the media.

IV. THE "OPENNESS" AND "NO INSTANCE OF PREJUDICE" ARGUMENTS OF CAMERA PROPONENTS ARE DIVERSIONARY AND DO NOT DEAL WITH THE REALITIES OF TELEVISED COVERAGE OF COURTROOM PROCEEDINGS AND TV'S USURPATION OF INDIVIDUAL RIGHTS AND PRIVACY INTERESTS

Since, after a ten-year experimental period, the media has not been able to demonstrate the public benefits which audiovisual coverage of court proceedings was to provide, it has tried to recast the grounds for debate in a form they could manipulate more easily.

Thus, the media argues for the superior rights of TV cameras because of the "openness" they provide, and it seeks to downplay the rights and interests in privacy of the trial participants by arguing that there are no instances of an individual case in which a party was able to show that the usurpation of those individual rights of a citizen had a prejudicial effect on the outcome of the case.

The media's "openness" argument is a rhetorical attempt to give TV cameras a Constitutional right they don't have. And, televising courtroom proceeds does have a significant effect on the dynamics of the proceedings. As the Committee's Judicial Survey, its Voter Survey and testimony of communications scholars makes clear, the presence of cameras is qualitatively and quantitatively different than a reporter with a pen.

A. Our New York courts are open, as they were before 1987 and have continued to be

The argument that TV coverage provides needed "openness" fails for a number of reasons. First, with references to the First Amendment, the argument is framed as though not allowing a camera in the courtroom is the same as not allowing reporters in the courtroom. TV reporters are allowed to attend open proceedings as are any other members of the press.

There is no constitutional right, New York or United States, to have TV cameras in the courtroom. Section 52's prohibition of the televising of court proceedings, to assure Privacy Rights under Article 5 of the Civil Rights Act, was not unconstitutional and will not be unconstitutional upon its reinstatement after the expiration of Section 218.

Our courts are open. We do not have star chambers. The right of members of the public and the press (including television reporters) to be present in our courtrooms continues to serve us well as it has for over 200 years.

Some claim that cameras provide access for those who are too busy to get to court. The submission of the "Committee for Modern Courts" gives as a reason for allowing TV cameras in the courts the fact that because "newly-constructed courtrooms are often tiny, television provides a minimally intrusive means of providing public access."

If the size of our courtrooms is truly a problem, which seems doubtful, then the problem ought to be addressed directly. Most likely the size of courtrooms is a problem only in high profile celebrity or other sensational trials where spectators may have to stand on line to get in. But in New York's large cities and small towns alike, our courtrooms are open and mostly uncrowded— for the routine workings of our judicial process. The State of New York certainly should not have a policy of allowing TV cameras in the courts because its easier to sit at home and watch the tube than to stand on line at the courthouse for a celebrity trial.

As to the suggestion that for some of the voters who watch TV footage related to our courts it may be the only information they have about New York's judicial system: (i) there is no way to tell whether that is so or not; (ii) it is condescending to presume that it is so; and (iii) even if it were so, it would not necessarily be a good thing and something which the Legislature should encourage. Citizens should be encouraged to learn about trials by serving on juries when called, as almost all voters are.

Moreover, greater access by TV to our courts does not necessarily make our courts more open or assure enhanced public understanding. Television coverage is incremental only, giving a different kind of access and information. The claim of a constitutional right to television access suggests that a TV camera is no different than a reporter with a pen. But the public information provided by cameras (images on a screen) can be and often is misleading, particularly insofar as the viewer is given the impression that the viewing experience is the same as the "firsthand" experience of being in the courtroom.

In reality, what is shown on commercial television in no way replaces actual presence at a proceeding. Unlike someone in the courtroom, the home viewer:

- may see only portions of a trial and probably will not see and hear all of the evidence;
- does not see all of what is going on in the courtroom (among other things, quite correctly, the home viewer will not see the jury); and
- has no interaction with others in the courtroom (certainly no experience like that of jurors interacting as they seriously deliberate).

Most important, as testimony from George Gerbner, Dean Emeritus, Annenberg School of Communications, University of Pennsylvania, makes clear, the experience of watching a trial in one's living room is a misleading and incomplete experience, unlike the real "firsthand" experience of being in the courtroom. On this point, Dean Gerbner noted:

> ... most deceptive is the illusion of actually seeing it, when in fact, what you are seeing is camera angles, camera selections, editing, et

cetera. And therefore, because they're unaware of the fact that they're seeing a pre-edited, pre-selected, pre-directed version of events, it is even more deceptive than reporting it in print. That addition itself is a dubious contribution, because that is probably least informative, that is what the parties of the trial look like, how they act, whether they're embarrassed, or whether they like to speak on camera. (October 29, 1996 Hearing, Tr. 54–55.)

B. TELEVISED COVERAGE DOES AFFECT COURT PROCEEDINGS, SUBORDINATING THE RIGHTS AND PRIVACY INTERESTS OF PARTICIPANTS TO THE RIGHTS OF THE TV CAMERA

The "no prejudice" argument pretends that televised coverage of court proceedings has no significant effect on the participants or the dynamics of the proceedings. As the Committee's Judicial Survey, the Marist Poll, and testimony of media scholars makes clear, such a claim defies common sense and ignores the realities of television.

The pretense that the televising of proceedings has no effect on them—that it is just a passive, non-intrusive camera—is belied by an argument of camera proponents themselves, that on the occasions when a camera is in the courtroom judges and lawyers straighten up and behave properly. It is disingenuous for the media to argue that the only adverse effect of television coverage of court proceedings which counts is one which can definitively be shown to have a prejudicial effect on the result of a case, when they rely on equally unprovable claims of positive effects.

Not unexpectedly, the Committee was advised of only a few specific instances of "abuses that occurred during the program," insofar as that description relates to the camera's having had a negative effect in a particular proceeding. The basic prejudicial effect with which the legislature should be concerned is not a matter of individual instances of provable effect. Rather, it is that the presence of TV cameras and the TV audience in the courtroom itself changes everything.

As attorney Jack T. Litman testified before the Committee, even though the matter of prejudice may be very real, it is all but impossible to prove (October 29, 1996 Hearing, Tr. 44-45). Litman cited Chief Justice Warren's concurring opinion in *Estes v. Texas*, 381 U.S. 536, 578-579 (1965):

> The prejudice of television may be so subtle that it escapes the ordinary methods of proof, but it would gradually erode our funda-

mental conception of trial. A defendant may be unable to prove that he was actually prejudiced by a televised trial. . . . How is the defendant to prove that the prosecutor acted differently than he ordinarily would have, that defense counsel was more concerned with impressing prospective clients than with the interest of the defendant, that a juror was so concerned with how he appeared on television that his mind continually wandered from the proceedings, that an important defense witness made a bad impression on the jury because he was "playing" to the television audience or that the judge was a little more lenient or a little more strict than he usually might be? And then, how is petitioner to show that this combination of changed attitudes diverted the trial sufficiently from its purpose to deprive him of a fair trial?

And it is even harder for a defendant to show possible future prejudice when opposing an application for televising a trial (Tr. 50-53).

(1) The Adverse Effects on Defendants in Criminal Trials

First and foremost is the likely effect of television coverage on the rights of defendants in criminal trials.

Given that the data provided by the Office of Court Administration reveal that in 94% of cases media applications for court coverage involve criminal cases, a critical concern for the Legislature should be the likely effect of television coverage on the fair trial rights of criminal defendants.

The statutory prohibition of unconsented-to television of arraignment and suppression hearings is a reflection of New York's continuing concerns about defendant rights. Beyond that, there ought to be real concerns about such matters as television coverage which gets involved with prejudicial matters which a jury cannot hear or consider but which (i) could become known to an unsequestered jury, or (ii) become a basis for public second-guessing disapproval of a jury's not guilty verdict.

While ideas as to the limitation of defendant's rights are becoming increasingly popular (a Yale Law School professor has gone so far as to suggest limitations on Constitutional protections against self-incrimination), traditional American sensitivity to defendant's rights still exists in New York—with the Legislature and with the majority of citizens: 62% of the voters surveyed in the Marist study thought television cameras in the courtroom get in the way of a fair tria. (MS Q4).

A very disturbing aspect of the position of camera proponents is its disregard of the additional burdens that TV coverage places on defendants in criminal trials. The sense of that situation is well understood by the average New Yorker, as seen in the response of 69% of the voters in the Committee's Marist survey who indicated that they would not want their trial to be televised if they were criminal defendants (MS Q 11).

In normal circumstances the experience of being a defendant in a criminal case is traumatic and nerve-wracking; but imagine how you would feel if you were a defendant and, in addition to normal trial concerns, you had to make decisions based on how the trial would be affected by TV coverage. Rather than strictly concentrating on your case, will your attorney be more concerned about how he/she appears on TV and about possible criticism by TV attorney commentators? Will your nervous image appearing in close-ups on the TV tube be seen as showing guilt?

Putting oneself in the shoes of a criminal defendant, would not the prospect or fact of television coverage be a factor in deciding whether to avoid a trial and public humiliation by taking a plea? Or in deciding whether to take the witness stand?

Or how would you feel if you knew that your reputation and chances to be cleared would rest not only on the jury and judge but also with thousands of people sitting in their living rooms or barrooms watching you on their TV tubes and making personal and emotional judgments as to your character, whether they like you, and whether they think you are bad and guilty regardless of the jury's verdict? If innocent, the court's record must be sealed; but the trial tapes could be used over and over to convict you in the court of public opinion.

I am particularly troubled by the disregard of substantial concerns raised by the criminal defense community in the face of TV's obsession with criminal proceedings. That this voice is ignored reflects an insensitivity to the rights of defendants, and exhibits a more general public and judicial disdain for such rights and a popular approval of the massive loading of men and women into our prisons.

An example of this anti-defendant attitude is the testimony of one witness who opined that lawyers who represent defendants in criminal cases are opposed to televised trials because most of their clients are guilty and the lawyers don't like to lose their cases in front of large TV audiences. Another is the notion that witnesses in civil cases do not need the same right to obscure their faces during testimony as do witnesses in criminal cases because in the latter instance the protection is necessary to protect witnesses from the presumptively dangerous defendant.

That the media are allowed to exploit this situation concerns me, as a trial lawyer mainly for defendants in criminal cases and as a citizen who believes in the fragile jury system and in the importance of preserving the independence of our court proceedings. The fair administration of justice requires courtrooms where decisions are reached after conscientious deliberations based on the evidence before the court and only that.

The Federal courts are absolutely correct in forbidding any televised criminal trials. New York should not be less sensitive to the rights of defendants in criminal trials.

(2) Effect on Trial Participants

On the general question of whether television coverage changes the trial atmosphere and the perceptions and conduct of participants and judges, the record suggests that the honest answer has to be: of course it does. Even if it were not so, the general perception that it *is* so can undermine confidence in the courts and the fairness of TV trials.

We cannot lightly regard or easily dismiss the survey responses of ordinary citizen voters, who live in a television dominated culture, and of judges, who also live in that culture and the day-to-day courtroom world in which they serve.

Nor can we lightly regard or easily dismiss the considered position of the Federal judges who have strongly opposed the intrusion of television into their judicial processes. Rights of defendants, jurors, judges, parties, and witnesses are no less important in our New York State courts than they are in our Federal courts. Considerations of the independence and integrity of our courts and the importance of logical and orderly deliberations (without concern about the reactions of non-participating audiences) should weigh no less in New York State courts than they do in Federal courts.

Both the Marist survey responses and answers to the Judicial Survey demonstrate that the Legislature should be concerned about the adverse impact on trial participants. The surveyed voters indicated that televised coverage would make 43% of them less willing to serve as a juror (MS Q6), 45% less willing to testify as a witness in a non-criminal case (MS Q8), and 54% less willing to testify as a witness in a criminal case (MS Q13).

These figures mirror the concerns of New Yorkers revealed in a 1991 survey conducted by Northeastern University's College of Criminal Justice, in which 48% of respondents said they would be less willing to testify in a criminal proceeding if cameras were present.

The Marist Survey also showed that 70% of voters would not want to have their trial televised if they had a civil lawsuit (MS Q7), and 68% of the voters indicated that they would not want the trial to be televised if they were a crime victim (MS Q12). Sex crime and domestic violence victims' rights advocates echoed this concern about the camera's negative impact on victim witnesses.

These responses are not surprising. After all, who would like the idea of abandoning all privacy and being judged by thousands of people sitting in their living rooms or in barrooms and finding entertainment in deciding who the good and bad guys are and whether the jury is right or wrong?

The validity of the voter's responses to the Marist questions was strongly confirmed by the testimony of trial attorneys Litman and Moschetti. From their very considerable experience with cameras in the courtroom, these attorneys confirmed the reality that a television camera in the courtroom does have an inhibiting effect on the presentation of evidence—that witnesses are reluctant to testify, that defendants are prejudiced, and that all participants are affected by the televising of trials. And 40% of judges who responded to the Judicial survey agreed that witnesses were more nervous in the presence of cameras.

Regarding the camera's affect on judges, particularly striking and disturbing was the response to one question in the Judicial Survey: 37% of the judges agreed that television coverage "tends to cause judges to issue rulings they might otherwise not issue" (JS, Q 4(g)). This is, of course, a subject which the Legislature has specified in the statutory mandate to the Committee; and we can see the wisdom of those concerns.

The testimony provided to the Committee by trial lawyers, jurors, and professional jury consultants demonstrates that the Legislature should be concerned about the impact of cameras on jurors as well. The issues raised included the effect on jurors of knowing that their verdict is subject to second-guessing by the viewing public; how coverage of only a portion of a trial inappropriately draws greater significance to that aspect of the proceeding; and how knowledge that a case will be televised negatively affects the jury pool by decreasing among some potential jurors the desire to serve and increasing it with others.

A particular area of concern was the affect on non-sequestered jurors when they go home knowing that their trial is going to be on television that night. Can they be told that they can't watch TV? Realistically, can they be expected not to watch to review what they saw in court? Or not to listen, when their friends or family give their views on what they saw on TV? Or, to be safe, should these jurors be sequestered throughout the trial? Such jurors would certainly be imposed on, one way or the other. Where does the State have the right or moral authority to impose such burdens on its citizens in the interests of commercial TV?

It is, it seems to me, unacceptable, demeaning, and wrong to give the TV media the right to make the participants in a trial be involuntary performers for the entertainment of TV viewers and the enrichment of TV companies and their advertisers.

(3) The testimony of media experts confirms the adverse effect of television on court proceedings

The results of the two Committee surveys are completely in line with the insightful testimony of Dean George Gerbner of the Annenberg School of Communications. Dean Gerbner, testifying about the potential effect of televising criminal trials, said that ". . . the difference between that kind of transmission and all other forms of recording is essentially [the difference] between a creek and a tidal wave. . . . The qualitative difference is that it simply adds the audiovisual elements, and it is visual" (October 29, 1996 Hearing, Tr. 56). Dean Gerbner went on to note that the quantitative addition of television coverage to the trial dynamic is immense. He gave his expert opinion that:

> . . . if you change the audience, you change the performers. There is no way that a national or global audience watching and viewing and listening would not affect [the participants in a trial], whether they know it or not. . . . when you know that the entire community is mobilized emotionally, an entire community to which you have to return[—]as a judge, you have to be reelected or ap-

pointed[;] as a juror, your neighbors, your friends, your associates, your boss, [are all] injected into that kind of environment, [and] there is no way that your own future will not weigh as heavily [as] the specific facts of the case. (*Id.* at p 59).

Again, the Committee's witnesses and the Committee's surveys confirm the correctness of the Legislature's concerns which underlie its cautious and restrictive approach to television coverage of court proceedings. With no demonstrable benefits, the adverse effects are there; and now is the time to take the next required, logical step of banning all audio-visual coverage of court proceedings.

V. THE COMMITTEE MAJORITY RECOMMENDATION AND ITS REJECTION OF ADDITIONAL MODEST SECTION 218 "SAFEGUARDS" REFLECTS AN INCORRECT ASSUMPTION THAT TV CAMERA RIGHTS SHOULD BE SUPERIOR TO INDIVIDUAL RIGHTS AND PRIVACY INTERESTS

The Committee Majority recommends that Section 218 be enacted on a permanent basis in its present form, with one "safeguard" addition: the requirement of a defendant's consent to audio-visual coverage of bail hearings.

In addition to the recommendations as to the statute, the Committee offered some precautionary admonitions to judges (to be vigilant in addressing the safety and privacy concerns of witnesses) and suggestions for the Office of Court Administration (should actively monitor camera-covered proceedings, should develop an enhanced judicial training program, and should not have any separate rules for death penalty cases).

While I dissent from the recommendation that Section 218 be made permanent, what I feel is most objectionable is making it permanent without adding "safeguards" which were advanced for their consideration by others in the majority but were rejected. As I indicate below, the approach the Committee Majority followed does not portend well for the future of its proposed "permanence" of Section 218 with all existing protections.

Preliminarily, I start with the belief that, given the concerns about camera coverage as reflected in the record, the "safeguards" aren't all that much in the first place. Thus, under Section 218, any defendant (or prosecutor) in a criminal case and any party, plaintiff, or defendant in a civil case can be forced, over their objection, to have their courtroom proceedings televised. And any witness, victim, or juror can be forced, over their objection, to have the courtroom proceedings in which they are participants televised.

The possible recommendations for additional "safeguards" which the Committee Majority considered and rejected related to:

(i) specifying that on applications for camera coverage, the trial judge shall give consideration to objections by parties, witnesses, and victims;

(ii) specifying that on applications for camera coverage, the trial judge shall give great weight to the fact that any party, witness, or victim is a child;

(iii) providing that, in divorce and custody cases, camera coverage shall be excluded where it is not in the best interests of a child or where the private nature of the proceeding outweighs its public benefits;

(iv) requiring that in rape, sexual assault, and domestic violence cases, the trial judge consult with the victim before granting an application for camera coverage of the proceeding;

(v) requiring defendant's consent to camera coverage of the sentencing phase of a death penalty case;

(vi) providing for the protection of the privacy of witnesses in civil cases;

(vii) providing specifically that there is no presumption for or against granting cameras access to the courtroom.

Recommendations (i) and (ii) are covered by the present implementing rules promulgated by the Chief Administrative Judge, 22 NYCRR 131.4. Recommendation (i) was specifically proposed "in order to make more explicit what may be implicit in the statute" and "*to strengthen the role of the trial judge in the exercise of his or her discretion . . . to take into account all objections to camera coverage, whether those objections are raised by parties, their counsel, prospective witnesses or crime victims*" (emphasis added). But the Committee rejected the recommendations on the basis that judges should be relied upon to know the rules and exercise their discretion appropriately.

Similarly, recommendations (iii) and (iv) were an effort to strengthen the trial court's ability to exercise discretion in ruling on camera applications. Unlike the first two recommendations, these areas are not specifically covered in the Court Rules; recommendation (iii) was proposed in response to testimony from victims' rights advocates that the concerns of victims were not adequately being considered. Nonetheless, the Committee rejected these recommendations, based on the notion that trial judges will take these concerns into account in generally assessing harm to a participant.

The rejection of (v), requiring consent of the defendant in the penalty phase of a capital prosecution, seems unduly harsh. It has an undertone of an unhealthy desire to see the guilty person sweat as he awaits his fate and squirm when he is condemned to death. The next logical step for the advocates would be to argue their right to televise the execution.

In criminal cases *all* witnesses (not just those for whom safety is a concern) have an absolute right to have their faces obscured on the television tube. But the Committee rejected recommendation (vi), which would have accorded the same rights to witnesses in civil trials. The justification behind this decision was that civil trials are different and the rights and privacy concerns of witnesses in civil trials (e.g., concerns that the televising of their face might injure their reputation or livelihood) were not as important as those of witness in criminal trials where "heightened safety concerns" might exist (in effect, making a kind of presumption of guilt in criminal cases).

By far the most unexplainable act of the Committee in its rejections of recommendations put before them for consideration was the rejection of a recommendation, (vii), that the statute be amended "to clarify that the statute contains no presumption for or against camera access."

The Committee rejected making such a recommendation even though (a) everyone one on the Committee agreed that Section 218 contained *no* specific presumption of camera access, and (b) they knew that a substantial percentage of the trial judges' responses to their Judicial Survey indicated that they were under the mistaken impression that there *was* a statutory presumption of access.

In rejecting the proposed clarifying presumption language (a statement like that which appears in the California camera-in-the-courts statute), the Committee rejected the reasons advanced for consideration of the recommendation:

Judicial discretion is central to the operation of New York's cameras in the courts law. That discretion must be broad. There must be a level paying field on which the First Amendment right of public access is accorded equal weight with the defendant's Sixth Amendment right to a fair trial. One way to achieve that equipoise among the conflicting constitutional rights is for the statute to explicitly state that there shall be no presumption for or against camera access.

If the Committee accepted the idea that the right of public access by a TV camera is to be accorded equal weight with a defendant's right to a fair trial, as it apparently does, then how could they have failed to make a recommendation which would help to assure that the playing field was level?

The rejection of the presumption recommendation certainly was a victory for Committee members who advocate the least restrictions possible. They cannot have helped but sense from the Judicial Survey that, in fact, the existing language of the statute could be interpreted to imply a presumption in favor of cameras in the courtroom.

The surveyed judges' impression that there is a presumption *for* camera access was certainly not unreasonable. Section 218 (5) (a) provides that "Audio-visual coverage of judicial proceedings, except for arraignments and suppression hearings, shall not be limited by the objections of counsel, parties, or jurors, except for a finding by the presiding trial judge of good or legal cause."

Without the addition to Section 218 of a strong clarifying statement that there is no presumption for or against camera access to the courtrooms, the playing field will remain uneven, and rights of TV cameras will continue to be given predominance over the rights of individual participants in the court proceedings.

A. The Committee's recommended permanence of Section 218 with all existing safeguards will quickly be eroded

The recommended permanence of Section 218 with all existing safeguards will not last. The present opposition to any amendment of Section 218 which would add safeguards or clarify the rights and privacy interests of participants in court proceedings, as well as the surface appeal of the media's "public interest" and "openness" arguments, foreshadows future erosion of such rights. Once the public gets used to having television entertainment values take over its courts, then, in the purported interests of "The

Public" and "Openness," the media will insist on and likely obtain more rights for the TV media with the removal of the safeguards for individual rights and privacy interests.

Camera proponents' opposition to anything which might provide additional safeguards to defendants in criminal trials, or to individual victims, witnesses, or civil trial parties, is very telling. For example, the Committee's rejection of increased protection for civil trial witnesses make sense when we recognize that the TV media wantsto get as much exposure as possible so that the public watching the TV tube can find the case more entertaining. In fact, Court TV has in the past refused to televise civil trial witnesses whose faces are obscured.

As soon as the media believe a reluctant public has become accustomed to televised trials, lobbyists and lawyers will be at the Legislature's door asking it to stop "over-regulating" their clients and to allow the faces of victims, witnesses, and, eventually, jurors to appear on the television tubes without being obscured. Their argument will be that the public has a right to know what is really happening in the courtroom, not just a part of that "reality."

The likelihood of success of such future media campaigns is very high. There is no organized opposition. Newspapers and newsmagazines which are controlled by corporations in the TV business will weigh in on behalf of less regulation and more "Public Trials." As before, liberal newspapers and their columnists will speak out for freedom of the press and the primacy of the public's right to know over individual rights and privacy concerns; and conservative newspapers will line up with them.

But our courts should not be given over to the media. The media have had their chance to prove by the experimental law, which was originally passed at the media's behest, that having televised trials will be a public benefit, and they have not proven their case.

VI. CONCLUSION

New York should take the lead among the states in reasserting the importance of an independent judicial system, and, as the federal judiciary has done, ban televised court proceedings

The New York Legislature has done itself proud in resisting powerful commercial interests and in proceeding very carefully, and increasingly more restrictively, in dealing with the profound issues relating to television cameras in the courtroom. It has shown that the Federal courts are not alone in their concerns about the commercialization of courtrooms and the rights and privacy interests of our citizens.

It is respectfully urged that the Legislature can now take definitive action to uphold the integrity of our judicial system and, as the Federal courts have done, bar television cameras from New York State courtrooms.

In a TV-saturated culture, we have had to get used to many changes, and in a way we have been powerless to resist the power of television and its effects on traditional values in our society. It would be nice to think that television is going to improve, that things are going to get better, that there will be no more O. J. Simpson Roman Circuses, and that TV will become more responsible and educational. But in our hearts we know that won't happen. Indeed, it's likely that the TV media people expected that once they got their foot in the door with an experimental program, we would get used to cameras in the courts as being a normal part of the TV culture and we would not care that the experiment never showed what they said it would.

But now New York does have a great opportunity. We may not be able to resist much of what TV does to our culture and the values of our society, but we do not have to join with and help those forces by turning over our independent courts to the TV media.

We do not need TV coverage of our courtroom proceedings. We did not need TV coverage before 1987, and we do not need it now. That should be abundantly clear when, after ten years, there is an increasing degree of concern about the wisdom of cameras in the courts.

Though the media invoke their service to "The Public," New Yorkers, judges, and ordinary citizen voters have not accepted that argument. The Committee's Judicial Survey and Marist Poll show where New Yorkers stand: they see what televised court proceedings are and they are unconvinced of the value of that coverage. The majority of surveyed judges and voters who believed that televised court proceedings are more for entertainment than for education about the judicial process were making a perfectly sensible assessment. For the very reason television producers want the right to coverage, and favor criminal trials, is because the immediacy and sensational makes it entertaining.

As it is, New York should be proud of its conservatism on the matter of cameras in the courts, insisting on experimental periods and safeguards for participants in the televised proceedings. Of course, the TV media have mobilized a campaign to discredit that conservatism. Thus, Richard N. Winfield, a member of the 1994 Committee whose recommendations the Legislature failed to adopt, calls the Legislature "too blunt an instrument and too political a branch of government to regulate the press," and expresses his annoyance at the Legislature for granting a "sequence of short-term leases . . . , each extension more restrictive than the last" (*Courtroom Cameras: A Final Word*, New York State Bar Journal, February 1997).

New York's citizens have no organized lobbies to match those of the media. They can only rely on their Legislature and expect that they will do the right thing and lead the way for other States to protect the integrity of their courts.

The involvement of the viewing public with television coverage is a threat to the goal of fairness in courts and trials that are independent of public pressure—where verdicts are to be reached on the law and the evidence and are not to be influenced by public opinion, no matter how many people may want a particular result. There is no "public right to know" that justifies giving up that independence.

The State of New York should be, and so far has been, less concerned about the passive mass viewer audience looking for good entertainment on the television tube than about the citizens who are in the courtrooms as witnesses, jurors, parties, judges, attorneys, and interested spectators. Those real people should be able to go about their business, the routine workings of the judicial process, without having to worry about being unconsenting "performers" for thousands of viewers watching selected parts of the trial.

The Committee Majority Report data, as opposed to its rec-

I am grateful for the volunteer work of Richard Sexton, who participated in the drafting, word-processing, and editing of this report. Mr. Sexton is retired Vice-President and General Counsel of SCM Corporation and is now engaged in private practice in New York City. Without his help, this Minority Report could not have been completed.

ommendations, provides good reasons why the TV cameras in the court experiment should now be ended and TV cameras banned from intruding on the administration of justice in New York courts just as they have been banned from intruding on the administration of justice in the Federal courts.

Respectfully submitted,

LEONARD NOISETTE

www.ingramcontent.com/pod-product-compliance
Lightning Source LLC
Chambersburg PA
CBHW051422290426
44109CB00016B/1401